HOLLOW EARTH

HOLLOW EARTH

*THE LONG AND CURIOUS HISTORY OF IMAGINING STRANGE LANDS,
FANTASTICAL CREATURES, ADVANCED CIVILIZATIONS, AND
MARVELOUS MACHINES BELOW THE EARTH'S SURFACE*

DAVID STANDISH

DA CAPO PRESS
A MEMBER OF THE PERSEUS BOOKS GROUP

Standish, David.
   Hollow earth : the long and curious history of imagining strange lands, fantastical
creatures, advanced civilizations, and marvelous machines below the earth's surface /
David Standish. — 1st Da Capo Press ed.
        p. cm.
   Includes bibliographical references and index.
   ISBN-13: 978-0-306-81373-3 (hardcover : alk. paper)
   ISBN-10: 0-306-81373-4 (hardcover : alk. paper)   1.   Science fiction—History and
criticism. 2.   Earth—In literature. 3.   Civilization in literature.   I. Title.
   PN3433.6.S73 2006
   809.3'8762—dc22

                                                                2006011035

First Da Capo Press edition 2006

Published by Da Capo Press
A Member of the Perseus Books Group
www.dacapopress.com

Da Capo Press books are available at special discounts for bulk purchases in the
U.S. by corporations, institutions, and other organizations. For more information,
please contact the Special Markets Department at the Perseus Books Group,
11 Cambridge Center, Cambridge, MA 02142, or call (800) 255-1514 or (617) 252-
5298,
or e-mail special.markets@perseusbooks.com.

Set in Adobe Caslon
Design by Cooley Design Lab

1 2 3 4 5 6 7 8 9 — 09 08 07 06

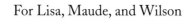
For Lisa, Maude, and Wilson

Be a Columbus to whole new continents and worlds within you, opening new channels, not of trade, but of thought. . . . What was the meaning of that South-Sea Exploring Expedition, with all its parade and expense, but an indirect recognition of the fact that there are continents and seas in the moral world to which every man is an isthmus or an inlet, yet unexplored by him, but that it is easier to sail many thousand miles through cold and storm and cannibals, in a government ship, with five hundred men and boys to assist one, than it is to explore the private sea, the Atlantic and Pacific Ocean of one's being alone. . . . It is not worth the while to go round the world to count the cats in Zanzibar. Yet do this till you can do better, and you may perhaps find some "Symmes' Hole" by which to get at the inside at last.

—Henry David Thoreau, *Walden*

CONTENTS

ACKNOWLEDGMENTS

In roughly chronological order, I would like to thank Senior Editor Kathleen Burke at *Smithsonian* magazine for giving me the go-ahead to do an article on the hollow earth for them, which got me started on this, and my apologies for going crazy and turning in a manuscript far too long. Great thanks, too, to my wonderful agent, Leslie Breed, for believing in the idea and finding a home for it. Senior Editor Ben Schafer at Da Capo stuck with the book despite many opportunities to bail out, given my turtle-like pace, fondness for digression, and writerly crabbiness. I am also grateful to several friends who read the manuscript in progress, offering both encouragement and helpful critiques—Scott Guthery, Beth Meredith, Chris Miller, and Lucie Singh. Medill School of Journalism graduate students Keith Chu and Michael Andersen were resourceful and persistent in tracking down source material and fact-checking. And a number of people provided invaluable assistance in sharing art and photography for the book's illustrations: Klaus-Peter Gelber of the Mineralogical Institute at the University of Würzburg for Athanasius Kircher engravings; Rick Loomis of Sumner & Stillman Antiquarian Booksellers (www.sumnerandstillman.com) for pictures of early Jules Verne editions; Michael Widner, archivist for the Koreshan State Historical Site in Estero, Florida, for many photographs of the Koreshan community; Bill and Sue-On Hillman, proprietors of the ERBzine website (www.erbzine.com), for artwork from Edgar Rice Burroughs's Pellucidar novels; also the Frank Frazetta Museum (www.frazettaartgallery.com), for permission to use his terrific Pelludicar cover art from the 1960s and 1970s; and Jean-Luc Rivera for sending scans of sci-fi magazine covers from his extensive "Shaver Mystery" collection. And finally, I would like to remember John Weigel and Walter Havighurst, Miami University English professors whose influence on me proved both deep and lasting.

INTRODUCTION

Here's one:

What do Sir Edmond Halley, Cotton Mather, Edgar Allan Poe, Jules Verne, L. Frank Baum, Edgar Rice Burroughs, Adolph Hitler, Admiral Byrd, flying saucers, Superman, Mount Shasta, and Pat Boone all have in common?

If you answered the hollow earth, you're way ahead of where I was before I started looking into this.

Like most kids of my time, I first encountered the idea that the earth might be hollow in Verne's *A Journey to the Center of the Earth*—even though he seemed to take forever to get down there. Because my tastes were resolutely low-rent, tending toward rock 'n' roll and science fiction, as a teenager I also read several of Edgar Rice Burroughs's *Pellucidar* novels of wild adventures in a prehistoric world beneath the earth's crust, starting in the middle with *Tarzan at the Earth's Core*. As an undergraduate at Miami University in southern Ohio, I lived for a while in a dorm named for John Cleves Symmes, an early prominent settler in the area, and learned that he had a namesake nephew, a veteran of the War of 1812, who devoted the last years of his life to proselytizing for an expedition to the North Pole, where he expected to find a vast opening leading into the earth's interior, which, he believed, was hollow, and contained an unspoiled paradise just waiting, well, to be spoiled. And then in a grad school Poe seminar, I found out that he'd liked Symmes' peculiar idea enough to use it as an ending for one of his short stories, "Ms. Found in a Bottle," and as a motif in his only published novel, *The Narrative of Arthur Gordon Pym.*

Years pass. I'd stuck all this vital information into a corner of the attic I call my brain and pretty much forgotten about it, just as I'd figured the rest of the world had—since everyone knows that it's not hollow, right? Wrong. While surfing around on the Internet a couple of years ago, I came across a website for a newsletter called *The Hollow Earth Insider*—along with much else. It turns out that the idea is still alive and well, at least among a cadre of fringe devotees. Not a few claim they make regular astral-travel visits inside, where they find a New Age civilization of peaceful vegetarians. Type the phrase "Hollow Earth" into your favorite search engine, and prepare to be amazed at the amount of material that turns up. Google produced 2,100,000 hits the last time I looked.

The hollow earth has had a long history. Right down to the present, the idea has been used again and again, changing and evolving in ways that suit the needs and concerns of each succeeding time.

Virtually every ancient culture worldwide, and most religions, has shared a belief in some sort of mysterious subterranean world, inhabited by strange and powerful creatures, right beneath our feet. These underworlds were myriad. The Sumerians believed in a vast netherworld they called Ki-Gal; in Egypt, it was Duat; in Greece and Rome, Hades; in ancient Indian mythology, it was Naraka; certain schools of Buddhism believed in a worldwide subterranean labyrinth called Agartha; in Japan, there was Jigoku; the Germanic people had Hellheim; the Inca called it Uca Pacha, while to the Aztecs it was Mictlan, and to the Mayans, Mitnal. And of course, to the Christians, it's good old Hell, toured most elegantly by Dante in the fourteenth century in his *Inferno*. The near-universality of these underworlds isn't surprising. They're the dark terrain of the unconscious given tangible form and structure, embodiments of the boogie-man who ran howling through our nightmares when we were kids.

But such mythic/religious ideas started to take on a scientific cast in the seventeenth century, beginning with English astronomer and mathematician Edmond Halley, best remembered for his famous comet. He gave us our first scientific theory of the hollow earth—in his formulation, consisting of independently turning concentric spheres down there, one inside the other. Halley arrived at this notion, which he presented to the prestigious Royal Society of London, to account for observed variations in the earth's magnetic poles. His true imaginative leap, however, lay in the additional thought that these interior spheres were lit with some sort of glowing luminosity, and that they might well be able to *support life*. Generations of science fiction writers have been thankful to him for this ever since.

Although the distinction between "hollow" and "riddled with subterranean labyrinths" is sometimes unclear, I have leaned as much as possible toward truly "hollow," and so haven't discussed such popular underground realms as Alice's Wonderland or Tolkein's Middle Earth—they have been looked at again and again, anyway. What I have tried to do here is trace the permutations on Halley's idea from his time down to the present. The story weaves in and out of literature and what passes for real life, and veers over into the charmingly delusional more than once. It includes writers major and minor, scientists, pseudo-scientists, religious visionaries and cranks, explorers, evil dictators, New Agers, scam artists, and comic book characters.

One thing I found fascinating was the hollow earth idea's continuing elasticity—it has been equally useful as a late-seventeenth-century scientific theory, an expression of early-nineteenth-century Manifest Destiny, a vehicle for mid-nineteenth-century musings on paleontology and Darwin, late-nineteenth-century religious utopianism, Teddy Roosevelt–style imperialism, a perfect creepy vehicle for 1950s Cold War paranoia, and a cozy home for dreamy contemporary New Age utopias.

There have been many books recently about important ideas or commodities that have changed the world. This one, I am happy to say, traces the cultural history of an idea that was wrong and changed nothing—but which has nevertheless had an ongoing appeal.

1

HOLLOW SCIENCE

THREE TIMES LATE IN 1691 EDMOND HALLEY stood before the London
Royal Society to read papers proposing that the earth is hollow, or nearly so. In a
carefully elaborated hypothesis based on principles expressed in Newton's landmark
Philosophiae naturalis principia mathematica (which Halley had helped bring to publication in 1687), he suggested that three concentric spheres lay beneath the surface,
turning independently on a north–south axis, each smaller than the next, all nesting
within one another, rather like *matrushkas,* those adorable Russian dolls. He theorized further that there might be life inside, supported by a source of light like that
of the sun itself.

Here was a new sort of thinking about the earth's interior, qualitatively different from all earlier ideas. Not the dark flowering of fearful, gloomy meditation on
death; not conjecture about the eternal reward or punishment of fragile, ineffable
souls; not mythology or religion or metaphysics, but science. A serious stab at it, at
any rate.

(opposite) Portrait of Edmond Halley at age eighty in 1736. He is holding one
of his drawings of the earth's interior spheres. (Reproduced by permission of
the President and Council of the Royal Society)

Why was he thinking these peculiar thoughts?

Scientific curiosity, certainly, but a curiosity driven by commerce as well.

Today Edmond Halley is known only for the comet of 1682, which he predicted would return in 1758. Until the late seventeenth century, comets were little understood and greatly feared, omens of terrible portent, an alarming anarchic presence in the otherwise orderly heavens. Their motions had been a great mystery. In 1680, a comet had for weeks cut a brilliant path through the night sky, seemingly hurtling toward oblivion on a collision course with the sun. The following year yet another came catapulting in the opposite direction through the solar system on its way to some unimaginable destination. Halley determined that these were not two comets, but one, traveling an epic ellipse on a regular circuit, as did the comet posthumously named for him. Its interval of seventy-four to seventy-nine years (occasional close swipes with the gravitational pull of Jupiter and Saturn slightly alter the timing) means it had been visible at Agrippa's death in 12 B.C.E., Attila's defeat at Chalons in 451 C.E., and the Norman conquest of England in 1066 (it's shown blazing across a section of the Bayeux Tapestry, with a group of frightened onlookers pointing skyward at it). Maybe there was something to the idea of portents, after all. It has been repeatedly suggested that the Star of Bethlehem was a comet—perhaps Halley's.

Halley would be important to the history of science if only for his influence on Newton's *Principia*. The train of thought leading to it was triggered by discussions Halley provoked with Newton about planetary orbits, and Halley not only nudged Newton along during the three years he spent writing it, he also served as editor and publisher, carefully reading and correcting page proofs. *Principia* appeared under the imprint of the Royal Society, but the money to pay the printer came out of Halley's own pocket. At every stage he shepherded it along.

It seems fitting, then, that Halley's hollow earth theory was the first scientific hypothesis to draw on Newton's revolutionary ideas, and it wasn't as off the wall as it may seem.

Throughout his life Halley pursued far-ranging interests and scientific investigations. Elected to the Royal Society in 1678 at the age of twenty-two, over the years he presented papers to that body on a hodgepodge of subjects. "The annals of the Royal Society are littered with enterprising papers by Halley," writes Lisa Jardine in *Ingenious Pursuits,* "on everything from the global patterns of trade winds, to the mechanics of diving bells, the rise and fall of mercury in the barometer, compass variation, and the beneficial effects of opium-taking." Of the last, he tried it and liked it. "Instead of sleep," he wrote in his January 1690 paper, "which he did design to procure by it, he lay waking all night, not as if disquiet with any thoughts but in a state of indolence, and perfectly at ease, in whatsoever posture he lay."

Such catholicity of interest was true to the idea of the Royal Society at its founding in 1660. One member, Henry Oldenburg, described the group as "a Corporation of a number of Ingenious and knowing persons—for improving Naturall knowledge, whose dessein it is, by Observations and experiments to advance ye Contemplation of Nature to Use and Practice."[1]

Members included Isaac Newton, Robert Hooke, Robert Boyle, and Christopher Wren. These were some of the chief laborers constructing a new machine. Together and separately they were fashioning the first cogs and wheels of that whirring rational device, the Enlightenment. The dreamy romanticism that had passed for thought until then—magic, alchemy, astrology, even religion—was being buried, and a shiny new mechanical creature was being put together piece by piece: the universe, newly seen!

The first tangible signs of the Enlightenment-to-be came early in the seventeenth century, with the initial stirrings of what became known as the scientific revolution. Francis Bacon kicked things off by overturning Aristotle and proposing a search for knowledge not through antiquarian study but by firsthand investigation—the basis for the scientific method. This was accompanied by a technological revolution still going full tilt in Halley's time. Dutch eyeglass maker Hans Lippershey had registered the first known patent for a telescope in The Hague in October

---

1. Quoted in Alan Cook's *Edmond Halley* (Oxford 1998). Note reads: First Minute Book: Oldenburg to Richard Norwood, 6 March 1664, Oldenburg Corresp, Vol. 2, p. 146.

1608, and not a year later Galileo began pointing one of his own construction at the night sky, soon observing mountains on the moon and sunspots, discovering four satellites of Jupiter, and confirming Copernican theories about a heliocentric universe. Sir Isaac Newton first gained notice in 1671 by presenting the Royal Society with a reflecting telescope of his own design. Meanwhile Robert Hooke was looking in the opposite direction through compound microscopes he devised to peer into previously invisible worlds. His self-illustrated *Micrographia,* an early "coffee table" book published in 1665, inspired Samuel Pepys to buy a microscope and encouraged Anton van Leeuwenhoek, a merchant in Holland, to make his own microscopes from lenses he ground himself. Van Leeuwenhoek began sending to the Royal Society his exquisite drawings of the creatures he was discovering in ordinary drops of water: "an incredible number of very small animals of divers kinds."

Major advances in precision clock making were also ticking along, another component in this surge of technical innovation and an important part of the scientific revolution itself, since much of what was being studied depended on accurate measurement of time—especially in relation to astronomy, navigation, and surveying. Clocks before the seventeenth century were large, crude devices that never kept anything close to true time. The minute hand wasn't added until 1670. In 1582 Galileo had observed the timekeeping properties of pendulums, and in 1656 Dutch astronomer and physicist Christian Huygens applied this principle to clock making with notable results. In 1675 he had one of those eureka! moments, thinking of a way to regulate a clock using a fixed coiled spring. This innovation led to smaller watches (though the often contentious Robert Hooke complained that he'd made a spring-regulated clock ten years earlier) that could be used onboard ships, since calculating exact time was the crucial missing component in the search to establish accurate longitude.

Much of this new scientific activity, especially in regard to astronomy and improvements in clock making, was being driven by economic and military interests, as were Halley's speculations on the hollow earth.

In the seventeenth century England became a true maritime power. From the time of the Restoration (1660) onward, English shippers began rivaling the Dutch, the world's greatest traders. In the many tangled wars that bloodied the century (between 1650 and 1700, for instance, the English fought three wars against the Dutch and were allied with them in a fourth against the French), the sceptered isle was duking it out with rivals on the open seas and putting together a colonial empire with far-flung holdings the world over. (One notable addition came in 1664, when they seized New Amsterdam from the Dutch and renamed it for the duke of York.) This meant more and more ships crisscrossing the oceans. Naturally they all had to know where they were and where they were going, as any miscalculation could lose money and lives. All those sunken wrecks full of lost plunder are tribute to what was at stake.

Determining latitude was a breeze, achieved by taking an angle on the sun or the polestar. But longitude was a bitch. Theoretically the easiest way to determine longitude was to establish a universal time at a prime meridian and then compare that to local time, applying a simple formula to calculate the distance from the prime meridian. But accurate clocks wouldn't exist until well into the next century, when John Harrison developed his famous watch and finally, after much cheap dodging on the Royal Society's part, won the celebrated Longitude Prize of £20,000 (about $12 million today), which had gone begging for fifty years. Until then, the next best thing was fanatically detailed astronomical tables.

In the seventeenth century, astronomy was a weapon in the national arsenal. For example, in 1675 King Charles II was persuaded to okay funding for the Greenwich Observatory. He did this because the sneaky, underhanded French had built one, and he didn't want England to be faced with an observatory gap! The first scientific institution in Great Britain, it was essentially built as a military installation. The money came from the budget of the Ordnance Department, which, as Lisa Jardine observes, was the Restoration equivalent of the Pentagon. The goal was greater accuracy and detail in astronomical charts—pinpointing the positions of the stars, the moon, and even the moons of Jupiter. Prior to trustworthy seagoing chronometers, celestial bodies were the most reliable way of determining longitude, distant clocks shining in the nighttime sky.

In 1676 twenty-year-old Halley left Oxford without graduating and eagerly journeyed to the island of St. Helena, a patch of land belonging to the East India Company located 1,200 miles west of Africa's southwestern coast. Arriving in 1677, there he spent a year mapping the night sky, returning in 1678 to produce a catalog of the celestial longitudes and latitudes of 341 stars—the first of its kind for that hemisphere and a considerable aid to navigation. As we'll see, navigational concerns led Halley to his theory of the hollow earth, as he attempted to explain variations in the earth's magnetic poles.

The magnetic compass had come into use during the twelfth century; and while valuable in a general way, sailors soon found that compasses had the annoying habit of significantly deviating from true north. Worse, there was no evident pattern or consistency to the magnetic variation. The lines of the earth's magnetism bend away from true north, and at any given place these variances themselves vary over time. Understanding the causes might lead to the ability to predict variation and thus compensate for readings that had been misleading sailors for centuries. (Another difficulty lay in New World real estate; territorial boundaries established with simple compasses caused constant legal wrangling as magnetic variation shifted.)

Here was a problem as significant as that of establishing accurate longitude.

Halley had more than a passing interest in magnetic variation. He had investigated the puzzle for years before presenting his 1691 papers and spent several years afterward at sea, primarily mapping magnetic variation in the South Atlantic. Understanding its causes promised potential long-term rewards, but detailed chapter-and-verse charts of current observed deviation were of immediate pragmatic value. His 1701 magnetic charts of the Atlantic and the Pacific were the first such published, as well as the first to connect points on the oceans with the same variance, using lines now called isogonic lines—also the first published.

He had made his first observations on magnetism as a sixteen-year-old schoolboy and continued them four years later during his long excursion to St. Helena. Magnetism was one of the great unknowns. It had been recognized as a force since ancient times, but nobody had a clue what it was. Sailors, for example, believed the powerful fumes given off by garlic somehow interfered with the proper working of the compass, and they wouldn't allow the stuff onboard.

The earliest scientific ideas about magnetism came from William Gilbert, eventual physician to Queen Elizabeth, who in 1600 published *De Magnete* after eighteen years of study and experimentation. In it he suggested that the earth is a vast magnet, explaining for the first time why compasses point north. Descartes had a go at a theory of magnetism in his 1644 *Principia philosophiae,* involving his famous fluids and vortices, but it was as wrong as it was ingenious.

The major work on the subject was Athanasius Kircher's 1641 *Magnes,* both exhaustive and a little cuckoo, a perfect emblem of the man himself. Kircher, a German Jesuit born in 1601, combined polymath erudition and intellectual eccentricity in ways far beyond those of mortal men. He is often mentioned as a candidate for "the last man to know everything," from obscure archaic languages and literatures to the latest in science to the most fantastical absurdities then in currency, all in heaps in the measureless attic of his remarkable mind. He was, as we used to say in the 1960s, a trip. He wrote forty-four books on subjects ranging from Egyptian hieroglyphics to possible causes of the bubonic plague, constructed strange objects (including an automatic organ), and assembled in Rome what was arguably the first natural history museum.

Kircher's *Magnes,* as one account describes it, "contains all that was known in his day on the subject of electricity and magnetism . . . filled with curiosities, both profound and frivolous. The work does not deal solely with what modern physicists call magnetism. Kircher discusses, for example, the magnetism of the earth and heavenly bodies; the tides; the attraction and repulsion in animals and plants; and the magnetic attraction of music and love. He also explains the practical applications of magnetism in medicine, hydraulics, and even in the construction of scientific instruments and toys. In the epilogue Kircher moves from the practical to the metaphysical (and Aristotelian) when he discusses the nature and position of God: the central magnet of the universe."[2]

Here is the weltanschauung of a man standing astride two continents of thought, one of them sinking fast. Despite his scientific instincts, Kircher resolutely wrapped his investigations, and especially his conclusions, in the theological fabric that had dominated intellectual pursuits for hundreds of years, one sun setting and another rising in a single mind. The end-of-an-era quality of his work is probably why he is little known now—that and the fact that he contributed virtually no original thought to the new science. But at the time his books were widely read and discussed, and Halley was certainly aware of *Magnes*. (Four of Kircher's books were listed in the inventory of Halley's library at his death.)

Another of his books had a certain relevance to Halley's hollow earth theory, the encyclopedic two-volume *Mundus subterraneus,* published in 1665 and something of a best seller in scientific circles—a work that Halley and the other Royal Society fellows would have known intimately. As *Magnes* compiled everything under the sun that Kircher could find or dream up about magnetism, *Mundus subterraneus* was a massive miscellany of knowledge and speculation about the earth's interior that included many knockout etchings by Kircher himself illustrating his theories.

Kircher's interest in things below stemmed from a long visit to Sicily, where in March 1638 he had close-up views as the famous volcanoes Aetna and Stromboli erupted. On returning to Naples, the enterprising priest arranged to have himself lowered into the crater of Vesuvius, active at the time, to see what he could see. One thing led to another. Nearly thirty years later, *Mundus subterraneus* gathered in eight hundred pages everything that was known about geography and geology, along with discourses on, for example, underworld giants, dragons, and demons; the spontaneous generation of insects from dung; mining and metallurgy; sections on poisons, astrology, alchemy, fossils, herbs, weather, gravity, the sun and

---

2. From the Spark Museum website at www.sparkmuseum.com/RADIOS.HTM.

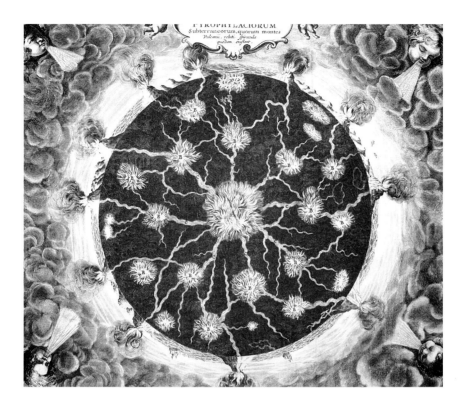

the moon, eclipses, and fireworks. In addition to his writing, Kircher claimed to have performed palingenesis by restoring a plant from ashes to its original form.

Amid this swirl of observed data and charming crackpottery was at least one speculation closer to truth than not: his notion about pockets of fire down below and the idea that the earth has a fiery center. If he wanted to put underworld giants down there too, he was simply carrying on a tradition that went back to Dante and beyond. His drawings of the earth's interior were probably the first visual cross-sections attempting to suggest in a scientific way what it might be like inside.

Kircher's thoughts regarding the world's hydraulics take a cue from a thirteenth-century encyclopedist known as Bartholomew of England, who believed

(above) Illustration by Athanasius Kircher showing pockets of interior fire scattered in a network beneath the earth's surface. (Reprinted with permission of the Mineralogical Institute, University of Würzburg, Germany)

a huge whirlpool opening existed at the North Pole. Kircher envisioned the earth as a sort of vast hot water tank. Icy water from the ocean poured in at the North Pole in a great vortex, percolated southward through the earth's interior, heated by a cen-

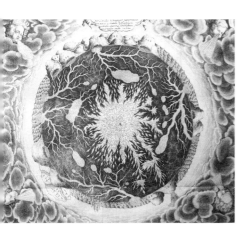

tral fire (provided by alchemical cosmic rays), and emerged on the surface, comfy as bathwater, at the South Pole—a system of heating and circulation he believed kept the oceans from either freezing or turning putrid. As Jocelyn Godwin points out in *Arktos,* Kircher offers two reasons for thinking this. "The first is scholastic," she writes, "for he states that everything in the universe has to be in motion, or else it will stagnate and die." The second is "through analogy . . . with human anatomy": it functions as a sort of digestive system. "The elements in the sea-water are extracted by this process, to be used for generation of metals. The undigested remains are then expelled at the nether end, the South Pole. As a further analogy with animal anatomy, Kircher likens the circulation of waters to the recently-discovered circulation of the blood. Thus he implies that the earth is constructed and behaves like a living creature." His drawings illustrating this system (including subterranean lakes and rivers) are probably the earliest attempt to show global patterns of ocean circulation. Although it didn't figure in Halley's theory, the motif of polar openings leading inside appears again and again in the history of the hollow earth.

Another book about the earth's interior that enjoyed wide readership in Halley's time was *The Sacred Theory of the Earth* by Thomas Burnet. The original Latin edition appeared in 1681, with an English translation following in 1684. Stephen Jay Gould called it "the most popular geologic work of the seventeenth century." As the new science jolted the existing Christian worldview—the biblical

(above) Illustration by Athanasius Kircher showing global patterns of ocean circulation. (Reprinted with permission of the Mineralogical Institute, University of Würzburg, Germany)

account of the universe—attempts to reconcile science and theology began to appear. Burnet's *Sacred Theory* proved one of the most notable, a pioneering effort in creationist thinking. Burnet (1635–1715) was an English divine who served on the faculty at Christ's College before becoming royal chaplain to King William III. As Gould wrote of him, "Burnet was a rationalist, upholding the primacy of Newton's world in an age of faith. For Burnet's primary concern was to render earth history not by miracles or divine caprice, but by natural, physical processes."[3]

Today his ideas read like fanciful daydreams. One main purpose of his *Sacred Theory* was to explain Noah's flood in a "scientific" way. No carny show miracles on God's part after the creation, but natural (and explicable) processes at work. Burnet dismissed the idea that the flood was a local phenomenon exaggerated over time to worldwide dimensions. His reading of Scripture made him believe that the entire globe was inundated. When he calculated that the volume of water in the world's oceans was insufficient to do the trick, he came up with a theory. Prior to the flood, the earth was unblemished as an egg:

> The face of the Earth before the Deluge was smooth, regular, and uniform, without Mountains, and without a Sea.... In this smooth Earth were the first scenes of the world, and the first generation of Mankind; it had the Beauty of Youth and blooming Nature, fresh and fruitful, and not a Wrinkle, Scar or Fracture in all its body; no Rocks nor Mountains, no hollow Caves, nor gaping Channels, but even and uniform all over.

A perfect expanse. Nor did it lean slightly lopsided on its axis as it does now, but stood up nice and straight. This meant there were no seasons. At certain latitudes perpetual spring prevailed. Thanks to this eternal spring, both humans and animals had a far better time of it, as well as longer lifespans. The prelapsarian paradise!

According to Burnet, the flood threw the earth so off kilter that along with

---

3. See the chapter "The Reverend Thomas' Dirty Little Planet" in Stephen Jay Gould's *Ever Since Darwin* (1979).

other dire results, its axis tilted, and it was goodbye, eternal spring. This idea had a
certain currency in the seventeenth century. Milton expresses it in book ten of *Paradise Lost* (1667), though he attributes the change to a deliberate act of God, who
sent angels with celestial crowbars as a wrecking crew to undo Eden by wrenching
the earth's axis askew:

> Some say he bid his Angels turne ascance
> The Poles of the Earth twice ten degrees and more
> From the Suns Axle; they with labour push'd
> Oblique the Centric Globe . . .
>   . . . to bring in change
> Of Seasons to each Clime; else had the Spring
> Perpetual smil'd on Earth with vernant Flours.

After the flood the world became as it is today—what Burnet calls a
"hideous ruin" and our "dirty little planet." In his view, how did this happen?

According to his theory, similar to one proposed by Robert Hooke in 1668,
from the original liquid chaos things settled out according to their densities, the
heaviest forming the core, with the "liquors" of the earth rising toward the top,
rather like a global parfait. The greater part of these liquors were "volatiles," chiefly
air, but with a considerable amount of minuscule crud mixed in: "The great regions
of the Air would certainly have their sediment too; for the Air was as yet thick,
gross, and dark; there being an abundance of little Terrestrial particles swimming in
it still." Gradually these settled, precipitated out of the foul air, until "they compos'd
a certain slime, or fat, soft, and light Earth, spread upon the face of the Waters.
This thin and tender Orb of Earth increas'd still more and more, as the little Earthy
parts that were detain'd in the Air could make their way to it." Over time an even
crust formed over a planet largely consisting of water, like scum congealing on a
cold pot of stew. He cites Psalms in support of this idea: "God hath founded the

Earth upon the Seas, and to him that extended or stretched out the Earth above the Waters."

Burnet quotes Moses in regard to what happened next: "The fountains of the great Abyss were broken open." This was "sixteen Hundred and odd years after the Earth was made." The culprits were three: the earth standing up so straight and unwavering on its axis, the tender crust covering the watery abyss, and the relentless sun. "Consider the effect that the heat of the Sun would have upon it, and the Wa-

ters under it; drying and parching the one, and rarifying the other into vapours." At the hottest latitudes it would be "continual Summer, the Earth would proceed in driness still more and more, and the cracks would be wider and pierce deeper." Eventually the sun boiled our earthly egg until it cracked. "When the appointed time was come, that All-wise Providence had design'd for the punishment of a sinful World, the whole fabrick brake, and the frame of the Earth was torn in

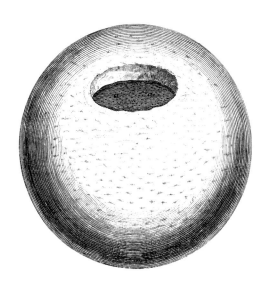

pieces, as by an Earthquake; and those great portions or fragments, into which it was divided, fell down into the Abysse, some in one posture, some in another." All fall down. And the world's face today is the horrible ruin that remained after the floodwaters subsided.

Oddly, given his belief that the sun beating endlessly on equatorial regions put this catastrophe in motion, Burnet places the breaking point near the North Pole, providing a diagram showing an unaccountably regular circular hole in the

(above) Thomas Burnet understood the earth's surface as solidified scum atop a liquid interior; as a result of the sun beating down on it, a hole appeared—pictured here. (Reprinted with permission of the Northwestern University Library)

crust, as if it had been attacked by a cookie cutter rather than blown up by subterranean oceans boiling through ruptured cracks. The proximity to the North Pole makes one wonder if he had been poring over Kircher's popular *Mundus subterraneus,* which appeared in 1665, sixteen years before Burnet's *Sacred Theory.*

Unfortunately for his career, in the end Burnet seems to have been overly influenced by the new science. In 1692—the same year Halley's paper about the hollow earth was published in the *Transactions* of the Royal Society—Burnet produced *Archaeologiae philosophicae,* suggesting that the Mosaic account of creation may have simply been an allegory. This is a common liberal interpretation today, of course, but at the time it was just a little too hip for the room. King William took considerable heat over having someone with such scandalous views as his court chaplain and had Burnet fired, ironic since *Archaeologiae philosophicae* was dedicated to William.

Such was the intellectual landscape when Halley proposed his hollow earth theory. Newton's *Principia* had provided a paradigm of the new science's accomplishments. But the scientific revolution did not one day simply appear full-blown, Athena out of Zeus's head. The late seventeenth century was a transitional time. Old theological certainties were now questions to be answered anew, but a belief in God as the great architect of the universe, evident in the work of Kircher and Burnet, continued to be expressed by such paragons of the new science as Newton himself. Indeed, belief in divine Providence led Halley to several of the more remarkable components of his theory.

The full title of his 1692 publication was *An Account of the cause of the Change of the Variation of the Magnetical Needle; with an Hypothesis of the Structure of the Internal parts of the Earth; as it was proposed to the* Royal Society *in one of their late Meetings.*

Halley begins with a rather touching mea culpa, saying that "some years since" (in 1683) he had published "a Theory of the Variation of the Magnetical Compass," proposing "that the Globe of the Earth might be supposed to be one great Magnet, having four Magnetical Poles." But on reflection, he continues, "I found two difficulties not easie to surmount, the one was that no Magnet I had ever seen or heard of, had more than two opposite poles; whereas the Earth had visibly four, and perhaps more. And secondly, it was plain that those Poles were not, at least all of them, fixt in the Earth, but shifted from place to place, as appeared by the great changes in the Needles direction within this last Century." He says of these problems, charmingly, "these difficulties had wholly made me despond, and I had long since given over an inquiry I had so little hopes of." They depressed him and he quit thinking about them.

But then he had a flash: "In accidental discourse, and least expecting it, I stumbled on the following Hypothesis." He doesn't tell us what triggered the new thinking. He's aware that what he's about to propose may at first blush seem wild and crazy and so he cautions, "If I shall seem to advance any thing that looks like Extravagant or Romantick, the Reader is desired to suspend his censure till he have considered the force and number of the many Arguments which concur to make good so new and so bold a Supposition." Next he marshals magnetic readings taken between 1580 and 1688 from many parts of the world—London, Paris, the southern Cape of Africa, St. Helena, Cape Comorine in India—to establish the general drift to the west of the magnetic needle over time. "The Direction of the Needle is in no place fixt and constant, tho' in some [places] it change faster than in others." So *something* is moving down there to cause this shift, and "this moving thing is very great, as extending its effects from Pole to Pole." Further, "the motion thereof is not *per saltum* [by fits and starts], but a gradual and regular Motion." Fine. But, he continues, given "the structure of our *Terraqueous* Globe," it is hard to imagine that anything can move inside it "without notably changing its Centre of Gravity and the Equilibre of its parts." It would disturb the rotation of the earth on its axis, "occasion strange alteration in the Sea's surface, by Inundations and Recesses thereof, such as History has never yet mentioned." So what's the answer? That "this moving internal substance be loose and detached from the external parts of the Earth." If it were attached, "the whole must necessarily move together." But it doesn't. The solution—and his great inspiration—"the External Parts of the Globe may well be reckoned as the Shell, and the internal as a *Nucleus* or inner Globe included within ours, with a fluid medium between."

Placing another sphere, with its own magnetic poles, turning slowly inside our own, solves the problem of the four magnetic poles. The disparity in rotation is slight—"in 365 Revolves the difference is scarce sensible." But it is enough to account for the gradual westward drift found in magnetic readings.

Alas, there will be scoffers. After urging "all Masters of Ships and Lovers of natural Truths" to continue collecting data and forward it to the Royal Society, he says, almost with a sigh, "in order to explain the change of the variations, we have adventured to make the Earth hollow and to place another Globe within it: and I doubt not but this will find Opposers enough." He next tackles possible objections—some with more success than others. There is nothing like this in nature. The inner globe would bang against the outer. The seas would leak into it. And, given the metaphysics of the time, even if it were possible, "yet it does not appear of what *use* such an inward Sphere can be of, being shut up in eternal Darkness, and therefore unfit for the Production of Animals or Plants." (Italics mine.)

He dismisses the first objection by pointing to Saturn surrounded by its rings. The nature of gravity would keep the inner globe from "chocking" against the outer. The seas wouldn't drain into it because, well, "the Wisdom of the Creator has provided for the Macrocosm by many more ways than I can either imagine or express." (God still came in handy when needed.) "What Curiosity in the Structure," he continues, "what Accuracy in the Mixture and Composition of the parts ought not we to expect in the Fabrick of this Globe?" And the very nature of "the Magnetical Matter" might help here. Invoking Newton's *Principia*, he says that gravity is also such that the particles on the underside of the "Terrestrial parts of our Globe" would over time "molder away or become loose" to "fall in, and with great force descend on the Internal [sphere], unless those particles were of another sort of Matter." And what might that be? "Why then may we not suppose these said

Arches to be lined throughout with a Magnetical Matter, or rather to be one great Concave Magnet, whose two Poles are the Poles we have before observed to be fixt in the Surface of our Globe." It's all done by magnets! The magnetical matter would pull everything upward and patch up any holes that might form, like a puncture-proof tire.

Again he turns to Newton, this time in regard to the relative densities of the earth and moon. Newton had calculated that "the Moon be more solid than the Earth as 9 to 5." Since the earth consists of the same materials and is so much larger, Halley asks if it isn't then logical to suppose "four ninths thereof to be Cavity?" As it happens, Newton's calculation of the moon's density was one of the few major errors in the *Principia* (the real ratio is 1 to 81), but no one knew that at the time.

Now we get to the good part. What possible *use* might these inner spheres have?

He first allows "that they can be of very little service to the Inhabitants of this outward world, nor can the Sun be serviceable to them, either with his Light or Heat." But he has answers to this objection. What follows next is a neat conflation of science and religion. He says that "it is now taken for granted that the Earth is one of the Planets"—the Copernican view of the universe—"and that they all are with reason supposed Habitable, though we are not able to define by what sort of creatures." This too was a popular idea at the time. A book published in 1686 by French scientist Bernard le Bovier de Fontenelle, *Conversations on the Plurality of Worlds,* a chatty account of the latest scientific news that helped further acceptance of the Copernican system, appeared in not one but two English translations in 1688. "I shou'd think it very strange," he wrote, "that the Earth shou'd be inhabited as it is; and the other Planets shou'd be so entirely desolate and deserted." He enumerates the vast variety of life on earth, down to those "thousands of small living Creatures" seen through the microscope, and then asks, "After this, can you believe, that Nature, who has been fruitful to Excess as to the Earth, is barren to all the rest of the Planets?"

This notion of an "abundant Providence," the idea that creation must be as copious as possible because that would logically be part of the Creator's plan, was a commonplace in seventeenth-century theology. Halley uses it, seemingly taking inspiration from de Fontenelle to make an argument for a more abundant creation *within* the earth:

> Since we see all the parts of the Creation abound with Animate Beings, as the Air with Birds and Flies, the Water with the numerous varieties of Fish, and the very Earth with Reptiles of so many sorts; all whose ways of living would be to us incredible did not daily Experience teach us. Why then should we think it strange that the prodigious Mass of Matter, whereof this Globe does consist, should be capable of some other improvement than barely to serve to support its Surface? Why may not we rather suppose that the exceeding small quantity of solid Matter in respect to the fluid Ether, is so disposed by the Almighty Wisdom as to yield as great a Surface for the use of living Creatures as can consist with the conveniency and security of the whole.

An inner sphere would provide more room for life.

But, he notes, ever aware of skeptics, some will say there can be no life down there without light "and therefore all this *apparatus* of our inward Globes must be useless." He admits he doesn't have a solid response to this one and says, a bit defensively, "To this I answer that there are many ways of producing Light which we are wholly ignorant of," and offers some possibilities: the medium itself may be "luminous after the manner of our *Ignes fatui.*" This is the Latin term for the phosphorescent light that hovers over swampy ground at night, sometimes known as will-'o-the-wisp. Seems like a stretch. A better possibility comes next: "The Concave Arches may in several places shine with such a substance as invests the Surface of the Sun." But he does not suggest what the substance may consist of and ultimately falls back on the unknown: "Nor can we, without a boldness unbecoming a Philosopher, adventure to affect the impossibility of peculiar Luminaries below, of which we have no sort of *Idea*." There may be a source of light down there beyond guessing about up here. Gently parodying the common academic appeal to ancient authority, he adds that "the Poets *Virgil* and *Claudian* have gone before me in this Thought, inlightning their *Elysian Fields* with Sun and Stars proper to those infernal, or rather internal, Regions." He quotes two lines from book six of the *Aeneid*:

> *Largior hic campos aether et lumine vestit*
> *Purpureo; Solemque suum sua Sidera norunt.*

> Here a more copious air invests the fields, and clothes with
> purple light, and they know their own sun
> and their own stars.

And three from book two of Claudian's *The Rape of Proserpine*:

> *Amissum ne crede diem, sunt altera nobis*
> *Sidera, sunt orbes alii, lumenque videbis*
> *Purius, Elysiumque magis Mirabere Solem.*

> Don't think that the way things are now, is the way
> they're going to be. We have other stars, other
> worlds; and you will see a purer light and marvel more
> intensely at the Elysian sun.

Halley comments, wryly: "And though this be not to be esteemed as an Argument, yet I may take the liberty I see others do, to quote the Poets when it makes for my purpose."

One way or another, there is light down there sufficient to support life.

Somewhere along the way in this argument—after many readings I still find it difficult to pinpoint—truly warming to his subject, he raises the number of these interior spheres from one to three. He now refers the reader to a diagram appended to the end of the paper. Describing it, he says, "The Earth is represented by the outward Circle, and the three inward Circles are made nearly proportionable to the Magnitudes of the Planets *Venus, Mars* and *Mercury,* all of which may be included within this Globe of Earth, and all the Arches sufficiently strong to bear their weight."

There it is. Three independently moving spheres inside, well-lit and capable of supporting life. The paper concludes on a brave note, though tinged with a defensive twitch or two:

> Thus I have shewed a possibility of a much more ample Creation, than has hitherto been imagined; and if this Seem strange to those that are unacquainted with the Magnetical System, it is hoped that all such will endeavor first to inform themselves of the Matter of Fact and then try if they can find out a more simple Hypothesis, at least a less absurd, even in their own Opinions. And whereas I have adventured to make these Subterraneous Orbs capable of being inhabited, 'twas done designedly for the sake of those who will be apt to ask *cui bono* [What is the good of it?], and with whom Arguments drawn from *Final Causes* prevail much. If this short Essay shall find a kind acceptance, I shall be encouraged to enquire farther, and to polish this rough Draft of a Notion till hitherto not so much as started in the World, and of which we could have no Intimation from any other of the *Phenomena* of Nature.

It should be noted that except for the life and light he posited down there, for which science fiction writers have been thanking him ever since, but about which, per the above, he obviously had certain reservations—his ideas regarding the causes of the earth's magnetism and the complicated shifts in the magnetic poles were quite prescient and not far in principle from current thinking. According to recent Halley biographer Alan Cook, "he showed an understanding of the essential structure of the Earth's magnetisation." The earth does consist of separate spheres of a sort: the outer crust; the mantle, which accounts for two-thirds of the planet's mass; a dense liquid layer of magma consisting chiefly of molten iron that's about half the earth's radius in extent; and a solid inner core inside that. The layer of molten metal is circulating—like Halley's internal Sphere—which creates electrical currents, which in turn create magnetic fields. The earth can be thought of as a great electromagnet. Even today all of this isn't entirely understood. But Halley was closer to being on the right track than it might seem at first blush.

In 1716, England was treated to a spectacular aurora borealis display—another phenomenon little understood at the time, and not completely so now. This came at the end of the "maunder minimum" in Europe and England, a period of low sunspot activity lasting from 1645 to 1715 that coincided with a near absence of the northern lights. Halley observed the display and wrote a paper offering an explanation for it that involved his theory of the hollow earth. He rightly supposed that the earth's magnetic field played a part in creating the aurora. Alan Cook comments that "his analysis of the structure of aurorae and their correspondence with the Earth's magnetic field remains impressive after nearly three hundred years." Halley further speculated—incorrectly—that the source of the particles reacting to the magnetic field to create the aurora might be the "medium" between the shell and the first internal sphere leaking out into the atmosphere. It might tend to leak more at the poles because, as Cook puts it, he believed that there "the shell is thinnest on account of the polar flattening of the earth."

At the age of eighty, Halley sat for what would be his last portrait. It is far different from the earliest known portrait of him at about age thirty, with long black hair dropping to his shoulders, in which he looks rather remarkably like a young Peter Sellers, with an expression on his face combining determination with a gleam of mischief in the eyes. In this later portrait his long wavy hair has gone white, he's added a few pounds, and his face shows patient resolve, like he'd rather be anywhere else than sitting still for this portrait painter. He's wearing a black velvet scholarly robe with lacy white shirt cuffs poofing out of the sleeves, and he seems to be standing in his library, with a number of large volumes on shelves behind him. It would be unremarkable but for the large sheet of paper he holds in his left hand, angled so the viewer can see what's on it—a drawing of spheres within spheres, almost identical to the one appended to his 1692 paper on the hollow earth in the Royal Society's *Philosophical Transactions.* Of the hundreds of projects he'd involved himself in, with accolades given for his work in dozens of areas, he remained fond and proud enough of his hollow earth theory to have it memorialized in what he must have suspected would be the last official portrait done of him. Those natural philosophers, the Beach Boys, would approve: Be true to your school!

Halley would probably have been flattered, amused, and appalled at the uses to which his theory would be put in the years to come.

Drawn by John J. Audubon Aug —
Witten Museum

2

SYMMES' HOLES

THE NEXT MAJOR HOLLOW EARTH EVENT BEGAN MODESTLY on April 10, 1818, in St. Louis, then the westernmost town of any size on the American frontier. Founded in 1764, the former French trading post had grown from a muddy backwater into a booming crossroads, becoming the stepping-off point to the West. The Lewis and Clark expedition embarked from there in 1804, the year after the Louisiana Purchase, an 827,987-square-mile tract of land that doubled the size of the country, bought from Napoleon at the bargain-basement price of a little under three cents an acre. In 1805 St. Louis was made the Territory of Louisiana's seat of government, and then in 1812, capital of the Territory of Missouri. Between 1810 and 1820 the population increased 300 percent. When the War of 1812 concluded in December 1814 (not counting the belated Battle of New Orleans), people began pouring in there, whether seeking boomtown opportunity or simply stopping to take a few deep breaths and buy some (overpriced) pots and pans before heading farther west. One of the new steamboats first put in there in 1817, beginning a traffic that would give St. Louis a prominence in the West that would last until the coming of the railroad in the 1840s and 1850s, when previously piddling Chicago would eventually steal its thunder. In the years immediately after the War of 1812, St. Louis was ripping and roaring.

One of those who landed there after the war was Captain John Cleves Symmes.

On April 10, 1818, he commenced handing out a printed circular of his own composition. It was his bold mission statement:

CIRCULAR

Light gives light to discover—ad infinitum

ST. LOUIS, MISSOURI TERRITORY, NORTH AMERICA
April 10, a.d. 1818

To all the World:

I declare the earth is hollow and habitable within; containing a number of solid concentric spheres, one within the other, and that it is open at the poles twelve or sixteen degrees. I pledge my life in support of this truth, and am ready to explore the hollow, if the world will support and aid me in this undertaking.

JNO. CLEVES SYMMES
Of Ohio, late Captain of Infantry

N.B.—I have ready for the press a treatise on the principles of matter, wherein I show proofs of the above positions, account for various phenomena, and disclose Dr. Darwin's "Golden Secret."

My terms are the patronage of THIS and the NEW WORLDS.

I dedicate to my wife and her ten children.
I select Dr. S.L. Mitchill, Sir H. Davy, and Baron Alexander Von Humboldt
as my protectors.

I ask one hundred brave companions, well equipped, to start from
Siberia, in the fall season, with reindeer and sleighs, on the ice of the
frozen sea; I engage we find a warm and rich land, stocked with thrifty
vegetables and animals, if not men, on reaching one degree northward
of lattitude 82; we will return in the succeeding spring.[1]

J.C.S.

This wasn't a stray brainstorm that occurred to him during a nightmare
brought on by a bad fish or after getting a little too corned up at the tavern. He had
been thinking and thinking on this. How he came to these conclusions—and how
he came to believe so passionately and persistently in them—is a mystery. But until
he died in 1829 at age forty-eight, the hollow earth was his obsession, his only
dream, his tragedy.

Born in Sussex County, New Jersey, in 1780, Symmes was named for a
prominent uncle whose generosity would figure in his future. The older Symmes
was a Revolutionary War veteran and chief justice of New Jersey, who in 1787 put
together a corporation to buy a 330,000-acre tract of public land in the southwestern corner of the present state of Ohio, between the Big and Little Miami rivers,
north of the Ohio River, a deal sometimes known as the Symmes Purchase.

His younger namesake started out well enough. His father, Timothy
Symmes, was a Revolutionary War veteran and a judge in New Jersey who married
twice and had nine children altogether. John Cleves was the oldest in the second

---

1. As reprinted in James McBride's *Pioneer Biography: Sketches of the Lives of Some of the Early Settlers of Butler County, Ohio*, 2 vols. (Cincinnati: R. Clarke & Co., 1859–1861).

crop of six. He had the usual semi-haphazard elementary education. Years later he recalled reading, at age eleven, "a large edition of 'Cook's Voyages,'" which his father, "though himself a lover of learning, reproved me for spending so much of my time from work, and said I was a book-worm."[2] He added that at "about the same age I used to harangue my playmates in the street, and describe how the earth turned round; but then as now, however correct my positions, I got few or no advocates." Poor Symmes. Already a visionary pariah in grade school.

He joined the army as an ensign—the lowest officer rank—at age twenty-two and was commissioned as captain in January 1812, months before war was declared against Great Britain. He did most of his service on the western frontier near the Mississippi River.

Symmes was at Fort Adams fifty miles below Natchez in 1807, as the final act in Aaron Burr's delusional scheme of personal empire was unfolding near there. Another dreamer! Burr was on his way down the Mississippi with an armed flotilla, rumored to be planning to seize New Orleans, in cahoots with the territorial governor, James Wilkenson. But Wilkenson got cold feet, ratted Burr out to President Jefferson, and rushed additional troops to several forts along the river, including Fort Adams, ordering those stationed in New Orleans to prepare for an attack. Burr got wind of this betrayal and went ashore north of Natchez, where he was arrested. Managing to fast-talk his way out of the charges, he masqueraded as a river boatman and melted into the wilderness on the eastern side of the river, making his way toward Spanish Pensacola. But as additional information about his schemes came to light, he was rearrested near Mobile and taken to Richmond, where he was tried for treason before Chief Justice John Marshall—and, somehow, acquitted.

Symmes became involved in his own drama at this time. He described it in detail in a long letter to his brother, Celadon, dated Fort Adams, June 28, 1807. When a fellow officer named Marshall declared Symmes was "no gentleman," Symmes sought him out to publicly "wring his nose" and provoke a duel. Duels

---

2. This is from a long marginal note by Symmes in a copy of *Symmes's Theory of Concentric Circles*, written by his friend, James McBride, and published as "By A Citizen of the United States" (Cincinnati: Morgan, Lodge and Fisher, 1826).

were a capricious business, given the primitive state of the weapons and the dubious skill of the duelists, and this was no exception. With their seconds at hand, the two faced off ten paces apart, standing sideways. "Are you ready?"

"Yes!"

"Fire!"

> We raised our arms together deliberately, from a hanging position. My intention was to aim at his hip; his (I learn) at my breast. Consequently, I got the first fire, which drew his shot somewhat at random, though it must have passed within a line of the lower part of my belly, as it pierced through my pantaloons, shirt-tail, and the bone of my careless hanging wrist, close to the joint. He received my ball in his thigh. I wanted to know if he desired another shot, and being informed in the negative, left my second and surgeon attending to him, and, with my handkerchief wrapped around my wound, went home and ate a hearty breakfast.

So Marshall just barely missed shooting off Symmes' privates, the shot ripping through his pants and underdrawers and striking his wrist. The wound at first seemed trivial, "little more than a scratch," but it refused to heal properly, causing him pain, fever, bloating in his feet and legs, and a bout of dysentery lasting six or seven weeks. A biographical sketch in an 1882 history of Butler County includes this letter and says that "Captain Symmes never fully recovered the use of his wrist. It was always stiff and a little awry." Marshall suffered lasting consequences as well. The wound "disabled him so that he carried the effects of it through life." But, the sketch writer adds, "he was afterward befriended by Captain Symmes, who always spoke of this duel with regret."[3]

Symmes had married Mrs. Mary Anne Lockwood on Christmas Day 1808 at Fort Adams. She was the young widow of an army captain and brought five

---

3. *A History and Biographical Cyclopaedia of Butler County Ohio, With Illustrations and Sketches of its Representative Men and Pioneers* (Cincinnati, Ohio: Western Biographical Publishing Company, 1882).

daughters and one son to the marriage. To this brood they added four more children, including a son named Americus, born in 1811, who carried his father's hollow earth banner into the 1880s, giving interviews, writing a book summarizing his theories, and putting up a memorial to him in a Hamilton, Ohio, public park, with a hollow stone globe at the top. It is still there today.

Symmes left the army in 1816 and worked as a trader in St. Louis, providing supplies to government troops stationed at forts on the Upper Mississippi and trading with the Fox Indians under special dispensation from the governor of Missouri Territory. He probably spent considerable time at Fort Osage, which sat high on a bluff overlooking the Missouri River, both a fortification and an "Indian factory"—a sort of early Wal-Mart filled with goods attractive to the Indians, who would trade deerskins, furs, and other hides for them. Deerskins were so common in the region that they were accepted as currency in lieu of the real thing.

Two years into this life as a trader, at the age of thirty-eight, Symmes printed up his circular announcing that the earth is hollow and offering to lead an expedition inside to claim the glorious lands lying within for the United States.

No one seems to know where he got this notion.

His friend James McBride wrote an explanatory book published in 1826 called *Symmes's Theory of Concentric Spheres* and says in the preface, "During the early part of his life he received what was then considered a common English education, which in after-life he improved by having access to tolerably well-selected libraries; and, being endued by nature with an insatiable desire for knowledge of all kinds, he thus had, during the greater part of his life, ample opportunities to indulge it." But McBride offers no specifics on his reading.[4] Similarly, his son Americus writes in *The Symmes Theory of Concentric Spheres*, published in 1878, nearly fifty

---

4. The book was published anonymously, as written by "A Citizen of the United States," but it's generally recognized that McBride was the author. Born in Pennsylvania in 1788, McBride migrated to the "Symmes Purchase" at age eighteen, where he made enough money as a merchant to become a historian of the Miami country's early white settlement and accumulated arguably the most extensive library in the area—of which, presumably, Symmes generously availed himself. It has been suggested by one writer, in fact, that McBride was the brains behind Symmes's hollow earth theory, directing his reading and thinking, and, puppetmaster-like, putting Symmes out there as the front man for it. But this seems unlikely.

years after his father's death, "During his boyhood and early life he received a good common English education, which, in after life, he greatly improved through his great fondness for reading and an insatiable desire for knowledge. He cultivated particularly mathematics and the natural sciences, and at an early age studied out the curious theory through which he became so widely known." Seems Americus may have cribbed a bit from his dad's pal.

What's most puzzling, if Americus is right that he figured out his theory of concentric spheres at an early age, is why he waited until he was nearly forty to spring it on the world. Could this be as deep and simple as a midlife crisis? Bookish, dreamy, he found himself with a mob of children, stuck bouncing around the frontier on horseback doing nothing more elevated than buying and selling, and for what? Mere profit? And not even much of that? Polite as they tried to be, all the biographical sketches written about him in the fifty years or so after his death mention that he wasn't getting rich as a trader. ("Captain Symmes's trading experience did not result in a pecuniary benefit to him.") Stuck in a boring dead-end job in St. Louis while continuing lifelong dreams of exotic places and great achievements, suddenly he has a visionary bailout plan.

But where had he gotten it?

One good possible starting point is Cotton Mather.

This will perhaps seem unlikely to those who think of Mather only as the arch-Puritan, the incarnation of all that was intellectually ugly and unappealing about American Puritanism in the late seventeenth and early eighteenth centuries, often pointed to as the chief villain in the Salem witch trials of 1692—*that* Cotton Mather? Yes.

Born in 1663 into one of Boston's most prominent families, Mather was not only the strongest voice of old-guard Boston Puritanism and a prolific writer on things ecclesiastical (he and his father, Increase, accounted for 30 percent of the books published in New England during the 1690s), he was also an interested and serious scientist. He read widely in the new science, corresponded with men such as

Roger Boyle, performed his own observations, and was named a member of the Royal Society in 1713. Like Burnet and others in England, Mather at first saw no threat in the new science; to the contrary, it seemed to him a tangible further articulation of God's plan. He welcomed it and routinely wove it into his sermons. The same Cotton Mather who embodied the worst medievalism in New England Puritanism was also an enlightened early advocate for smallpox inoculation. He produced two major works on "natural history," as the new science was generally called. The first, *Curiosa Americana*, grew out of a series of letters he had sent to the Royal Society starting in 1712, reporting on a variety of homegrown phenomena.

Mather's *The Christian Philosopher*, a considerable amplification organized by subject into chapters, appeared in 1721. Mather biographer Kenneth Silverman calls it "the first general book on science written in America." It enjoyed great and ongoing popularity and was almost certainly studied by John Cleves Symmes, since the book had become a staple in popular scientific literature by Symmes' day. It summarized the best current knowledge on various subjects in order to show "that Philosophy [read: Newtonian science] is no Enemy, but a mighty and wondrous Incentive to Religion." Maybe. As Perry Miller observes, toward the end of his life, a certain desperation creeps into Mather's writings, a growing realization that the Enlightenment may be the enemy of religious fervor, after all. Miller writes in *The New England Mind: From Colony to Province:*

> Mather was no Pascal, but he was imaginative enough, or tormented enough, to realize along with Pascal that the experimental philosophy had opened up an infinity on either side of finite existence, that man was now poised between the mathematical extremes of microscope and telescope, that he no longer stood in the center of a symmetrical system, that he had become a thinking reed hemmed in by two massive enigmas.

But in *The Christian Philosopher* Mather reveals no doubts or fears. Instead, there is a certain exuberant delight here, both in all these terrific new ideas and findings and in demonstrating the ways this marvelous complexity absolutely *demands* a marvelous God behind it all. The chapter on magnetism is the most relevant to Symmes' theory. Mather begins:

> Such an unaccountable thing there is as *the MAGNETISM of the Earth.* A Principle very different from that of *Gravity.* The Operations of this amazing Principle, are principally discovered in the communion that *Iron* has with the *Loadstone*; a rough, coarse, unsightly Stone, but of more Value than all the *Diamonds* and *Jewels* in the Universe.

A historical survey of advances in knowledge about magnetism follows, from the "Antients" to Roger Bacon to Henry Gellibrand (who discovered the drift of magnetic variation around 1634) to Edmond Halley. Mather devotes nearly three pages to summarizing Halley's 1692 paper in *Philosophical Transactions*, not failing to mention that

> Sir *Isaac Newton* has demonstrated the *Moon* to be more solid than our *Earth*, as nine to five; why may we not then suppose four Ninths of our Globe to be Cavity? Mr. *Halley* allows there may be Inhabitants of the lower Story, and many ways of producing *Light* for them.

Mather concludes the chapter with a certain glee. Given all this knowledge and theorizing about magnetism, he says, practically chuckling, the truth is, "*Gentlemen Philosophers*, the MAGNET has quite *puzzled* you." And its mysterious force leads directly to God. We "see much of Him in such a wonderful *Stone* as the MAGNET. They have done well to call it the *Loadstone*, that is to say, the *Lead-stone: May it lead me unto Thee, O my God and my Saviour!*"

Though Halley's paper was reprinted in the century or so after its appearance, *The Christian Philosopher* seems the likeliest place for Symmes to encounter his ideas. But Halley makes no mention of large holes at the poles, the most singular feature of Symmes' theory. Symmes may have known Kircher's *Mundus subterraneus,* which, as already noted, picked up on the ideas of a medieval geographer in positing a great watery vortex at either pole; but this too is far from the huge gaping "verges" theorized by Symmes. And Kircher's globe, while having a central fire and other pockets of vulcanism, plus a complex network of subterranean waterways, was primarily solid.

Many of the articles summarizing hollow earth ideas found on the Internet—and there are plenty of them, ranging from the fairly accurate to the delusional, just like the rest of the Internet—attribute the idea of polar openings and other hollow earth notions to Leonhard Euler. He's considered one of the eighteenth century's most important mathematical thinkers, and was until recently on the face of Switzerland's ten Franken bill. Students of calculus and trigonometry can blame him for their headaches. He didn't invent calculus (Leibniz and Newton did, independently, in the 1680s), but Euler "carried [it] to a higher degree of perfection," as the *Encyclopedia Britannica* puts it, adding, "He did for modern analytic geometry and trigonometry what the *Elements* of Euclid had done for ancient geometry."

The earliest mention of Euler in connection with the hollow earth appears in James McBride's *Symmes's Theory of Concentric Spheres* (1826), the first extended and (fairly) coherent explication of Symmes' ideas. Symmes himself never did manage to produce a single document elaborating and putting them in order. Instead he wrote many short shotgun blasts about aspects of his theory that appeared as scattered newspaper articles, and he presented them in a series of ill-advised lectures from 1820 until his death in 1829. So the McBride book is the definitive source regarding his thinking.

After citing Halley's theory, McBride says that Euler was also an advocate but differed "as to the nature of the nucleus." He continues: "Euler believed it to be a luminous body formed of materials similar to the sun, and adapted to the purpose of illuminating and warming the interior surface of the crust, which he supposed might be inhabited equally with the exterior surface."

As the UnMuseum website has it, "In the eighteenth century Leonhard Euler, a Swiss mathematician, replaced the multiple spheres theory with a single hollow sphere which contained a sun 600 miles wide that provided heat and light for an advanced civilization that lived there."[5] And a 1909 article about Symmes in the *Ohio Archaeological and Historical Publications* journal by Cincinnati lawyer John Weld Peck says Euler "accepted Halley's theory and went further in asserting that the inner sphere might be luminous and thus light and warm the inner surface of the outer crust, and he further inferred that the interior might be inhabited." Certain (presumably) more reliable writers make similar assertions, such as science popularizers L. Sprague DeCamp and Willy Ley in *Lands Beyond* (1952). But they don't cite primary sources for their claims regarding Euler's beliefs in interior suns and advanced civilizations, and I have been unable to turn up any such proof. Indeed, in *Letters to a Princess of Germany,* his widely read popularization of current science that appeared in three volumes between 1768 and 1772, Euler is categorically opposed to Halley's ideas about the earth's magnetism and the moving interior spheres that he suggests to account for it.

Another candidate offered as a likely source of Symmes' inspiration is Sir John Leslie (1766–1832), a Scottish physicist and mathematician best remembered for his studies of capillary action and as the creator of the first artificial ice in 1810. Leslie had his own convoluted hollow earth theory that derived from his theory of the "compression of bodies." As Duane Griffin, assistant professor of geography at Bucknell University, explains it, "The theory is based in part on an experiment by British physicist John Canton that Leslie believed established the compressibility of water, an idea Leslie believed his peers had dismissed prematurely (they were actually correct—water is uncompressible). The theory of the compression of bodies holds that the density of any substance is a function of its particular elastic properties and its distance from Earth's center."[6] This would produce an "almost inconceivably dense" Earth, far denser than it has been calculated to be. The answer to this problem? Leslie says, in *Elements of Natural History* (1829 edition), "Our planet, must have a very widely cavernous structure. We tread on a crust or shell whose thickness bears but a very small proportion to the diameter of its sphere." Further, since there couldn't be a vacuum down there, it must be filled with something besides air, since it too would compress. "The vast subterranean cavity," wrote Leslie, "must be filled with some very diffusive medium, of astonishing elasticity or internal repulsion among its molecules . . . [the] only fluid we know possessing that character is LIGHT itself." He adds, with such verve you can practically hear the stirring organ chords ascending behind it: "The great central concavity is not that dark and dreary abyss which the fancy of Poets had pictured. On the contrary, this spacious internal vault must contain the purest ethereal essence, *Light* in its most concentrated state, shining with intense refulgence and overpowering splendor."

This is, however, contrary to another idea about interior lighting that is often attributed to him, one that seems to be another hollow earth equivalent of an urban legend. The UnMuseum again: "Scottish mathematician Sir John Leslie proposed there were two inside suns (which he named Pluto and Proserpine)." And a website reliably named Professor Fringe says, "John Leslie would place 2 suns in hollow earth—named Pluto and Proserpine."[7] These two supposed interior suns of Leslie's turn up frequently. But if he actually suggested them, neither Professor Griffin nor I have been able to locate the primary source.

So these are the likely influences. But somewhere along the way, Symmes made the huge leap he is chiefly remembered for—those vast holes at the poles. The originality and boldness of the idea no doubt contributed to Symmes' reticence about announcing it to the public, if, as his son claimed, it had come to him at an early age. The scientific world at the time had no shortage of wacky explanations for

---

6. "What Curiosity in the Structure: The Hollow Earth in Science" by Duane Griffin is an excellent, short historical paper surveying scientific thinking about the hollow earth, down to the present. Quite readable though aimed for an academic audience. It is available online at www.facstaff.bucknell.edu/dgriffin/Research/Griffin-HE_in_Science.pdf.

7. http://www.professorfringe.com/he.htm.

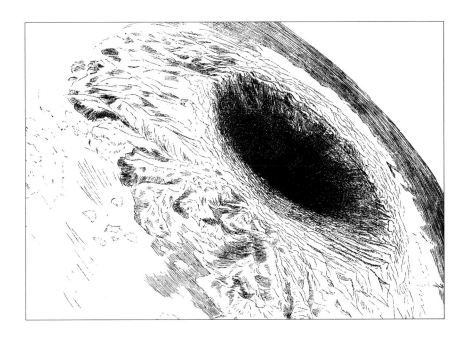

just about everything, but these Symmes' Holes were still pretty far out there. He must have sensed the ridicule he was in for even before he ever opened his mouth.

But he had worked out the theory in minute detail and amassed mountains of data to support it. The whole thing rested on Symmes' "proof" of a universal imperative toward hollow concentric spheres, from planets down to the molecular level. As McBride summarizes the theory in his book, "The Earth is composed of at least five hollow concentric spheres, with spaces between each, an atmosphere surrounding each; and habitable as well upon the concave as the convex surface. Each of these spheres are widely open at the poles. The north polar opening of the sphere we inhabit, is believed to be about four thousand miles in diameter, the southern above six thousand."

Tortured logic lies behind this.

In part it involves an "improvement" on Newton's ideas regarding gravity.

(above) Illustration of the northern polar "verge" as if seen from the moon.
(*Harper's New Monthly Magazine*, 1882)

If larger objects exert a greater pull on smaller, Symmes asks, why hasn't everything in the universe collected into a single huge glob? He has a couple of answers. First, the hollow concentric molecules making up everything exert a "repulsive" force on one another; and second, all of space "is filled with microscopically invisible hollow spheres of aether—which by their elasticity hold the planets of the universe in place," as Peck tries to explain it in his 1909 article. Peck continues: "In other words, we live in a sort of rubber ball universe in which the elastic hollow spheres of aether are so pushed as by their elasticity to hold in place the heavenly bodies. This expansive quality in the molecules which constitutes the aerial fluid creates a *pushing* instead of a *pulling power* which is the real principle of gravity."

If this makes much sense to you, you're ahead of me.

The other operative—and more understandable—principle involved in creating the hollow earth is centrifugal force. Here his argument owes something to the primeval liquid sphere postulated by Burnet and others. To Symmes, this whirling viscous first chaos would generate a hollow center by propelling all the heavier material inside the earth out toward the edges, like a cosmic potter's wheel. This centrifugal flinging of the earth's heaviest material would in turn create mountain ranges and other great surface irregularities by unevenly pushing this weighty stuff outward, until it cooled and solidified into the untidy surface as we know it. This process would also produce a landscape on the inside that roughly mirrors the one on the surface, including oceans.

But wouldn't the water be sucked down to the center by gravity, not to mention any people or creatures inside? No. Here Symmes conveniently returns to Newtonian thinking about gravity. Since centrifugal force has flung most of the earth's mass toward the outer parts of the sphere, the earth's true center of gravity lies in some middle ground between the outer surface and the surface of the landscape within, much nearer the edge than the geographical center. No danger of falling off once you're inside.

He doesn't suggest an interior sun. The holes, or "verges," are cut at slight angles, twelve degrees off from being parallel with the equator. The descent into them is gradual, so that a traveler might not at first realize that he has crossed the threshold and is on the way inside. Since they're angled and several thousand miles across, regular sunlight can get in, and according to some complicated calculations he's made about refraction of light in the "cold, dense air" of the poles, more is *bent* downward, so that together there's enough light to support plant and animal life inside. His prosaic analogy here is a room in a house that only gets northern light; the sun never shines directly into the room, but still it is bright.

Symmes and his subsequent interpreters marshal bushels of evidence pointing to the existence of the polar openings, mostly drawn from accounts of Arctic expeditions—details these earlier explorers had no idea were verifications of polar openings, incidentally. He cites observations of animals and birds heading north at the onset of winter, which he takes to mean that they are heading for the opening, presumably to overwinter in the cozy interior; similarly, he quotes sightings of great numbers of animals appearing from the north in springtime, heading south, fat and happy, as if from nowhere—returning, he knew, from their winter vacation below.

Georges Buffon, the celebrated French naturalist of the eighteenth century, is invoked by P. Clark in an 1873 *Atlantic Monthly* article, regarding his report that "immense shoals of herrings in good condition come down from the polar seas and are never known to return." This, Clark says, "renders the solution of the migration of fishes from the north more difficult. If they return [to the north] in the spring, why are they never observed as well as when they go south?" Clark, channeling Symmes, answers "that they make the annual circuit of the earth, over the exterior and interior surfaces and through both openings at the poles." They were making the same circuit suggested by Kircher two centuries earlier. Symmes and his supporters also note reports of great piles of driftwood found along the northern coasts of Iceland, Norway, and Siberia, which have "every appearance of a tropical production" and are taken to have been produced inside. And not just trees.

Clark again: "Vegetables of singular character, and flowers of peculiar fragrance and color, unknown to botanists, are sometimes found in this drift." The implication, of course, is that these mysterious specimens come from the paradise within.

Symmes, McBride, and others insist that the zone of fierce cold and ice near the poles is merely a frozen ring to be traversed. Beyond it, things warm up, and there is an open polar sea leading to the interior. Again, the anecdotal experiences of many explorers, both north and south, are offered as evidence—among them British explorer James Weddell, who did indeed encounter ice-free conditions on his third voyage into Antarctic waters in 1822–1824, which allowed him to penetrate to seventy-four degrees fifteen minutes south in the sea later named for him, beating Captain James Cook's 1774 record in the *Resolution* by more than three degrees. Clark, in his *Atlantic Monthly* article, offers this typical evidence: "One navigator, Captain Ross, when in high latitude beyond the verge, speaks of the Arctic Sea as being calm and clear of ice, while south of him was a wide belt of ice.[8] He describes the currents of air coming from the north as being so warm as to dissolve the snow and ice around him and far to the south."

This insistence on an open polar sea was far from being the private hobbyhorse of Symmes and his defenders. It had widespread currency, largely because people *wanted* it to be true. Others didn't add the imaginative twist about an interior world, but they believed, especially in regard to the Arctic, in part because it kept alive the old dream of a shortcut to Asia—the long sought Northwest or Northeast Passage, a dream that motivated explorers well into the middle of the nineteenth century. As late as 1873, P. Clark's article about Symmes in the *Atlantic Monthly* glibly states that "it is now generally conceded that a vast open ocean exists in the polar regions."

An open sea at the top of the world had been an appealing idea for hundreds of years. No one had actually seen this remote part of the earth, so why not a handy, easily navigated ocean? Greek mythology put the earthly paradise of

---

8. Sir John Ross, whose second arctic expedition (1829–33) in search of the Northwest Passage discovered and surveyed Boothia Peninsula and King William Island in Canada's Northwest Territories. His nephew, James Clark Ross, part of the expedition, located the north magnetic pole.

Hyperborea there, a warm, inviting place of perpetual sunshine hidden behind the back of Boreas, the North Wind, untouched by his chill. Apollo spent his winter vacations there. Even this seems an antecedent to Symmes' ideas, suggesting that the far north is somehow beyond the cold.

A Greek named Pytheas made the first recorded voyage to the north in the fourth century B.C.E. In a work since lost he told of an island six days' sail beyond England, on the Arctic Circle, which he called Thule. Though his accounts were later dismissed as fantasy, the idea of a fog-shrouded land at the end of the earth captured imaginations for centuries afterward. In the 1930s it was neatly folded into strange Nazi mythology about a pure Aryan homeland in the north (all that *white* probably attracted them).

The next known northward incursions came around 800 C.E. as Irish monks fled the marauding Vikings. They made their way north (possibly as far as Iceland and Greenland) to establish brooding monasteries on isolated windswept promontories, where they meditated and kept fragile hold on knowledge. They were

(above) Animals apparently migrating northward.
(*Harper's New Monthly Magazine*, 1882).

also searching for the Land of the Blessed, a mythical northern place where grapevines produced fruit twelve times a year, and there was peace—the unlimited grape supply (all that wine) arguably being as attractive as the idea of peace. One of those Vikings, Erik the Red, was the first colorful character associated with these northern lands. When he was banished from Iceland after killing some of his neighbors, Erik headed west and found a large barren island four hundred miles distant. He poked around there for a few years and then returned to Iceland in 985 with rosy upbeat real-estate-salesman accounts of the land he'd found (he was the first European to make landfall). With a true promoter's instinct, he named it Greenland. Twenty-five ships set out, and the fourteen that made it established a colony that lasted almost three hundred years, gradually dying off as Europe's Little Ice Age began in the fourteenth century. Erik's son, Leif Eriksson, was probably the first European to set foot on the North American continent about 1000 C.E., though some scholars dispute this.

The next round of northern exploration commenced within a few years of Columbus's epochal (if mistaken) voyage of 1492. As is well known, he was aiming for Cathay, the spices and other profitable exotica of the Orient. Instead he slammed into a New World quite inconveniently in the way. Dreaming of a passage to India, when he reached Cuba he was convinced it was mainland China and sent a full dress party that included an authorized representative of the pope into the interior expecting to find some grand city, and of course he insisted on calling the inhabitants Indians. This was the first attempt in an ultimately futile search that would last another 350 years for that tantalizing shortcut to Asia.

The idea of an open polar sea got a boost when Gerardus Mercator's revolutionary—and beautiful—world map appeared in 1569. It rendered the earthly sphere into rectangular grids for easier use by navigators, even though the proportions got pretty weird in the north and south, with Greenland looming like Godzilla over puny North America cringing beneath it, one-tenth its size. Showing the arctic regions according to this scheme proved impossible, so Mercator drew another map of the Arctic, from a point of view in outer space above the planet. He combined several traditional elements—including an open polar sea—primarily drawing on a fourteenth-century text, now lost, called *The Travels of Jacobus Cnoyen of Bois le Duc.* It contained a summary account of travels to the north by an English friar who had gone there for King Edward III and written a book about it, *Inventio Fortunatae,* also now lost. But Mercator read Cnoyen's book, and wrote a long letter about it to John Dee, Queen Elizabeth's astrologer, in which he says the friar, using "magical arts," claimed to have seen this utmost northerly place in 1360. The friar said that four arms of the sea rushed as torrential rivers between Arctic landmasses to form an ocean at the top of the world. These rivers crashed together at the pole, forming a terrible maelstrom that plunged into an abyss, the foaming water sucked down into the center of the earth. And so Mercator drew it in his polar map. Mercator places as his centerpiece at the pole a dark craggy rock—the legendary *Rupes Nigra* or Black Precipice, the lodestone mountain toward which all compasses presumably pointed.[9] The projection suggests a broken donut, with an inner sea as the hole and plenty of ocean space for navigation between the four northern landmasses and the known continents to the south. Thus his map of polar regions inadvertently served as an advertising poster for the open polar sea and a shortcut to Asia—and one that Symmes certainly knew.

Symmes insisted on this open sea for his own purposes, of course. It was additional "proof" of his polar openings and the idyllic interior that beckoned. But Symmes' polar dreams were in the mainstream zeitgeist. True, he took his polar fascination one toke over the line, but it was going around. A polar mania in the form of voyages of exploration, both north and south, reasserted itself after 1815 and was going full tilt when Symmes offered his theory to the world and himself as the leader of an arctic expedition. Symmes and his polar holes influenced thinking

---

9. Mercator wrote in a letter to John Dee, Queen Elizabeth I's astrologer: "In the midst of the four countries is a Whirlpool into which there empty these four Indrawing Seas which divide the North. And the water rushes round and descends into the earth just as if one were pouring it through a filter funnel. It is 4 degrees wide on every side of the Pole, that is to say eight degrees altogther. Except that right under the Pole there lies a bare rock in the midst of the Sea. Its circumference is almost 33 French miles, and it is all of magnetic stone. And is as high as the clouds, so the Priest said, [and] one can see all round it from the Sea, and that it is black and glistening."

about the hollow earth from then on. After Symmes, ideas about the hollow earth, in real life and in fiction, become inextricably linked with the poles and polar exploration, right down to the present.

Finding a shortcut to Asia from Europe through a Northwest Passage had initially appealed to the English because the known routes to the Orient—around Africa and South America—had been monopolized by the Spanish and Portuguese. Over time the monopoly crumbled, but dreams of finding the passage lived on. The pursuit of it took on a certain frenzy during Symmes' lifetime and must have

(above) Polar projection from Gerardus Mercator's revolutionary
world map. (Collection of The Map House of London)

contributed to his polar visions. Many of the polar "authorities" Symmes invokes in support of his theory were involved in seeking this icy grail.

The archipelago lying above the North American continent proved both tantalizing and maddening to these explorers. Around every cape might lie an open sea and a straight shot to Asia—or more bays that finally gave way to a shoreline, more large islands to navigate around, or a wall of ice. But great rewards lay at the end of the labyrinth if it could be found. The names of those who tried and failed ornament the map of northern Canada, a cartographical necropolis of brave futility. They include John Cabot, Jacques Cartier, Henry Hudson, and James Baffin.

Samuel Hearne, a Hudson's Bay Company employee who made several heroic treks through the Canadian north between 1769 and 1772, became the first European to walk overland from Hudson's Bay to the Arctic Ocean—and back!—thereby establishing that there was no sea passage through continental North America. His 1795 account of his adventures, *Journey from Prince of Wales Fort in Hudson's Bay to the Northern Ocean,* makes stirring reading even today, and is cited repeatedly by James McBride in support of Symmes' theory, particularly in regard to the abundance of wildlife Hearne encountered, taken as testimony of a mild interior where these creatures presumably overwintered.[10]

Noted naturalist Daines Barrington published *The Possibility of Approaching the North Pole Asserted* in 1775. It was reprinted with new material in 1818, the same year Symmes produced his first circular, and is another of the polar authorities McBride quotes in support of Symmes.[11]

In 1789 Alexander Mackenzie, working for the North West Company, rival to the Hudson's Bay Company, made an epic hike comparable to Hearne's

---

10. McBride in *The Theory of Concentric Spheres*: "Hearne, who travelled very high north and northwest on the continent of America, details various facts in his journal, which strongly corroborate Symmes's position . . . he states that large droves of *musk-oxen* abound within the arctic circle . . . white or arctic foxes are, some years, remarkably plentiful, and always come from the north. . . . We should conclude that the internal region of the earth is as much more favourable to the support of animal life, as the rein-deer is larger than our deer, and the white bear larger than our bear . . ."

11. McBride enlists the aid of the book half a dozen times, saying of it, "there is an extensive collection of instances cited, where navigators have reached high northern latitudes. . . . It is almost uniformly stated, that in those high latitudes, the sea is clear of ice, or nearly so, and the weather moderate."

nearly twenty years earlier, from Lake Athabaska in present northeastern Alberta, to Great Slave Lake, where he encountered the beginnings of the river now bearing his name, following it over five hundred miles northwest to its mouth in the Beaufort Sea, above the Arctic Circle. In 1793 he crossed the Canadian Rockies and reached the Pacific; both journeys provided further verification that no continental passage existed. His *Voyage from Montreal on the River St. Lawrence, Through the Continent of North America, to the Frozen and Pacific Oceans, in the Years 1789 and 1793* was published in 1801, yet another resource McBride picked over in defending Symmes.[12]

Exploration of the far north had almost died out in the early nineteenth century—until about the same time Symmes published Circular 1. Oddly, renewed interest in the Arctic resulted from the end of the Napoleonic Wars and the January 1815 Treaty of Ghent, which concluded the American–British War of 1812. In fighting these wars on almost worldwide fronts, the British had built up a huge naval fleet with hundreds of ships and thousands of sailors. Suddenly they had no one to fight. The result was massive layoffs (just as Symmes had been mustered out shortly after war's end), officers reduced to half pay, and a splendid fleet lying idle. What to do with all those ships and well-trained officers? Second Secretary of the Admiralty John Barrow had a plan to keep at least some of them busy. Arguing that unlocking the secrets of the north had virtually become a matter of British honor, Barrow set several expeditions in motion that began a renewed effort that ended in 1854 with the first successful navigation of the Northwest Passage, 350 years after the first attempts. However, the route was so far north that it was useless commercially. Barrow, also a founder of the Royal Geographic Society, proselytized for and hyped this ambitious enterprise. In 1818 his *A chronological history of voyages into the Arctic regions; undertaken chiefly for the purpose of discovering a north-east, north-west, or polar passage between the Atlantic and Pacific: from the earliest periods of Scandinavian navigation, to the departure of the recent expeditions* appeared and sold rapidly.

---

12. Arguing Symmes' case for greater refraction of light in polar regions, McBride quotes Mackenzie in a footnote as stating "'that sometimes the land *looms*, so that there may be a great deception in the distances.' —*Mackenzie's Voyage*, p.11, New York, 1802."

Four Royal Navy ships left England in April 1818—the same month Symmes began handing out his circular, offering to lead his own polar expedition— two in search of the Northwest Passage and two in an effort to reach the pole. Commander David Buchan headed the polar voyage, which was a complete bust. North of Spitsbergen they ran into horrific winds and wall-to-wall pack ice. They were back in London drinking hot toddies by October. The other expedition, led by Captain John Ross and Lieutenant William Parry, made some headway, though the explorers turned around for home due to what proved to be a major delusion on Ross's part. The well-outfitted ships reached the west coast of Greenland by June, rediscovering Baffin Bay and naming Melville Bay just south of Thule. In early August, in far northwestern Greenland, they came upon a small band of Inuits, who were moved and amazed at these majestic creatures—the ships, which the Inuits were convinced must be alive. Awestruck, curious, they approached and addressed the ships, asking them, "Who are you? Where do you come from? Is it from the sun or the moon?" A crew member who spoke their language tried to explain. "They are houses made of wood." The Inuit refused to believe him, saying, "No, they are alive, we have seen them move their wings."[13] It is the most touching passage in all the arctic annals.

These were just the beginning of a succession of voyages mounted by the Royal Navy for the next three decades. Symmes must have ground his teeth in frustration at being left out of all this arctic exploration, to be on the sidelines watching. He was in many ways simply a product of the times, as things polar had captured the popular imagination. Eleanor Ann Porden, on meeting John Franklin aboard his ship just before his first voyage, was moved to lyrical ecstasies, publishing *The Arctic Expeditions: A Poem* in 1818. So moved, in fact, that on his return, she married him. In Scotland, a billboard-sized panorama—those scenic paintings on a roll that were slowly unspooled in theaters to music and commentary, a low-tech precursor to the movies—called *The Arctic* was playing to a packed house in Glasgow,

---

13. This story appears in *A Fabulous Kingdom: The Exploration of the Arctic* by Charlies Officer and Jake Page (New York: Oxford University Press, 2001).

described as *Messrs. Marshall's grand peristrephic panorama of the polar regions,*
which displays the north coast of Spitzbergen, Baffin's Bay, Arctic Highlands, &c. : now
exhibiting in the large new circular wooden building, George's Square, Glasgow: painted
from drawings taken by Lieut. Beechey, who accompanied the polar expedition in 1818;
and Messrs. Ross and Saccheuse, who accompanied the expedition to discover a northwest
passage. Journals and memoirs by arctic explorers became a growth industry in
Symmes' lifetime, and they must have rankled. What to do? Try even harder to get
that expedition going.

Symmes left St. Louis in 1819. The country was experiencing its first serious economic depression, remembered as the Panic of 1819, a postwar slump compounded by a flaky unregulated banking system and greatly reduced foreign
commerce. He gave up on Indian trading and moved his family to Newport, Kentucky, just across the Ohio River from Cincinnati. There is no information about
what he did for a living there during the two years before he hit the lecture trail,
how he supported that crowd of children. McBride says that he completely occupied himself with working out his theory.

He had already gained a bit of a reputation. Some zealous heartland
boosters, eager to claim the frontier contained more than yahoos and grifters,
had taken to calling him "Newton of the West." He could be found some days at
the new Western Museum in Cincinnati, hanging out with other esteemed scientists including John James Audubon, who worked there briefly and made a sketch
of Symmes in 1820 for *Western Magazine.* In it he sits sideways at a table salted
with several scientific instruments and a journal, a few fat volumes on a shelf,
and a large globe with the North Pole cut off behind him. He wears a dark frock
coat and a lighter collared vest, collar up, his thinning black hair combed forward to
combat a deeply receding hairline, nose a little pointy, eyes a little squinty, brows
beetley, mouth a little soft. He radiates a certain innocence and otherworldliness.
Symmes shared Audubon's interest in birds. He wrote a note for the *National*
Intelligencer in 1820 about purple martins, largest of the American swallows, whose

nests were everywhere in Cincinnati, so they clearly "delight in the society of man," but they "migrate in a peculiar manner. It appears to be unknown from whence they come, and whither they go." His speculation was that they migrated to somewhere else that people congregated.[14] Naturally he had a plan to find out— by banding them.

Birds had been banded for centuries. A falcon of French King Henry IV's is the first on record, lost in 1595, turning up a day later in Malta, 1,350 miles away. Audubon had been the first in America to do so, tying silver cords to the legs of fledgling phoebes in Philadelphia in 1803 and identifying a few when they returned the next year. Symmes gave specifics about these martin bands: they should contain the date and "a rough drawing of a ship, with the national flag, and drawings of some of the animals of the climate, as a sort of universal language; also, a request for the reader to attach a similar label about the time of the return of the birds in the spring, and to publish the circumstance in a newspaper of the country. If we do not by such means learn, soon or late, where the martins go, it will be inferable that they go to some unlettered people or unknown country." Sly old Symmes. What unknown country and what unlettered people? He adds, "The more reasons we find for presuming there are unknown countries, the more we will be disposed to exert ourselves in research." Even sitting on the porch of the Western Museum, idly musing on where martins go in winter, his thoughts turned ever back to the hollow earth.

During this time in Newport, 1819–1820, he did accomplish one thing, and it was, in its way, a landmark, though one quickly forgotten. He wrote a novel called *Symzonia: Voyage of Discovery*. It bore the byline Captain Adam Seaborn, but is universally attributed to Symmes. Seaborn calls the land he discovers inside the earth Symzonia. Lavish praise is heaped on Symmes throughout ("That profound philosopher, John Cleve Symes"). The novel seems a long, sweet dream by Symmes of what he might find and accomplish if only he were permitted to do so. But it is more than that. According to Victoria Nelson in her 1997 *Raritan* article,

---

14. In fact most martins winter in South America, from southeastern Brazil as far west as Colombia.

"Symmes Hole, Or the South Polar Romance," *Symzonia* was the very first American utopian novel.

All utopian novels ultimately derive from Plato's *Republic*, but the term comes from Thomas More's *Utopia*—which means Nowhere—published in 1516. Between More and Symmes, many dozens of utopian fictions and treatises had been inflicted on an imperfect world. A *selective* New York Public Library bibliography lists 153 of them as appearing between 1516 and 1820. But *Symzonia* seems to be the first homegrown American utopian fiction.

It wasn't the first fiction set in subterranean realms. There had been a scattering of these during the eighteenth century, from several countries. The earliest was *Relation d'un voyage du pole arctique au pole antarctique* (1721), which recounts a Kircherean roller-coaster ride on a whaling ship sucked into a vortex somewhere north of Greenland, racing through the watery bowels of the earth from North to South Pole, where an extraordinary island floating under the Antarctic is found. Luxuriant vegetation reigns among warm-water lakes and waterfalls; the voyagers witness battles between polar bears and seals, encounter giant fish, a volcano, a pyramid with fiery reflections, and a structure of white stones before setting sail for the Cape of Good Hope. Another French novel, *Lamekis, ou les voyages extraodinaires d'un egyptien dans la terre interieure* (1734), took its characters to a roomy subterranean world beneath Egypt.

In 1741 came the first novel of an underworld with real literary merit, Baron Ludvig Holberg's *Journey of Niels Klim to the World Underground.* The preeminent Scandanavian writer of the Enlightenment, Holberg is claimed by both Denmark and Norway as a literary great. *Niels Klim,* first written in Latin, owes a considerable debt to *Gulliver's Travels* in spirit and shape. Niels enters a cavern and falls toward the center of the earth, thinking as he drops,

> I fell to imagining that I was sunk into the subterranean world, and that
> the conjectures of those men are right who hold the Earth to be hollow,
> and that within the shell or outward crust there is another lesser globe,

and another firmament adorned with lesser sun, stars, and planets. And the event discovered that this conjecture was right.

Instead of falling all the way, he finds himself suspended in orbit. On consideration, he decides that's fine—as a heavenly body he "would surely move with equal solemnity to a famished philosopher." But then a flying monster approaches, a menacing griffin a little like the one that gives Dante a ride in the *Inferno*. "So great was my terror that, unmindful of my starry dignity to which I was newly advanced, in that disorder of my soul I drew out my university testimonial, which I happened to have in my pocket, to signify to this terrible adversary that I had passed my academical examination, that I was a graduate student, and could plead the privilege of my university against anyone who should attack me." Niels' jaunty insouciance gives the novel considerable charm, though it suffers from the defect common to all utopian fiction: the story repeatedly stops dead in its tracks to explain one or another set of customs. Niels harpoons the griffin and both fall to the planet Nazar below, where he is bothered by a bull and climbs a tree to get away. The "tree" proves to be the wife of the chief magistrate in a nearby city, and Niels finds himself jailed for assault. The creatures are cousin to those in the Forest of Suicides in the *Inferno*—trees with human heads on top and little feet on which they creep about. Nazar is a topsy-turvy utopia, or rather a bunch of them, where prevailing values on the surface are overturned. Niels spends much of the book traveling from country to country, each one devoted to its particular idée fixe. The novel adds Holberg's voice to those of Montesquieu and Voltaire in their battle against religious fanaticism, the pious persecution and torture it leads to, doing so with humor, as Klim travels round the planet and encounters countries where the authorities cruelly suppress divergent views. The novel was quickly translated into French, English, German, Dutch, and Danish.

A whimsical sort-of-subterranean English novel, *The Life and Adventures of Peter Wilkins* by Robert Paltock, published in 1751, is, as a contemporary critic grumped in the *Monthly Review,* "the illegitimate offspring of no very natural conjunction betwixt Gulliver's travels and Robinson Crusoe; but much inferior to the meaner of these two performances, either as to entertainment or utility. It has all that is impossible in the one, or improbable in the other, without the wit and spirit of the first, or the just strokes of nature and useful lessons of morality of the second." Paltock probably figured that stealing from two best sellers at once doubled his chances at a hit, and *Peter Wilkins* has a certain mutant appeal. After seducing and marrying a servant girl—there are touches of *Tom Jones*, published two years earlier, as well—Wilkins signs on a ship, is taken as a slave by Portuguese in Angola, escapes with a resourceful black fellow slave, and has many adventures in Africa before stealing a ship with other English refugees.

They become lost sailing south, where the ship, reaching the Antarctic, is inexorably attracted to a black lodestone mountain—the looming shadow of Mercator—and all but Wilkins are swept overboard. He begins exploring in a smaller boat, which is caught in a current and yanked down the drain of a maelstrom, bobbing up into an enormous underground cavern. Coming upon a small island, he sets up housekeeping à la Crusoe. Far luckier than Crusoe, who had only unsexy Friday for company, Wilkins meets one of the locals, a beautiful winged young woman with skin like the down of a swan. They marry, after a fashion, and live together for many years as a happy couple, raising several children, until she decides to visit her family. Wilkins helps the king thwart a plot to overthrow him, asking as reward that slavery be abolished and reading introduced to the peasantry—a little utopian nod here at the end. At the last, his wife dead, Wilkins old, he begins longing for England. Borne aloft, homeward, by winged bearers, he is unceremoniously dropped into the sea when a passing ship fires a cannon at this unlikely sight and frightens them off.

Easily the oddest of these eighteenth-century subterranean novels, not to say the creepiest, is Jacques Casanova's five-volume *Icosameron*, published in 1788 and running to a little over 1,800 pages. The novel recounts the experiences of a teenage brother and sister who fall into the earth's interior through a watery abyss. There they find an inner world inhabited by many-colored hermaphroditic dwarves called Megamicres, who live in a color-coded social hierarchy with the red ones at the top of the heap. Their primary method of eating consists of sucking on each other's breasts. They're also nudists. Edward and Elizabeth promptly rip off their own clothes, declare themselves married, and set about propagating as fast as they can. Each year during their eighty-one-year stay, Elizabeth gives birth to twins, who in turn marry at age twelve and begin having their own twins. Finally Ed and Liz make their way back to London, leaving behind millions of offspring. Not only do they cause a population glut down there, they screw up a previously balanced society in other ways as well, introducing gunpowder and war, among other things.

Symzonia, published in 1820, was the first American hollow earth novel and set the pattern for many that followed, right down to the present. It established the usual structure for such books—the trip to the pole, discovery of a land and people/creatures inside, adventures and revelations while there, and a return home, usually to ridicule and disbelief. Later books described alarming dystopias down there, but *Symzonia* is a voyage into a utopian world—serving as a vehicle for social commentary as well as a 248-page ad for Symmes' theories. He begins:

> In the year 1817, I projected a voyage of discovery, in the hope of finding a passage to a new and untried world. I flattered myself that I should open the way to new fields for the enterprise of my fellow-citizens, supply new sources of wealth, fresh food for curiosity, and additional means of enjoyment; objects of vast importance, since the resources of the known world have been exhausted by research, its wealth monopolized, its wonders of curiosity explored, its every thing investigated and understood!

Far from being some pointless ethereal scheme, his reason for going is pragmatic, useful, and filled with the potential for profit. Symmes succinctly expresses the spirit of the times. One by one the great mysteries of the physical world were being figured out, the earth revealing its last geographical secrets. The poles, a few tangled, uncharted jungles here and there, the odd undiscovered island, were all that remained to be explored—or claimed by some country or other. Even the vast expanse of the American continent was filling up at a dizzying rate. Only three states had been added to the original thirteen by 1800, but by 1820 seven more had joined the ranks, with troublesome Missouri to be added in 1821—all of them, with the exception of Maine, carved out of what had been Indian land and

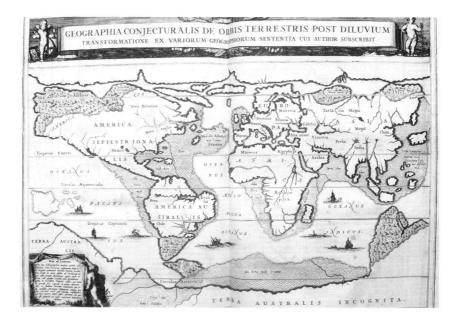

wilderness at the time of the American Revolution. Symmes had seen this happening firsthand after the War of 1812, with swarm after swarm of western settlers using St. Louis as their jumping-off point. One way of viewing this—as Symmes clearly did—was as ever-diminishing possibilities for great blue sky opportunity.

(above) World map from Athansius Kircher's *Mundus subterraneus* (1665) showing Terra Australis. (Mineralogical Institute, University of Würzburg, Germany)

The earth's interior promised virgin land, ripe fruit waiting to be plucked, an unclaimed Eden, and no competition.

Seaborn has invented a new sort of vessel for his voyage to the South Pole. Certain he will encounter that open polar sea near the verge, he also knows he'll have to penetrate the "icy hoop" barrier that will come first. His novel steamboat has a specially reinforced frame and powerful slanted paddlewheels capable of churning through the ice. This is a nice Yankee-ingenuity touch. Steamboats were ultramodern craft when Symmes was writing. Robert Fulton's experiments had introduced the first regularly scheduled steamboat between New York and Albany in 1807, cutting what had been a four-day trip to thirty-two hours. By an interesting coincidence, Symmes had a front-row view of Fulton's next effort, a steamboat built in Pittsburgh in 1811, which began regular service between New Orleans and Natchez in 1812, routinely chugging past the river forts where Symmes was stationed. But Seaborn's steamboat also has a design element that's a bow to the mythical past—no iron in the construction. "I remembered the misfortune of the discoverer SINBAD, whose ship, when he approached the magnetic mountain, fell to pieces," he explains, so Seaborn uses only "tree-nails" and copper bolts. It's an odd detail, in that Symmes/Seaborn goes to considerable lengths to seem scientific throughout, and suggests the power this ancient idea apparently still had.

In recruiting his crew, Seaborn wisely neglects to mention that he's planning a cruise *inside* the earth; instead he signs them on for a three- or four-year term on "a sealing voyage in the South Seas." Even though Symmes' real plans related to an expedition to the northern polar opening, he aims for the southern one in the novel. He probably did so because his story would seem less fantastical set there, since less was known about it.

Captain James Cook had made a couple of swipes at the Antarctic during his voyages of 1768–1771 and 1772–1775, seeking to prove or disprove the idea of a Terra Australis, the great theoretical southern continent placed on a map by Ptolemy and kept there by succeeding generations of cartographers, though no one had ever seen it. On January 17, 1773, Cook became the first to cross the Antarctic Circle but was stopped by an ice pack without seeing land. He did see one thing that prompted further exploration: seals beyond counting on the forbidding island of South Georgia, a thousand miles east of South America's southern tip, its dark barren mountains half buried in glaciers, an island Edmond Halley had seen in 1700 while mapping magnetic variation aboard the *Paramour*.[15] In the years after Cook's sighting, slaughter followed knowledge. The pursuit of seals led to more and more incursions into these "inexpressibly horrid regions," as Cook characterized them in his journal. Despite great hardship and danger, the smell of profit lured the sealers ever deeper into the southern ocean. Whales drew them as well. European and American homes were brightened at night by whale-oil lamps, and the northern whale fisheries were getting fished out. So the rush south was on. But these sealer/whalers weren't scientific explorers, ready to share the geographical details they were learning; to the contrary, they tried to keep their discoveries secret. The sealers especially, since their dumb wholesale methods—finding an island covered with seals, they would wipe out the entire population before moving on—required locating ever new sealing grounds among the more than two hundred islands strewn east and south of Tierra del Fuego.[16]

In masking his quest as a sealing voyage, Symmes was both timely and strategic. *Symzonia* is an early specimen of American sea fiction, preceding James Fenimore Cooper's *The Pilot* by three years. As the *Explorer* heads south, Symmes works hard at making the voyage realistic, providing specific detail that rings true. Until they reach the ice barrier, *Symzonia* might be another of the many seagoing

---

15. Today 95% of the world's southern fur seals—upwards of a million—jam South Georgia in summer, along with half the southern elephant seals, a quarter-million albatrosses, and penguins numbering in the millions.

16. As Walker Chapman writes in *The Loneliest Continent:* "Sealing was a brutal, cold-blooded operation, and the men who manned the ships were the toughest to go to sea since the days of the Elizabethan buccaneers. Sailing in ice-filled seas, gliding between uncharted rocks hidden by mist and snow, they made their landings on lonely, barren islands where thousands of friendly, harmless seals had come to mate. The seals offered no defense as the sealers went among them, clubbing them to death. The men worked caked with grease, wading in rivers of blood. It was cruel work, and attracted cruel men. . . . Island after island was stripped of its seals. One sealing vessel alone killed 100,000 seals in five years."

journals that had been published over the years. They round Cape St. Roche, put in at Rio for provisions, and then stop for a month at the Falkland Islands, where Seaborn says he needs to recover "from the debility occasioned by the vexations and anxieties of business in these retrograde times"—might Symmes be thinking about his struggle to make a living trading with the Indians?—"and the pernicious habits of living, common among civilized men, upon food rendered palatable by a skilful admixture of poisons." While cleaning up his system—to "regain the firm health so necessary to a man who undertakes great things," he explains, modestly—Seaborn does a bit of touristic exploring of these wild dramatic islands, pronouncing them "salubrious." A sealing party is dropped off on one of the outlying Jason Islands. When Seaborn returns two days later, he says, approvingly, that they had made good use of their time, "having cleared this island and all the neighboring keys . . . of the few seal which could be found." They're scarce because of other sealers before them. But no worries—there are many more farther south:

> I concurred in the opinion published by Capt. Symmes, that seals, whales, and mackerel, come from the internal world through the openings at the poles; and was aware of the fact, that the nearer we approach those openings, the more abundant do we find seals and whales. I felt perfectly satisfied that I had only to find an opening in the "icy hoop," through which I could dash with my vessel, to discover a region where seals could be taken as fast as they could be stripped and cured.

There's a huge colony here of Gentoo penguins (distinguished by a white head stripe from eye to eye, a red-orange beak and feet), whose eggs are just waiting to be stolen and packed into salt barrels, tasty bar snacks for the trip. Symmes, revealing his inner birdwatcher, goes on for several pages about the Gentoo's characteristics and habits, saying, "the contemplation of these orderly, discreet, and beautiful am-phibia, afforded me much pleasure, and gave rise to many delightful anticipations."

He's certain they're "visiters [*sic*] from the internal world." He notes their "remarkably gentle and harmless disposition," from which "I inferred that the inhabitants of the internal world . . . must be of a remarkably pacific, and gentle disposition."

The restorative month of R & R over, they're once more heading south. They cruise by South Georgia Island but don't stop because Seaborn is itching to get to the "verge." He takes this interval as an opportunity to anticipate what they'll find, per Symmes' theories, of course. How seven months of sunlight and that greater refraction will make the pole warm. "I think if we can but find our way to the polar region, we shall be in much more danger of being roasted alive, than of being frozen to death." Many of the crew buy into this, but Symmes provides his narrative with that most useful of stock characters, the grumbling doubter, in the form of Mr. Slim. He's not having any. All previous expeditions have been stopped by *ice*, dammit! Seaborn explains at great length why, according to "that profound philosopher, John Cleve Symmes," the "icy hoop" exists, and why he is certain that beyond it lies smooth sailing—the only trick is finding a way through. "We shipped with you, sir," cries Slim, "for a sealing voyage; not for a voyage of discovery. You have no right to hazard our lives." Slim says that even if we get through the icy hoop, what if we can't get back? "We must in such a case all perish, and our blood would be upon your head."

Seaborn wisely forbears telling Slim his real purpose, "of my belief of open poles, affording a practicable passage to the internal world, and of my confident expectations of finding comfortable winter quarters inside; for he would take that as evidence of my being insane." That he would—just as most people did on hearing Symmes' theories. Slim isn't satisfied, and soon he's busy drumming up interest in a mutiny. But just as they confront Seaborn, land is sighted, a large island crawling with seals. Its lee side provides a permanent break in the icy hoop. Seeing this, Slim backs down—for the moment. By acclaim this new country is named Seaborn's Land. "The existence of a continent near the south pole, was thus fully established." Chalk up another of the world's mysteries solved by Seaborn. Two parties go ashore,

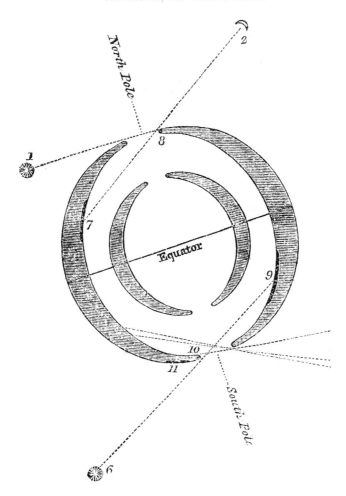

SECTIONAL VIEW OF THE EARTH.

SHOWING THE

OPENINGS AT THE POLES.

Map of the interior world from the original 1820 edition of *Symzonia*.

one to spend several days exploring, the other to start sealing. When the exploring party gets back, having found timber, a mighty river, and a strange, enormous animal, the sealers have already racked up seven thousand skins and counting. Before leaving, Seaborn formally claims his new country for the United States. The claiming ceremony is all-American. He draws up a manifesto proclaiming that on November 5, 1817, he "did first see and discover this southern continent." But then to assure permanency, "I had it engraved on a plate of sheathing copper, with a spread eagle at the top, and at the bottom a bank, with 100 dollar bills tumbling out of its doors and windows, to denote the amazing quantity and solidity of the wealth of my country."

All who can be spared go ashore, taking musical instruments, two pieces of cannon, wine, and grog. They bury the copper plate, covering it with a large stone engraved with "Seaborn's Land, A.D. 1817," put up a "liberty pole," and Seaborn orders "a salute to be fired of one gun for every State." What follows is a light commentary on the galloping Union circa 1820:

> "How many will that be, sir?" asked Mr. Boneto, adding, that they came so fast he could not keep the run of them. Slim said it was twenty-one. I objected to that number, as being the royal salute of Great Britain, and settled the matter by telling them to fire away until they were tired of it, and finish off with a few squibs for the half-made states.

Then it's on to the interior. Because the declivity of the "verge" is so gradual, the crew at first doesn't realize they're steaming into the interior world, and Seaborn is keeping his mouth shut. "No one knew which way we were steering but myself." They lose sight of land, the compass goes crazy, and the sun sets briefly, causing alarm among the crew, but "the weather had been for some days so hot that a little night was very desirable." They are inside. "We continued running due north, *internal,* three days." At last, on November 28, they discover land, but to Seaborn's disappointment, it is an island inhabited only by "terrapins of a monstrous size, some few seals, penguins, and numerous sea fowl." But no people. "The great number of turtles was satisfactory evidence to my mind, that there were no human beings on the island." Had there been, he implies without elaborating, all the turtles would have been eaten.

The crew is delighted and "complained of nothing but the excessive heat." It's almost too much for Seaborn. "The next morning I was quite sick, in consequence of the heat." It becomes almost a running gag in this section, Symmes rubbing in the idea that it's really warm at the pole. How hot is it? Seaborn becomes alarmed that the "excessive heat" may put them all in "great danger of the yellow fever making its appearance." Reasoning that things will get cooler the farther in they go, he's preparing to move on as fast as possible when the remains of a ship are discovered, a "wreck of some outlandish vessel" put together using "a white elastic wire" of an unknown substance. Seaborn plucks out some samples of "this singular material" and with them "fired the imagination of my people, by representing to them the enormous wealth we should acquire, could we obtain a cargo of it to carry to our country, where it would be more valuable than silver; and that the use to which it was applied was sufficient evidence of its being abundant where this vessel was built." Even if this is a ruse to calm the fearful crew by filling their heads with money, the mental leap from finding the elastic wire to visions of its profit potential is immediate and seamless.

For a week they cruise farther into the interior, when Slim has another go at mutiny. We must be in some great hole in the earth, and the sun will disappear entirely—we will be engulfed in total darkness and never find our way out again! We have to turn back to Seaborn Land! If you refuse, we will throw you overboard! But Seaborn plays hard poker with them. If you do, he asks, who among you can find his way back? Oops. He assures them that he has no desire to perish in a sea of darkness either, that if they press on they can winter in a region far more pleasant than Seaborn's Land. Let's give it another two weeks; if we find nothing, we'll turn back. But "should they persist in their mutinous course, I would break my instruments, throw my books overboard, and leave them to help themselves as they could." All relent, Slim still grumbling.

Five days later they see a strange, five-masted ship and follow it into port. As the light is fading, Seaborn decides to anchor offshore until morning. Through his telescope he can see "buildings and moving objects on the land, which assured me that the country was inhabited." Seaborn is nearly giddy with anticipation. He reflects:

> I was about to reach the goal of all my wishes; to open an intercourse with a new world and with an unknown people; to unfold to the vain mortals of the external world new causes for the admiration of the infinite diversity and excellence of the works of an inscrutable Deity.

But then Symmes pulls back the curtain a little too far, revealing more than really might have been prudent, if understandable given the ridicule he suffered:

> I was about to secure to my name a conspicuous and imperishable place on the tablets of History, and a niche of the first order in the temple of Fame. I moved like one who trod on air; for whose achievements had equalled mine? The voyage of Columbus was but an excursion on a fish pond, and his discoveries, compared with mine, were but trifles . . . His was the discovery of a continent, mine of a new World . . . I compared my doings and my sensations with those of that swarm of sordid beings who waste their lives in Wall-street, or in the purlieus of the courts intent on gain, and scrambling for the wrecks of the property of their unfortunate fellow beings, or hiring out the efforts of their minds to perform such loathsome work as their employers would pay them for;—men who feel themselves ennobled by their wealth; who think themselves superior to

the useful classes of society; from whom I had often heard the scornful observation, "he is nothing but a shipmaster."

This seems an outpouring straight from Symmes' poor neglected heart, hidden away here deep in his manuscript. But if this is the prideful bitter nighttime of his soul, the next chapter opens with a sunrise, and with it a far rosier outlook. He awakes to see

> gently rolling hills within an easy sloping shore, covered with verdure, checquered with groves of trees and shrubbery, studded with numerous white buildings, and animated with groups of men and cattle, all standing in relief near the foot of a lofty mountain, which in the distance reared its majestic head above the clouds . . . here there was nothing wanting to a perfect landscape.

It's a scene that could have been lifted directly from Thomas Jefferson's dreams, an ideal pastoral nineteenth-century vista. And even before setting foot there, unconcerned that the locals might possibly have their own name for their country, Seaborn immediately christens it Symzonia, "out of gratitude to Capt. Symmes for his sublime theory." Can anyone doubt that Symmes wrote this?

Seaborn puts on his "best go-ashore clothes," and with the "stripes and stars waving over the stern of the boat," he goes to meet the Symzonians. Up until this point, *Symzonia* has been a passable adventure story; but now it becomes a utopian fiction, with all the attendant pitfalls—tedious patches devoted to a faux anthropological look at the perfect Symzonian society. The story grinds to a halt as we learn far more about their customs than we really need. Much of it seems inspired by Thomas More's *Utopia* (1516).

For an ideal people, they're a little short, averaging five feet tall. But they're tremendously athletic, able to leap thirty feet at a single bound—probably because of their natural, healthy diet, being strict vegetarians and teetotalers. True to the universal racism of the time, their utopian skin is whiter than white—fair-colored Seaborn resembles the "sootiest African" by comparison. Of course they're all handsome and beautiful. And they generally live to be two hundred years old. The Symzonian form of government is pure democracy, and the society is an uncorrupted meritocracy.

Seaborn's reaction to all this seems worth quoting at length, as it represents Symmes' critique of America at the time:

> This state of things appeared to me at first to be beyond the limits of possibility in the external world. . . . My mind was for some time occupied by reflecting upon the extraordinary difference in the *natural* condition of the internals and externals. . . . I perceived that the greater part of the labour of the externals was devoted to the production of things useless or pernicious; and that of the things produced or acquired, the distribution, through defects in our social organization, was so unequal, that some few destroyed, without any increase of happiness to themselves, the products of the toil of multitudes. . . . Instead of devoting our time to useful purposes, and living temperately on the wholesome gifts of Providence, like the blest internals, so as to preserve our health and strengthen our minds, thousands of us are employed in producing inebriating liquors, by the destruction of wholesome articles of food, to poison the bodies, enervate the minds, and corrupt the hearts of our fellow beings. Other thousands waste their strength to procure stimulating weeds and narcotic substances from the extreme parts of the earth, for the purpose of exciting diseased appetites. . . . Still greater numbers give their industry and their lives to the acquistion of mere matters of ornament, for the gratification of pride, an insatiable passion, which is only stimulated to increase its demands with every new indulgence. . . . I saw that the internals owed their happiness to their rationality, to a conformity with

the laws of nature and religion; and that the externals were miserable, from the indulgence of inordinate passions, and subjection to vicious propensities.

But even Symzonia isn't entirely perfect. They do have their occasional criminals and degenerates. What do they do with them? Exile them to a far land near the northern polar opening, where they grow darker from the sun and become larger due to their gross habits. You guessed it. In ancient times, groups of them wandered over the rim onto the External world, and all of us are the descendents of these debased outcast misfits—thus all the rotten behavior prevailing out here on our side.

Soon the Symzonians conclude that they have to get rid of these Externals, lest their edenic society be infected by them. How do they decide this might happen? By reading our world's great literature! Seaborn has brought along all sorts of books—including the complete Shakespeare and Milton's *Paradise Lost*. The Symzonians have translated them into their own language, studied them carefully, and decided that the Externals are hopelessly corrupt. So Seaborn & Co. are peacefully 86'd and sent on their way. Rather than head home empty-handed, while still in the southern polar regions, they slaughter 100,000 seals for their skins, sail to Canton, exchange them there for "China trade" goods, which they bring home, sell, and become rich—briefly. Seaborn's broker cheats him and goes under, and he's broke, so he writes the book in hopes of recouping his losses via a best seller. It didn't work.

Few copies of *Symzonia* were sold, but still he kept at it. Little had changed since that first circular in 1818, which he delivered "to every learned institution and to every considerable town and village, as well as to numerous distinguished individuals, throughout the United States, and sent copies to several of the learned societies of Europe," according to the 1882 *History and Biographical Cyclopedia of Butler County Ohio*.[17] "It was overwhelmed with ridicule as the production of a distempered imagination," the entry continues, "or the result of partial insanity. It was for many years a fruitful source of jest with the newspapers. The scientific papers of Europe generally treated it as a hoax, rather than believe that any sane man could issue such a circular or uphold such a theory." Even so, Symmes continued to produce circulars and publish newspaper articles, and he wrote *Symzonia* as well. These seem only to have compounded the ridicule, but he wouldn't quit.

Writing about it didn't put his theory over, so in 1820, Symmes began lecturing. Probably no would-be public lecturer was ever worse equipped to do so. A contemporary said of him, "His voice is somewhat nasal, and he speaks hesitatingly, and with apparent labor."[18] A 1909 article by John Weld Peck in the *Ohio Archaeological and Historical Quarterly* says, "As a lecturer he was far from a success. The arrangement of his subject was illogical, confused, and dry, and his delivery was poor." Peck adds, "However, his earnestness and the interesting novelty of his subject secured him attentive audiences wherever he spoke." Train wrecks always draw crowds. Even his friend James McBride, in the biographical sketch appended to his book on Symmes' theory, admits his deficiencies.

> Captain Symmes's want of a classical education, and philosophic attainments, perhaps, unfits him for the office of a lecturer. But, his arguments being presented in confused array, and clothed in homely phraseology, can furnish no objection to the soundness of his doctrines. The imperfection of his style, and the inelegance of his manner, may be deplored; but, certainly, constitute no proof of the inadequacy of his reasoning, or the absurdity of his deductions.

Symmes began this unfortunate enterprise with lectures in Cincinnati and Hamilton, Ohio—his eventual home and burial place. Then for the next several

---

17. *A History and Biographical Cyclopaedia of Butler County Ohio, With Illustrations and Sketches of its Representative Men and Pioneers* (Cincinnati, Ohio: Western Biographical Publishing Company, 1882). This book is available online at http://www.rootsweb.com/~ohbutler/cyc/.

18. Quoted without naming the source in "Symmes and His Theory," by E. F. Madden, *Harper's New Monthly Magazine.* October, 1882: 740–744.

years he took the show on the road, lecturing wherever they'd have him, dragging along a globe customized to demonstrate his polar openings. These appearances seem painful even to contemplate.

In 1822 Symmes petitioned Congress to equip an expedition, with him as leader, to either of the poles to locate the opening there, urging both the great profit and glory that would derive from it. Somehow he persuaded Kentucky senator Richard M. Johnson to present it. After a few remarks the petition was permanently tabled. He tried again in December 1823, asking for an expedition to test the "new theory of the earth," adding that, theory or not, "there appear to be many extraordinary circumstances, or phenomena, pervading the Arctic and Antarctic regions,

(above) John Cleves Symmes' globe. (The Academy of Natural Sciences of Philadelphia)

which strongly indicate something beyond the Polar circles worthy of our attention and research." This met with similar result. In January 1824 he petitioned the Ohio General Assembly to pass a motion approving his theory and to "recommend him to Congress for an outfit suitable to the enterprise," according to the *Butler County* history. "On motion, the further consideration thereof was indefinitely postponed." Then in 1825, hearing of an arctic expedition the Russians were about to mount, he applied through the American minister to go along; approval was granted, but with no money attached, and he couldn't afford to do so—yet another disappointment in a life full of them.

He did make one notable convert in his lifetime—Jeremiah Reynolds. Nearly twenty years younger than Symmes, Reynolds had grown up in southwestern Ohio, attended Ohio University without quite getting a degree, and was editing the *Wilmington Spectator,* a paper he had started in that small Ohio city, when he met Symmes in 1824. He was so taken with his theory of concentric spheres that he quit his job to join Symmes on tour as a co-lecturer. Given his subsequent career, one has to wonder about his sincerity in this, whether he might not have simply been looking for the main chance, a way out of a small-potatoes job in a small-potatoes town. He's an intriguing figure, a major footnote in American literature due to his later influence on both Poe and Melville.

Reynolds, a natural promoter and entrepreneur, seems to have persuaded the reluctant, stay-at-home Symmes that they needed to take the show on the road, to embark on a national lecture tour to promote his theory. They set out lecturing together in September 1825, starting with a few dates in Pennsylvania.[19] Where Symmes was halting, often seeming confused, his new partner generally wowed skeptical audiences who had come to scoff. In Chambersburg, the editor of the local newspaper wrote that he'd considered Symmes' ideas "wild effusions of a disordered imagination." But on hearing Reynolds, he and the rest of the audience were "completely enchained" because Reynolds presented "facts, the existence of which will not admit of a doubt, and the conclusions drawn from them are so

---

19. The best account of this partnership is found in William Stanton's 1975 *The Great United States Exploring Expedition of* 1838–1842, to which I am indebted for the details here.

natural, so consistent with reason, and apparently in such strict accordance with the known laws of nature, that they almost irresistibly enforce conviction on the mind." In Harrisburg Reynolds spoke before the legislature, and, according to William Stanton, "fifty of the lawmakers responded with an enthusiastic letter that urged the government to equip an expedition, for the promise it held out was 'quite as reasonable as that of the great Columbus' and 'better supported by facts.'"

In Philadelphia, they had a major falling-out. Symmes' health was tricky, and Reynolds offered to take on the entire burden of lecturing—*his* way. Reynolds realized the tactical rewards in downplaying the wackier parts of the theory while stumping for a national polar expedition on its own merits, which he wanted to lead. But Symmes refused to compromise about how the theory should be presented, and the brief partnership ended. Symmes packed up his globe and went off lecturing on his own in the northeast and Quebec, giving several talks at Union College in Schenectady and even spoke to a group of students at Harvard University before ill health forced him to stop. Too sick to make it back home, he went instead to his birthplace in New Jersey, where he was the guest of an old friend of his father until he at last recuperated enough for the journey to Ohio. "When he reached Cincinnati in February, 1829," McBride's *Pioneer Biography* says, "he was so feeble that he had to be conveyed on a bed placed in a spring wagon, to his home near Hamilton"—the farm his namesake uncle, Judge Symmes, had given him a few years earlier. He died on May 29, 1829. He was forty-eight years old.

Of his many children, Americus, born at the Bellefontaine fort north of St. Louis in 1811, tried to keep his father's light burning. Americus arranged to have a monument built on his gravesite in Hamilton, Ohio, an obelisk surmounted by a stone hollow globe twenty inches across and open at the poles, and in 1878 wrote his explanatory apologia, *The Symmes Theory of Concentric Spheres, demonstrating that THE EARTH IS HOLLOW, HABITABLE WITHIN, AND WIDELY OPEN AT THE POLES*, a book that elucidated the theory with updated "evidence" from polar exploration that had occurred since his father's death. At seventy-one, he was still giving interviews in support of his father's theories, telling a *Harper's New Monthly Magazine* writer, "If my father's plan was adopted, the riddle of an open polar sea could soon be solved, the pole reached, and Symmes's new world found." Loyal to the end.

An article by B. St. J. Fry, in the August 1871 *Ladies Repository* says in summary:

> Captain Symmes deserves a tender remembrance, and his friends never failed to cherish his memory, and regret that his last years were so full of cheerless mortification. Had the opportunity been afforded him to penetrate the polar latitudes, his faith and courage would have made him one of the boldest adventurers, and he would scarcely have failed to return with useful information and the broader and more truthful views that are now held by intelligent men. No man of his day had studied the subject more thoroughly, and his plans for penetrating the icy North were those that later explorers have adopted with advantage. But his theory has so many of the elements that are woven into childish Munchausen stories, that few men could consider it with any degree of seriousness. But the men who so readily discarded them were for a time deceived by Locke's famous "moon hoax," which had as little common sense to recommend it, and which was less susceptible of proof. For many of Captain Symmes's surmises have been proven to be well founded, but they do not in any wise establish his theory.

3

POLAR GOTHIC:
REYNOLDS AND POE

AFTER PARTING COMPANY WITH JOHN CLEVES SYMMES in Philadelphia, J. N. Reynolds continued lecturing on his own for the remainder of 1825 and into the next year. Unlike Symmes, he had considerable success, often charging fifty cents a head—roughly the equivalent of ten dollars today—and usually packing them in.[1] But his delivery wasn't much snazzier than Symmes'. "According to our memory," wrote historian Henry Howe, "he was a firmly built man, of medium stature, with a short nose, and a somewhat broad face. His delivery was monotonous, but what he said was solid, and his air in a high degree respectful and earnest and withal very sad, as though some great sorrow lay upon his heart, which won our sympathy, and this without knowing anything of his history."[2] Reynolds's first book-length publication, *Remarks on a Review of Symmes' Theory,* appeared in 1827, so his association with Symmes' ideas continued for a time. But by degrees Symmes' Holes began to

---

1. It must have been pretty profitable to him. His first solo lectures in Philadelphia, according to a notice in *The Democratic Press,* drew "an auditory of from thirteen to fifteen hundred. . . . The lecture was intended and well calculated to remove prejudice against the theory of Capt. Symmes."

2. Henry Howe, *Historical Collections of Ohio* (Columbus, Ohio: The State of Ohio, 1891), 1:430–432.

close up or disappear in his talks, as increasingly he discarded Symmes' theory and warmed to his true subject: the country's vital need for a polar expedition. It is only a slight exaggeration to say that Reynolds was the one mainly responsible for churning up national enthusiasm for such an enterprise.

One eager enthusiast was Edgar Allan Poe.

There is continuing speculation regarding whether Poe and Reynolds knew each other personally. Their careers and interests intersected again and again. Poe took repeated literary inspiration both from Symmes' theory and Reynolds's speeches and writings, to the point of lifting certain passages from Reynolds wholesale. The question takes on extraliterary interest because of Poe's enigmatic final words. On the night of October 7, 1849, Poe lay writhing in fear and pain on his deathbed, a ruin at forty. Over and over as he died, a single word came repeatedly to his lips: "Reynolds . . . Reynolds . . . Reynolds . . ."[3] No one knows why. Whether they actually knew each other has never been established, though my guess is that they must have.

When Reynolds began barnstorming the eastern states, Poe was a sixteen-year-old living in Richmond. In 1826, he spent eleven infamous months at the University of Virginia, chiefly devoting his time to gambling, unsuccessfully. While Poe was at the university, Reynolds wasn't far away. "The center of Reynolds's activities at first appears to have been Baltimore," Robert Almy wrote in the February 1937 *Colophon*. "He delivered and repeated his course of lectures there in September and October 1826. At Baltimore Reynolds received not only a favorable press but offers of financial aid in fitting out an expedition to the South Pole."

Stealing a leaf from his erstwhile mentor, in 1826 Reynolds began agitating for a national polar expedition. His focus was now on the Southern Ocean. The Antarctic was the larger unknown and the promise both of scientific discovery and commerce the greater for it. Although the main goal of such an expedition would be scientific, the scientists might turn up commercially useful information, such as the whereabouts of more seals and whales. New sources were needed to maintain

---

3. As related in *Israfel: The Life and Times of Edgar Allan Poe* by Hervey Allen (1926).

the annual 4 million barrels of whale oil produced by New England. Almost 7 million whales had been killed by then, primarily to keep parlor lights burning on long winter nights.

Part of his campaign included speaking to state legislatures to persuade them to submit "memorials" to Congress—endorsements of the polar expedition idea urging government action. He also enlisted the interest of the open polar sea crowd. As already noted, the idea that open navigable sea lay beyond an icy rim was an ancient notion that continued to have great currency among prominent scientists and others you'd think would have known better. Like the Northwest Passage, it was an idea that people *wanted* to be true. Reynolds, like Symmes before him, mined the existing literature on polar exploration for anecdotal gems to place gleaming in his argument for the open polar sea and the bright possibilities it offered.

Finally, he called on national pride. The American republic itself was a green new enterprise, with many scoffers just waiting for it to fail; a national expedition would be a way to show the world what America was made of. There was no time to waste. Even this great southern unknown was beginning to give up its secrets to others.

The continent was first sighted in 1820, with three different contenders for the honor. Russians are certain it was their Admiral Bellingshausen, who was the first to circumnavigate Antarctica since Cook. The British are convinced it was Edward Bransfield and William Smith, who were on a mission to chart the South Shetland Islands. And Americans claim it was sealer Nathaniel B. Palmer, who in November 1820, as the twenty-one-year-old commander of the sloop *Hero,* sailed into Orleans Strait at about sixty-three degrees, forty-one minutes south and came within sight of the continent. The former teenage War of 1812 blockade runner is also credited with discovering the South Orkney Islands and later spent part of the 1820s transporting troops to help Simon Bolivar in South America. British sealing captain John Davis had made the first landing on Antarctica at Hughes Bay on February 7, 1821; but as there were no seals in sight, his party only stayed an hour and then split. That same year had marked the first Antarctic overwintering, when eleven men from the wrecked British ship *Lord Melville* toughed it out on King George Island. British explorer and sealer James Weddell, in three successive voyages—1819–1821, 1821–1822, and 1822–1824—was almost single-handedly turning the Southern Ocean into his private pond, having surveyed and named a number of the major Antarctic island groups, and, on the third voyage, encountering unusual ice-free conditions (more fodder for OPS believers), reaching seventy-four degrees, fifteen minutes south, beating Cook's record by more than three degrees, in the sea presently named for him. Even as Reynolds was stumping for an expedition, the French were preparing to mount one of their own.

Should the United States be left behind?

On May 21, 1828, a resolution passed the House asking the president to devote a government ship to exploring the Pacific—if it could be accomplished with no extra appropriation of funds. President Adams told Reynolds he was pleased it had passed. Reynolds was named a special Navy Department agent to round up all the information he could. He interviewed every whaling and sealing captain he could find and sought out scientists for the voyage. He oversaw the rebuilding of the war sloop *Peacock* at the New York Navy Yard, which was launched to great hoopla in September 1828. But then things started to go wrong. A tangled series of reverses followed, due largely to the Adams' administration's lame-duck status. On taking office in March 1829, after handily beating Adams in the 1828 election, Democrat Andrew Jackson killed it for political reasons. Not only was it a leftover from the old administration, but Reynolds had been outspoken about his pro-Adams views. The expedition was canceled.

But Reynolds had a backup plan. One argument against the expedition during the legislative backpedaling that killed it had been a minimalist construction of the Constitution: it wasn't the government's business to be sponsoring and paying for such tomfoolery. As the prospects of a government expedition curdled, Reynolds formed the South Sea Fur Company and Exploring Expedition and went about rounding up backers and interested scientists. He was helped in this by Edmund Fanning, a longtime sealer and explorer (several discoveries in the central Pacific are credited to him) who had been proselytizing for a national Antarctic expedition since before the War of 1812. President Madison had commissioned him to lead a voyage and the ships were about to leave when war was declared against England, putting an end to that idea. Too old now to join himself, Fanning nevertheless helped Reynolds stir up interest in a private expedition.

A wealthy New Yorker named Dr. Watson came to the rescue, putting up most of the money for outfitting a ship and two small tenders. The kicker was that he got to go along. The *Annawan* and the *Seraph*, both brigs, and the *Penguin*, a schooner, sailed in October 1829 with Reynolds aboard—he'd gotten his polar expedition. Nathaniel Palmer captained one of the ships. Benjamin Pendleton, who as a sealer had often sailed into the unforgiving Southern Ocean, skippered another. James Eights of Albany, an accomplished artist and scientist, was resident naturalist. In a voyage that proved thin on accomplishments, Eights's contributions stood out. In articles afterward he described a trilobite relative in the South Shetlands that wasn't described again for seventy years. As they sailed west of the Antarctic Peninsula, he observed erratic boulders that differed geologically from the local rock, correctly surmising that they had hitched a ride here embedded in icebergs sheared from the Antarctic mainland. Eights also discovered the first fossils in the Antarctic, specimens of petrified wood, and a peculiar creature, a pyncnogonid, a ten-legged sea spider, the first so described.

The trip began inauspiciously, and got worse. Planning to sail south together, the ships quickly lost sight of each other and didn't meet up again until they reached Staaten Island (Isla de los Estados), their rendezvous point just east of Tierra del Fuego. As they headed southeast for the South Shetlands, just north of the Antarctic Peninsula now partly named for Palmer, science and commerce found themselves at odds. The sailors had hired on for shares in the sealing take and became increasingly testy as the holds did not fill up. When they got to Antarctica, they found no sign of Symmes' welcoming verges, open water, and balmy temperatures: "They at length arrived in sight of land," Robert Way wrote shortly after the expedition, "which they afterward discovered to be a southern continent, which seemed completely blockaded with islands of ice."[4] They attempted a landing in a long boat, but in the rough, stormy water it went careening for a considerable distance, out of sight of the ship, before they could reach the shore. They found themselves stuck there, without provisions. "Starvation seemed to stare them in the face." Way continues:

> But behold! Providence seemed to provide the means of support in the sea lion. He exhibited himself at the mouth of a cave, and ten men, in two squads, were sent out to bring him in. They soon returned with his carcass, which weighed 1,700 pounds. His flesh was excellent eating. By an accurate astronomical observation, they found their latitude to be eighty-two degrees south, exactly eight degrees from the South Pole. After some ten days of anxious delay on land, the sea becoming calm, they put out to sea in their long boat to endeavor to discover the ships. They sailed on and on for nearly forty hours. At length, being very weary, late in the night, they drew their boat upon a high inclined rock. All, in a few minutes, were sound asleep except Reynolds and Watson. They stood sentinels over the boat's crew, and felt too anxious to sleep. About 2 or 3 o'clock in the morning, they saw a light far distant at sea. The crew was soon wakened, and all embarked in their boat and rowing with might and main for the ships. They soon arrived, and the meeting of the two parties was full of enthusiastic joy. They were convinced that they could not enter the South Pole, as it was blocked up with an icy continent; hence they were willing to turn their faces homeward. Here the seamen mutinied against the authority of the ship, set Reynolds and Watson on shore, and launched out to sea as a pirate ship.

---

4. This sketch of Reynolds is quoted in *The History of Clinton County Ohio* (Chicago: W. H. Beers and Company, 1882), 580–585.

Reynolds didn't seem to mind. For many months he traveled all over Chile, and earned himself a footnote in American literary history—one of several—by hearing a supposedly true story about a renegade white whale in the Pacific off Chile, which he later wrote up for the May 1839 issue of *Knickerbocker* magazine under the title "Mocha Dick, or the White Whale of the Pacific." Guess who read it?[5]

Reynolds finally joined the warship USS *Potomac* in October 1832 at Valparaiso, Chile, as the commodore's private secretary, remaining in that capacity during a two-year voyage and publishing a several-volume account of it in 1835 that made his reputation as an explorer and a writer.

In 1835 Poe was twenty-six years old and had already put together a pretty checkered track record. Born in Boston to a pair of itinerant actors, he lost his mother when he was two and then was bounced around from place to place. He attended the University of Virginia for eleven months in 1826, where he lost so much money gambling that his guardian yanked him out of school. Returning home, he learned that his sweetheart had dumped him and was engaged to another guy. In 1827 Poe landed in Boston, where he self-published a volume of poems, dripping youthful Byronic angst, called *Tamerlane and Other Poems,* to little notice. Dead broke, he enlisted in the army under an assumed name; his guardian apparently took pity on him, buying him out of the army and arranging an appointment to West Point. Poe got himself expelled by pulling a Bartleby and refusing to attend classes or drills. Before entering West Point, he'd published another volume of poems, *Al Araf, Tamerlane, and Minor Poems,* in 1829. After leaving West Point he went to New York City, where he published another volume, simply called *Poems.* These volumes contained some of his best work but nobody was buying, so he moved to Baltimore in 1831 and began to write stories.

---

5. Reynolds finds no metaphysics lurking in his story of the white whale, and, at the end of his tale, it's killed. Melville probably read the story as a young sailor aboard the *Acushnet.* In 1847, Melville bought a copy of Reynolds' *Voyage of the United States Frigate Potomac.*

By then he'd settled into the peculiar domestic arrangement that continued for many years—living with his devoted widowed aunt, Mrs. Maria Clemm, and his first cousin, her young daughter Virginia, whom he married in 1835 when she was thirteen years old. They had cramped barren rooms in a Baltimore boardinghouse and were desperately low on money. His aunt took in sewing to help pay the bills. Poe had long since begun his fatal dance with alcohol and opium. Certainly his brain was wandering through untraveled realms, but not of gold. His terrain was the "blackness of darkness."

And he found inspiration in Symmes' Hole.

Thanks largely to Symmes and Reynolds, the idea of the hollow earth had become linked with the fascinating mystery of the poles. Nobody had ever been there, at least to live and tell about it, so they offered complete artistic freedom, a tabula rasa on which anything could be written—made even more inviting by the imaginative addition of Symmes' Holes.

Poe entered a literary contest sponsored by the *Baltimore Sunday Visiter* in 1833. First prize was $50—the equivalent of $750 today. Instead of submitting just one story, Poe sent several, which he had bound together in a makeshift book. The youngest of the judges, delegated as first reader of the "slush pile," was so knocked out by one of the stories, "Ms. Found in a Bottle," that he insisted on reading it aloud to the others, who agreed that it was a winner. The prize was announced and the story published in the October 19, 1833, issue. It was reprinted in the December 1835 issue of the *Southern Literary Messenger.*

Passing strange, this little tale. The world-traveling narrator begins with a disclaimer, saying that he has "often been reproached" for "a deficiency of imagination"—to make his bizarre account the more believable. He sails on a ship from Batavia, Java, bound for the Sunda Islands, "having no other inducement than a kind of nervous restlessness which haunted me as a fiend." For days the ship is becalmed and then suddenly caught in the mother of all storms, a terrible "simoom"—"beyond the wildest imagination was the whirlpool of mountainous and foaming

ocean within which we were engulfed." Its first blast sweeps everyone on deck overboard and drowns those below, leaving only the narrator and an old Swede alive.
The storm rages ceaselessly for five days, driving "the hulk at a rate defying compu-
tation" ever south, toward polar seas, "farther to the southward than any previous
navigators." The sun disappears and all is black; the seas remain dizzying, towering
watery peaks and great chasms. While at the bottom of one, they spot a huge black
ship far above, hurtling downward right at them. The crash propels the narrator
into its rigging. He soon discovers the ship's crew to be ancient ambulatory zombies
who "seemed utterly unconscious of my presence" and "glide to and fro like the
ghosts of buried centuries." The floor of the captain's cabin is "thickly strewn with
strange, iron-clasped folios, and mouldering instruments of science, and obsolete
long-forgotten charts." This ship too races due south, borne by wind and a strong
current, "with a velocity like the headlong dashing of a cataract." And then, with
just enough time for him to pop his manuscript into a bottle and cork it, the end:
"Oh, horror upon horror! The ice opens suddenly to the right, and to the left, and
we are whirling dizzily, in immense concentric circles, round and round the borders
of a gigantic amphitheatre, the summit of whose walls is lost in the distance . . . we
are plunging madly within the grasp of the whirlpool—and amid a roaring, and
bellowing, and thundering of ocean and of tempest, the ship is quivering, oh God!
And—going down."

Poe's debt to Coleridge's *Rime of the Ancient Mariner* is evident, but he
owes his ending to Symmes' Hole, sending his unfortunate narrator to his reward
down its epic drain. Whirlpools seem to have been swirling through his mind at this
time because another of the stories he submitted to the contest was "A Descent into
the Maelstrom." In this one, the narrator and a Norwegian fisherman sit high on
a cliff's edge overlooking the sea in northern Norway, and the tale consists of the
fisherman relating how his ship was sucked down into the legendary maelstrom
just offshore from where they're sitting, and how he lived to tell the tale. Poe for
purposes of verisimilitude inserts into the narrative a long description by Jonas

Ramus, dating from 1715, which was reprinted in the 1823 edition of the *Encyclopedia Britannica.* The whirlpool here had long been noted by sailors, appearing on Dutch charts as early as 1590 and turning up on Mercator's 1595 atlas. The Lofoten Islands lie entirely within the Arctic Circle on Norway's northeastern shoulder, and a treacherous current, frequently whipped into a whirlpool, rushes between two of them, Moskenesøya (north) and Mosken (south). The hydrodynamics aren't entirely understood—seemingly a combination of the current slamming into tidal shifts, with high winds sometimes thrown in. Poe amplifies the whirlpool to mythic proportions in his tale and suggests it may be the opening to a great abyss—citing no less an authority than Athanasius Kircher: "Kircher and others imagine that in the centre of the channel of the Maelstrom is an abyss penetrating the globe, and issuing in some very remote part—the Gulf of Bothnia being somewhat decidedly named in one instance. This opinion, idle in itself, was the one to which, as I gazed, my imagination most readily assented." Kircher had argued that the maelstrom marked the entrance to a subterranean channel connecting the Norwegian Sea, the Gulf of Bothnia, and the Berents Sea, believing that such whirlpools were an important part of ocean circulation. "A Descent into the Maelstrom," for all its *stürm und drang,* is less exciting than its companion piece, possibly because the fisherman lives through it, something the reader knows at the beginning.

One of the contest judges had been Maryland congressman and author John Pendleton Kennedy, whose *Swallow Barn* had been published pseudonymously in 1832, and who would become "the Maecenas of Southern letters"—with Poe being the first notable recipient of his patronage. As a result of the contest, they struck up a friendship, and Poe wasn't shy about bemoaning his financial straits. Kennedy put him in touch with Thomas White, owner of the new, struggling *Southern Literary Messenger.* Poe began contributing to it. His first story appeared in March 1835 and more tales and poems followed. In August 1835, Poe moved to Richmond to become the magazine's editor. He also wrote reviews, essays, and stories, as many as ten an issue. Under his editorship the circulation quadrupled in a year to around five thousand.

Poe didn't last long as editor. Owner Thomas White fired him in January 1837 for erratic behavior caused by depression and drinking, though the parting probably had some mutuality to it. Poe had ideas about establishing a truly national magazine, and the natural place to try that was Philadelphia or New York. In late February, Poe, Virginia, and Mrs. Clemm had taken lodgings in an old brick building at Sixth Avenue and Waverly Place. Reynolds was also living in New York at this time. Poe contributed to the *Southern Literary Messenger* until he died; his final contribution, the poem "Annabel Lee," ran in the November 1849 issue, a month after his death.

During his tenure at the magazine, Poe's interest in Reynolds and things polar repeatedly showed itself. Before he took over as editor, in fact, a favorable review of Reynolds's *Voyage of the Potomac* appeared in the June 1835 issue. The anonymous reviewer remarks that Reynolds "will be remembered as the associate of Symmes in his remarkable theory of the earth, and a public defender of that very indefensible subject, upon which he delivered a series of lectures in many of our principal cities." Though apparently not a believer, the reviewer goes on to note that there's "very valuable information scattered through the book," and that "he writes well, though somewhat too enthusiastically, and his book will gain him reputation as a man of science and accurate observation. It will form a valuable addition to our geographical libraries." The August 1835 issue notes that Reynolds's *Potomac* has been "highly praised in the London Literary Gazette."

The "Critical Notices" in the December 1835 issue—almost certainly written by Poe—contain an extensive detailed summary of what's in the July 1835 issue of the *Edinburgh Review*, a standard practice of the time revealing both slim literary pickings to write about and the ongoing American inferiority complex regarding things British. One article summarized is a review of Sir John Ross's *Narrative of a Second Voyage in search of a North-West Passage, and of a Residence in the Arctic Regions during the years 1829 . . . 1833 . . . Including the Reports of Commander, now Captain, James Clark Ross . . . and the Discovery of the Northern Magnetic Pole.* The *Edinburgh* reviewer takes issue with calling it a "discovery," quibbling in regard to whether his observations are entirely accurate. Poe agrees: "The fact is that the Magnetic Pole is *moveable,* and, place it where we will, we shall not find it in the same place tomorrow." He adds:

> Notice is taken also by the critic that neither Captain nor Commander Ross has made the slightest reference to the fact that the Magnetic Pole is not coincident with the *Pole of maximum cold.* From observations made by Scoresby in East Greenland, and by Sir Charles Giesecké and the Danish Governors in West Greenland, and confirmed by all the meteorological observations made by Captains Parry and Franklin, Sir David Brewster has deduced the fact that the Pole of the Equator is not the Pole of maximum cold: and as the matter is well established, it is singular, to say no more, that it has been alluded to by neither the Commander nor the Captain.

This little tirade flaunts a flurry of knowledge about the subject—revealing an ongoing interest on Poe's part—and echoes Symmes, Reynolds, and others who believed in the warmer open polar sea at the top and bottom of the world, an idea that would figure greatly in *The Narrative of Arthur Gordon Pym,* his only published attempt at book-length fiction.

Another lengthy notice in the same issue, occupying three columns of eyestrain-size type, is a review of *A Life of George Washington, in Latin Prose,* by one Francis Glass, published by the reputable firm of Harper and Brothers, and edited, with a glowing introduction, by none other than J. N. Reynolds. One presumes that Poe had his tongue firmly planted in cheek when he wrote, "We may truly say that not for years have we taken up a volume with which we have been so highly gratified, as with the one now before us." Glass too was from southwestern Ohio—he'd been Reynolds's mentor. Poe has great (and uncharacteristically gentle) fun here, saying, "Mr. Reynolds is entitled to the thanks of his countrymen for his instrumentality in bringing this book before the public."

In the February 1836 issue, Poe had asked a number of literary lights to contribute samples of their autographs for sportive analysis; included among James Fenimore Cooper, Washington Irving, and John Quincy Adams was J. N. Reynolds.

A lengthy notice titled "South-Sea Expedition" appeared in the August 1836 issue, commenting on the publication in March of a "Report of the Committee on Naval Affairs, to whom was referred memorials from sundry citizens of Connecticut interested in the whale fishing, praying that an exploring expedition be fitted out to the Pacific Ocean and South Seas, March 21, 1836." The review enthusiastically endorses the idea, calling it "of paramount importance both in a political and commercial point of view," quoting Reynolds at length in several places. A news item appended to the end reports that the expedition has been given the go-ahead by the president, and that Reynolds has been named the expedition's corresponding secretary, which the anonymous reviewer (in all likelihood, Poe) says is "the highest civil situation in the expedition; a station which we know him to be exceedingly qualified to fill."

In April 1836 Reynolds had made a three-hour address to Congress offering reasons the country should underwrite such an expedition. He had shifted his public arguments to the economic benefits that would accrue. As far as the earth being hollow, "it might be so." He was no longer very interested in the question. His own "bold proposition" now was that there could be an icy barrier around both poles, but "being once passed, the ocean becomes less encumbered with ice, 'and the nearer the pole the less ice.'" In May 1836 Congress appropriated $300,000 for the enterprise. Reynolds's address was subsequently published as a book by Harper's, which Poe reviewed in a lengthy essay for the January 1837 issue of the *Southern Literary Messenger.* Again he heaps lavish praise on Reynolds—"the originator, the persevering and indomitable advocate, the life, the soul of the design." Poe says it is needed because the fishery is of such importance to the country, but "the scene of its operations, however, is less known and more full of peril than any other portion of the globe visited by our ships." The "full of peril" part suggests what is to come in

Pym: "The savages in these regions have frequently evinced a murderous hostility—they should be conciliated or intimidated" (though in *Pym* those savages will have other ideas). There follows a detailed history of Reynolds's efforts leading up to this, which notes that "the motives and character of Mr. Reynolds have been assailed." But "we will not insult Mr. Reynolds with a defense. Gentlemen have impugned his motives—have these gentlemen ever seen him or conversed with him half an hour?" This last is the strongest indication we have that Poe and Reynolds actually knew each other.

Unfortunately for Reynolds, these "gentlemen" had the final say. Before the sailing date, he was dismissed from the post, and did not accompany the expedition that was largely his creation. It had partly to do with an ongoing antipathy on the part of the Navy to having civilians of any stripe aboard their ships; also, as delay began to follow delay, with the appropriation rapidly dwindling, Reynolds had been making his opinions known a little too loudly, and got on the wrong side of Secretary of the Navy Mahlon Dickerson. But the dismissal also showed the hand of Charles Wilkes, the expedition's eventual leader, who had been clashing with Reynolds ever since the aborted 1828 effort.[6] From here on, perhaps understandably after such disappointment as a reward for such prolonged effort, Reynolds' interests shifted away from the sea. He continued to write about earlier adventures—two such pieces appeared in the *Southern Literary Messenger,* in 1839 and 1843, and "Mocha Dick" in *Knickerbocker* in 1839—but he devoted the rest of his life to law and politics.

In 1840 he hit the boards in Connecticut as a campaign speaker for the Whigs, and in 1841 began a law firm on Wall Street, where he worked primarily on maritime law. In 1848, ever entrepreneurial, he organized a stock company for a mining operation in Leon, Mexico. The sketch of Reynolds in *The History of Clinton County Ohio* concludes: "He was elected president of the company, and,

---

6. Nathaniel Hawthorne, then thirty-four years old, whose *Twice-Told Tales* had been published in 1837, had also applied for the job as Corresponding Secretary, seeking "a way out of despondency," as Robert Almy puts it, adding, "His friend Franklin Pierce advised negotiating through Reynolds, and himself talked with and wrote Reynolds in Hawthorne's behalf." But nothing came of it, and in 1839 Hawthorne took a position in the Boston Custom House instead.

after a few years of persistent effort, he made quite a success in the field; but his health soon failed, and he died near New York City in 1858, aged fifty-nine years. He was buried in that city."

Poe liked Reynolds and the address so much that he stole parts of it for *The Narrative of Arthur Gordon Pym*, whose opening chapters were published serially in the January and February 1837 issues of the *Southern Literary Messenger*. Poe also lifted details from Reynolds's earlier *Voyage of the Potomac*. Reynolds wasn't alone in the honor. Poe ransacked existing seagoing literature for his tale about Pym, appropriating left and right, and returned to Symmes' Hole for his big finale.[7]

Poe's timing in writing *Pym* showed his good commercial instincts—he was a magazine editor, after all. The voyage had captured the national imagination and was just under way when Poe's novel came out, which left him free to cook up the grisly possibilities he envisioned for his own Antarctic excursion. Even so, the book didn't sell very well, and Poe returned to the shorter work at which he was far more accomplished.

Literary historian Alexander Cowie summed up *Pym* as "a plotless, nightmare-ridden book." Right on both counts, but it nonetheless holds a certain fascination, however morbid. For all its faults, which are many, it is a lot of gruesome fun. A seeker of extreme sensation in life, it makes sense that Poe would push every boundary he could think of in his writing. One literary form of pushing limits is parody, and *Pym* is arguably that as well, a ghastly gothic send-up of that literary staple, the journal of a polar voyage. It bears an uncanny resemblance to one polar voyage in particular—*Symzonia*. A number of scholars have pointed to *Symzonia* as a likely model. In *Pilgrims Through Space and Time*, J. O. Bailey, citing a long list of parallels, suggests that it might have been called *Pymzonia*. But with all its debts to Symzonia—and Poe truly seems to have used it as a template for his own tale—*Pym* takes these elements to the outer limits. And it's all done deadpan,

---

7. Others he liberally pilfered from were Benjamin Morrell's *A Narrative of Four Voyages* (J. & J. Harper, New York, 1832); *The Mariner's Chronicle* (stories of true sailing disasters originally published from 1804 to 1812, reprinted as a collection by George W. Gorton, New Haven, 1834); and R. Thomas's *Remarkable Events and Remarkable Shipwrecks* (New York, 1836). Behind on getting material to his publisher, Poe resorted to using these as a bit of Novel Helper.

with a straight face. Poe admired *Robinson Crusoe* for its seeming verisimilitude, and all that ransacking of marine literature, with the occasional outright theft for good measure, at first gives the book the superficial aspect of being just another voyager's account of his travels; the realistic, matter-of-fact journalistic tone continues as events get more and more outrageous. Poe loved hoaxes, and he does his damnedest in *Pym* to carry it off.

But there are hints early on. Before the voyage is under way, the young narrator rhapsodizes about his hopes for the trip: "For the bright side of the painting I had a limited sympathy. My visions were of shipwreck and famine; of death and captivity among barbarian hordes; of a lifetime dragged out in sorrow and tears, upon some grey and desolate rock, in an ocean unapproachable and unknown." Mind you, this is what he *hopes* will happen. And does he ever get his wish!

Pym is sneaked onboard by his friend Augustus, deposited as a stowaway in a dark claustrophobic hold, from which he soon finds he cannot get out, beginning the voyage in a sort of burial alive, one of Poe's favorite terrors. While he's stuck in this fetid compartment, up on deck the crew is mutinying. For days he nearly starves and goes mad, and is threatened by man's best friend, a dog trapped in there with him. Finally Augustus springs him. Joined by thuggish-looking half-breed Dirk Peters, the three kill all the mutineers but one and retake the vessel. But, wouldn't you know it, a protracted gale reduces the ship to a floating wreck, kept from sinking by its buoyant cargo of oil. They can't get at the food in the hold, so it's either death by starvation or being washed overboard.

Then a ship approaches with what proves to be an *ex*-crew. "Twenty-five or thirty human bodies, among whom were several females, lay scattered about . . .

(above) Dirk Peters, as imagined by artist René Clarke, looking cheerfully sinister and ready to rock with his bottle of rum and shiv on his belt, in a 1930 edition produced by Heritage Press for the Limited Editions Club. (© 1930 by The Limited Editions Club [George Macy Companies, Inc.])

in the last and most loathsome state of putrefaction." On one sits a seagull, "busily gorging itself with the horrible flesh, its bill and talons deeply buried, and its white plumage spattered all over with blood." A tip of the hat to Coleridge for that scene. Another vessel comes by but doesn't see them.

Now they're *really* starving. They begin sizing each other up as possible entrees. They draw lots, and Parker, whose idea it was, gets the short straw. Dirk Peters, living up to his first name, stabs him. For the next four days the others nosh on Parker's diminishing remains. Finally Pym figures out a way to cut a hole into the storeroom, which is filled with water, so they have to dive repeatedly to bring up whatever they can—a bottle of olives, a bottle of Madeira, and a live tortoise. Augustus has injured his arm, which begins turning black, and he wastes away, a mere forty-five pounds when he dies. When Peters tries to pick him up, one of Augustus's legs comes off in his hands. Can things get worse? Of course. The hulk rolls over. But the three survivors manage to clamber up on it, and, in one of those ironies that made Poe smile, what do these starving men find on the hull? Plenty of nutritious barnacles. They catch rainwater in their shirts.

It's brutally hot, but they can't cool off in the ocean because of the sharks endlessly cruising around them. They're dying. But then another ship approaches, the *Jane Guy,* and this time they are saved—briefly. This whaler heads farther south, piercing the southern ice barrier into temperate seas. As the climate becomes increasingly warmer—just as it does in *Symzonia*—they come upon an island near the South Pole populated by seemingly friendly savages. But it turns out to be one of the strangest and most sinister islands in literature. Everything, every plant and creature, even the water, is black. The woolly-haired natives even have black teeth— and not from not brushing. White in any form is unknown to them, except for the strange white animal (with red teeth) they worship as a terrible totem. The natives come out to meet the *Jane Guy* in large sea canoes, greeting them with cries of *Anamoo-moo* and *Lama-Lama.* For a few days everything is swell. But then they set an ambush for the crew, killing them in a landslide; they head out in canoes to burn

the *Jane Guy,* which proves a miscalculation when the gunpowder in the hold explodes, sending body parts flying. All the crew are dead but Pym and Peters, fortuitously semi-buried alive (again) in a rock chamber during the landslide. They manage to escape in a native canoe, abducting one Nu-Nu to accompany them as a guide, but he proves useless, lying in the canoe bottom writhing in fear and dying a few days later. A persistent current draws their little craft ever southward. A gray vapor is seen rising above the horizon.

The seawater becomes hot to the touch and takes on a milky hue. "A fine white powder, resembling ashes—but certainly not such—fell over the canoe and over a large surface of the water." A day later, "the range of vapor to the southward

(above) Boat adrift. "The wind had entirely ceased, but it was evident that we were still hurrying on to the southward, under the influence of a powerful current."
(© 1930 by The Limited Editions Club [George Macy Companies, Inc.])

had arisen prodigiously in the horizon, and began to assume more distinctness of form. I can liken it to nothing but a limitless cataract . . . we were evidently approaching it with a hideous velocity." Not counting a short afterword, which Poe provides to continue the pose that this has been an actual nonfiction account, these are the final lines:

> Many gigantic and pallidly white birds flew continuously now from beyond the veil, and their scream was the eternal *Tekeli-li!* as they retreated from our vision . . . and now we rushed into the embraces of the cataract, where a chasm threw itself open to receive us. But there arose in our pathway a shrouded human figure, very far larger in its proportions than any dweller among men. And the hue of the skin of the figure was of the perfect whiteness of the snow.

Go figure. He says in the afterword that the final two or three chapters have been lost, regrettable because they no doubt "contained matter relative to the Pole itself, or at least to regions in its very near proximity; and as, too, the statements of the author in relation to these regions may shortly be verified or contradicted by means of the governmental expedition now preparing for the Southern Ocean."

Pym's abrupt ending has puzzled and annoyed readers and critics alike. Did Poe simply weary of a bad business, as many have suggested? Could be. But its very abruptness adds a final element of ambiguity missing from the rest of the book. Toward the end Poe begins toying with the symbolic possibilities of whiteness and, less happily, blackness. Critic Leslie Fiedler has argued persuasively that taking his white characters way down south to the all-black island represents southern racist dreaming, nightmare division, a macabre South Seas rendering of that deepest slaveholder dread—a slave insurrection. "The book projects his personal resentment and fear," says Fiedler, "as well as the guilty terror of a whole society in the face of those whom they can never quite believe they have the right to enslave."

Whiteness doesn't fare too well either. In *The Power of Blackness*, Harry Levin sees in that final whiteness "a mother-image." Levin says "the milky water is more redolent of birth than of death; and the opening in the earth may seem to be a regression wombward." But Fiedler finds in the engulfing womblike whiteness of the cataract a perverse twist on the great mother symbol. Clearly, despite the postscript, Pym and Peters are sucked down to their deaths, and Fiedler sees this final and fatal embracing whiteness as "the Great Mother as *vagina dentata*." Ouch! And Poe uses Symmes' Hole to chew up his hapless hero! "From the beginning," Fiedler says, "a perceptive reader of *Gordon Pym* is aware that every current sentimental platitude, every cliché of the fable of the holy marriage of males is being ironically exposed."

I would suggest an even wider reading—that *Pym* is also a send-up of the mania for polar exploration and the bright sunny possibilities being trumpeted by Reynolds & Co. Was Poe among the enthusiasts? Yes. Could he help seeing the dark humor in all this optimism? Or resist sticking it to the whole bunch, even though he admired Reynolds and thought the expedition was cool? It would seem not. The book's commercial failure may have had less to do with its gory excesses and/or artistic deficiencies (it really *is* better and more fun to read than it's supposed to be) than its naked subversiveness regarding this particular scene in the American Dream.

Interestingly, Poe found an ally in Henry David Thoreau, who also had something to say about the national enthusiasm Reynolds generated for exploration of the South Pole and about Symmes' Hole too, though his comments in the concluding chapter of *Walden* (1854) were typically contrarian and transcendental, making metaphysics of it all:

> What was the meaning of that South-Sea Exploring Expedition, with all its parade and expense, but an indirect recognition of the fact that there are continents and seas in the moral world to which every man is an isthmus

or an inlet, yet unexplored by him, but that it is easier to sail many thousand miles through cold and storm and cannibals, in a government ship, with five hundred men and boys to assist one, than it is to explore the private sea, the Atlantic and Pacific Ocean of one's being alone . . . It is not worth the while to go round the world to count the cats in Zanzibar. Yet do this even till you can do better, and you may perhaps find some "Symmes' Hole" by which to get at the inside at last.

Good old Henry, ever marching along to that different drummer. Explore the Symmes' Hole within you—it is more mysterious and profound.

A JOURNEY

TO THE

CENTRE OF THE EARTH.

4

JULES VERNE: A JOURNEY TO THE CENTER OF GEOLOGY

FROM HERE, THE HOLLOW EARTH IS A CAROM SHOT—from Poe to Baudelaire to Verne.

Poe died slowly, horribly, in Baltimore during the first week of October 1849. He had stopped there on his way from Richmond to Philadelphia, where he was to be paid $100 for editing a book of poems by Mrs. St. Leon Loud, such were his financial straits. Why he stopped in Baltimore isn't known, nor what he did for five days between leaving the packet boat until he was found by his friend Dr. J. E. Snodgrass in a barroom, a wreck collapsed in an armchair. "His face was haggard," Snodgrass later wrote, "not to say bloated, and unwashed, his hair unkempt and his whole physique repulsive." Snodgrass took him to the Washington College Hospital, unconscious. Poe woke in the middle of the night to a pitiless swarm of DT symptoms, sweating, quaking, gibbering in a "busy but not violent or active delirium, the whole chamber seethed for him, and with vacant converse he talked to the spectres that withered and loomed on the walls."[1] He lingered thus for days. Biographer Hervey Allen writes of his final hours:

---

1. This account is related in Hervey Allen's landmark 1926 biography, *Israfel.*

On that last night, as the shadow fell across him, it must have been the horrors of shipwreck, of thirst, and of drifting away into unknown seas of darkness that troubled his last dreams, for, by some trick of his ruined brain, it was scenes of *Arthur Gordon Pym* that rose in his imagination, and the man who was connected most intimately with them.

"Reynolds!" he called, "Reynolds! Oh, Reynolds!" The room rang with it. It echoed down the corridors hour after hour all that Saturday night. The last grains of sand uncovered themselves as he slipped away, during the Sunday morning of October 7, 1849. He was now too feeble to call out any more. It was three o'clock in the morning and the earth's shadow was still undisturbed by dawn. He became quiet, and seemed to rest for a short time. Then, gently moving his head, he said, "Lord help my poor soul."

His tormented body had found rest, but his reputation lived on for continued abuse. It began with a savage obituary by Rufus Griswold, a former colleague at *Graham's* magazine in the early 1840s whom Poe had unwisely chosen to be his literary executor. Griswold had been stewing over unkind things Poe had written in reviews of poetry anthologies Griswold had edited and began taking revenge in this *New York Daily Tribune* obituary published two days after Poe's death—establishing the view of Poe as little more than a drug-ridden degenerate that would be the prevailing version of him in America for many years. During his lifetime his writing never attracted a large popular audience. To the general public he was known chiefly for "The Raven," which was widely reprinted after it appeared in 1845. In a culture where "that d—-ed mob of scribbling women," in Hawthorne's famous frustrated phrase, sold the most books and stories, it is no wonder that Poe's weird dark vision wasn't welcome in the sunny optimistic America of the time, wormwood, not lemonade. And his scandalous personal habits made it even worse. For all his brilliance, he was an embarrassment, best forgotten.

At least in his own country.

But in France, Charles Baudelaire had discovered Poe in 1847—at the age of twenty-six—and found in him a kindred spirit, a lost twin. They even looked a little alike, though Poe before the wreckage commenced was the more handsome. The only surviving pictures of Baudelaire show an older, ravaged landscape tinged with a *soupçon* of William Burroughs, but the two men shared bold, swelling foreheads and intense, glowing black eyes.

Starting in 1848, Baudelaire began translating Poe's tales into French. These translations became a life passion that provided most of his paying literary work for many years. In 1856 some of the stories were collected as *Histoires extraordinaires,* followed in 1857—the same year his own *Les fleurs du mal* was published— by *Nouvelles histoires extraordinaires.* (These titles for the collected Poe translations seem significant in regard to Jules Verne, since the overall title he gave his many novels was *Voyages extraordinaires.*) In 1857 too came *Les Aventures d'Arthur Gordon Pym,* followed by *Eurêka* (1864) and *Histoires grotesques et sérieuses* (1865). They were of such high caliber that they continue to be the standard Poe translations in the world's French-speaking countries.

Why such dedication? In a letter to a friend Baudelaire wrote, with a certain exasperation, "They accuse me, me, of imitating Edgar Poe! Do you know why I so patiently translated Poe?—*Because he resembled me.* The first time that I opened a book of his I saw, with awe and rapture, not only subjects dreamed by me, but *sentences,* thought by me, and written by him, twenty years before."[2]

The parallels are striking. Like Poe, Baudelaire suffered familial disruption at an early age. His father, sixty-one at his birth, died when he was six, and little Charles had Mommy all to himself for a couple of years. But then she spoiled everything by marrying a career soldier Baudelaire quickly came to despise. The family moved to Lyon in 1832, and his stepfather promptly dumped Baudelaire into a military boarding school. At fifteen he was permitted to transfer to a prestigious high school. Moody, melancholic, he was expelled in 1839 and then took up the

---

2. This letter is quoted by Edna St. Vincent Millay, in her 1936 translation with George Dillon of *Les Fleurs du Mal.* She comments that "Baudelaire made it the patient and worshipful task of half his writing years to translate the prose of Poe into French, to present to the European public a writer whom he considered to be a genius unappreciated at home."

study of law, which primarily meant tireless bohemian carousing in the Latin Quarter. His excesses kept him broke, and it was presumably at this time that he contracted syphilis from a prostitute. In 1841, his parents put him on a boat to India; maybe large doses of sea air and sunshine would bring him to his senses. They didn't. Reaching the island of Mauritius in the Indian Ocean, he refused to go any farther and returned to Paris. Given all this, it seems remarkable that his stepfather then gave him an inheritance of 100,000 francs, but he did. Baudelaire blew half of it in two years on fancy clothes, fine wines, expensive meals, the right books and paintings, and, the better to enjoy it all, plenty of opium and hashish. His alarmed parents put him on a financial leash with a legal guardian to control his money, which failed to alter his unregenerate habits but left him struggling to get along most of the time, a situation exacerbated by debts to moneylenders that became a pit he never could climb out of—his chronic poverty being something he also shared with Poe.

In 1855, thanks to his growing reputation as a translator of Poe and an art critic, his poetry began to be published. He had great hopes for the 1857 collection of *Les fleurs du mal,* but instead it brought scandal and heartbreak. A scathing review by *Le Figaro* was followed by a trial that found thirteen of the one hundred poems an affront to public morality, heretical, obscene. Six were banned, a suppression not lifted until 1949.

The effects of syphilis increasingly showed themselves. He said he felt "the wind of the wing of imbecility" blowing over him. In 1864 he went to Belgium in hopes of persuading a publisher to bring out his complete works, staying there until 1866, when he suffered attacks of paralysis and aphasia. He spent his last year in a nursing home in Paris and died on August 31, 1867, at the age of forty-six, in his mother's arms.

(above) Charles Baudelaire (1821-1867). (Réunion des Musees Nationaux/Art Resource NY Musee d'Orsay, Paris, France)

Poor Baudelaire seems the unlikeliest possible vessel to carry the light of inspiration that would lead to the first best-selling novel about the hollow earth, from Poe to Jules Verne. Compared to tortured visionary Baudelaire, Verne was the picture of bourgeois normalcy. But he read Baudelaire's translations of Poe in various journals and newspapers (Verne knew almost no English), and they touched something in him. It was, however, something different from the deep solemn chord Poe had sounded in Baudelaire's heart. Verne responded chiefly to the cleverness, ratiocination, and up-to-date scientific trappings Poe wrapped his strange stories in. Both Poe's influence and their great differences are glaringly obvious in Verne's 1897 *The Sphinx of the Ice Fields*—his sequel to Poe's *Narrative of Arthur Gordon Pym*. That he was still thinking about Poe and his chopped-off novel this late in his life (Verne was sixty-seven when it was published) says a lot about how Poe remained with him. But he draws a lame "ending" completely lacking in the grand spiritual mystery Poe's final paragraphs suggest. Pym's body is found pasted to a loadstone mountain looming at the South Pole; Verne doesn't follow him down the cosmic drain clearly waiting in Poe's original. This is emblematic of a practical materialism very much in the regular daylight world, far from the spooky subterranean cosmos inhabited by Poe.

Verne was just a normal guy whose life gave little hint of the fantastic voyages that he would find within and that would make him the originator of the modern science fiction novel. He was born in 1828 in Nantes, France, then a fading entrepôt thirty-five miles up the Loire River estuary, 240 miles southeast of Paris. His father, Pierre, had a modestly successful law practice, and the family lived in one of the better neighborhoods, in a house overlooking a quay. Verne grew up watching ships coming and going from all over the world. As the firstborn son he was expected to follow his father's profession. In 1848, his studies took him to Paris, but apolitical young Jules did not join the revolutionary riffraff in the streets. Instead he found himself entranced with the theater. He started hanging out with the artsy bohemian set, actors and writers, becoming friends with Alexandre Dumas *fils,* four years his senior and already famous thanks to his novel *La dame aux camélias,* recently published when they met. They began collaborating on musical confections for the theater, the first of which, *Broken Straws,* went up in June 1850, produced in a venue newly and conveniently opened by Dumas *père.* The play had a decent run, but Verne's expenses while working on it equaled what money he got.

He spent the 1850s in a long struggling apprenticeship, inching crablike toward the new fictional form he would create. Hoping to generate some extra income, in 1851 he wrote the first of many pieces for *Musée des familles,* a magazine devoted to articles and fiction with an educational underpinning. These pieces needed to be solidly researched—even the fiction—and entertainingly didactic, both qualities he would bring to his novels. His theatrical work continued. For two years he became the secretary—unpaid—to the Théâtre Lyrique's director, which put him in the thick of things. But despite years of trying and occasional small successes, his theatrical writing never developed into much. He did gain a sense of shaping discrete scenes that carried over into the novels, and presumably his skill at writing dialog was honed as well. By 1856 he had given up the pretext that he would ever become a lawyer. He had also snagged a potential wife, Honorine, a young widow with two small children and an attractive dowry. He tried to persuade his father to pay 50,000 francs to buy him a share in a stock brokerage in Paris, where Jules would invest for his father and his father's friends, make everybody rich, and still have plenty of time for his writing. His father wasn't buying. In the end his father-in-law made a place for him in a brokerage office he was opening in Paris. Jules and Honorine were married on January 10, 1857.

In the meantime, he continued to write pieces for *Musée des familles,* gaining considerable facility in conducting detailed research—scientific, geographical, historical—taking meticulous notes and then synthesizing the information, threading it into an agreeably entertaining article or story. Whether he was aware of it or not, these pieces were moving him closer to becoming the "real" Jules Verne. He also made a friend who would be a great influence. Jacques Arago was an explorer, travel writer, artist, playwright, and theatrical impresario. Nearly forty years Verne's senior, Arago had traveled to the world's remotest parts and then written and illustrated books about his adventures. Blind and in his sixties when Verne met him, Arago embodied the been-there, done-it-all, know-everything character who would play the lead in so many of Verne's novels. He also had theories about writing that Verne listened to. "He argued that travel books," writes Herbert R. Lottman in his 1996 *Jules Verne,* "when the explorer avoided pedantry, were second only to memoirs as the most interesting of all books, with a minimum of description and a maximum of pithy dialogue."

In 1862 Verne began assembling the pieces of his long apprenticeship into the first of his *Voyages extraordinaires* series: *Five Weeks in a Balloon.* Its sources were disparate and spread over many years, not the least of which were two stories by Edgar Allan Poe, "The Balloon Hoax" and "The Unparalleled Adventure of One Hans Pfall." What came to be known as "The Balloon Hoax" had first been presented as fact, appearing as an extra edition of the *New York Sun* on April 13, 1844, under the headline

ASTOUNDING

NEWS!

BY EXPRESS VIA NORFOLK!

THE

ATLANTIC CROSSED

IN

THREE DAYS!

This account of a wayward balloon (named Victoria, just like Verne's) blown off course across the Atlantic during an attempted flight across the English Channel to France exactly mimicked the journalistic style of the time and was widely accepted as fact, for a day or two anyway. "Hans Pfall," while more fantastic—Hans constructs a balloon that takes him to the moon—also tries to present itself as an account of actual events.[3] Verne's *Five Weeks in a Balloon* achieves the same verisimilitude in recounting a balloon trip by three Englishmen across Africa, starting from Zanzibar and ending up in sub-Saharan Senegal. Just as Poe had played off the excitement surrounding the Wilkes expedition in *Arthur Gordon Pym,* Verne in *Five Weeks* was responding to the current fascination with Africa. Like the poles, it was a great unknown. Even as the novel was published in January 1863, John Speke was on his way home from having reached the long-sought-after source of the Nile in July 1862. He and Sir Richard Burton had made much-publicized African expeditions a few years earlier. Verne's novel, essentially an adventure-filled, low-flying travelogue, caught this buzz, overlaying a concurrent fascination with the possibilities of aviation, and was an immediate hit.

Part of its success was due to Verne's publisher, Pierre-Jules Hetzel. Verne dropped off the manuscript for him and returned two weeks later to a rejection—of sorts. Hetzel told him he had the makings of a great storyteller but needed to make some revisions. Verne knocked them off quickly, and they were in business. Hetzel was both sympathetic and helpful in working with him as a close adviser on his stories, offering encouragement and suggestions Verne almost always followed. Their collaboration lasted many years. In spring 1864 Hetzel began publishing *Magazin d'education et de récréation,* a bimonthly illustrated magazine for a younger audience, another publication that aimed to entertain while edifying. From the first issue it began serializing novel after novel by Verne before they appeared in book form, which was usually at year's end, just in time for the New Year's gift-giving then popular in France.

Verne's first serialized novel turned to another mysterious place—the North Pole. His longest effort to date, it was subsequently published as two separate volumes: *The English at the North Pole* and *The Desert of Ice,* which were then

---

3. While 7,254 miles above the North Pole, Hans makes an observation that the earth there becomes "*not a little concave*" and that the "dusky hue" of the Pole itself, "varying in intensity, was, at all times darker than any other spot on the visible hemisphere, and occasionally deepened into the most absolute blackness. Farther than this, little could be ascertained." This description, while deliberately elliptical, seems to be a definite allusion to a sighting by Hans of a Symmes' Hole up there.

combined under the title *The Adventures of Captain Hatteras.* During the 1840s and 1850s the world was captivated by the disappearance of legendary polar explorer Sir John Franklin; expedition after expedition was mounted to find out what had happened to him, and each one produced a fresh crop of polar narratives. Like Poe before him, Verne absorbed all such literature he could find, relying especially on Sir John Ross's *Second Voyage in Search of a North-West Passage* (1835), when Ross's nephew, James Clark Ross, discovered the magnetic pole. In Verne's story, Captain Hatteras veers from his search for the Northwest Passage toward the pole, driven to be the first to plant the British flag on it. This showed a characteristic instinct for timely prediction on Verne's part. From this time on the arctic focus shifted from pursuing the Northwest Passage to standing on the North Pole. In Verne's novel we naturally find that old standby, the open polar sea, but he adds a fresh twist by explaining it through the presence of volcanoes—one of which sits atop the pole. Verne never buys into Symmes' Holes, but in *The Desert of Ice* he does have Dr. Clawbonny observe:

> In recent times it has even been suggested that there are great chasms at the Poles; it is through these that there emerges the light which forms the Aurora, and you can get down to them to the interior of the earth.

So he knew about Symmes and his holes, but in *A Journey to the Center of the Earth* (1864) he found another way for his characters to get down there, courtesy of Athansius Kircher.

There were two French precursors to Verne's novel that he would have known. *Le voyage au centre de la terre* (1821) was written by Jacques Collin de Plancy, author of several books on vampires, ghosts, the living dead, that sort of thing. Clearly de Plancy's novel owes a great deal to Symmes and eighteenth-century novels by Holberg and Casanova, which Verne's doesn't. The characters embark on a voyage to Spitzbergen, where on winter's approach they nearly starve, but at the end of the first volume they find the *chute au centre de la terre* and head down into it. There they run into little people, *sauvages du petit globe,* and we're off into a litany of their habits, customs, religion, government, and so on. In volume 3, they visit a series of countries with varying peculiarities, emerging from the opening at the South Pole and heading home. It is a considerably more old-fashioned take on the hollow earth than Verne provides.

The other predecessor was by Alexandre Dumas *père,* a strange concoction called *Isaac Laquédem,* whose main character was the Wandering Jew, which Dumas had conceived on an epic eighteen-volume scale but never completed. It has never been translated into English. The first parts appeared in 1852–1853. As Arthur B. Evans describes it in *Science-Fiction Studies* (July 1996), "In *Isaac Laquédem,* the hero Laquédem is guided to the center of the earth by Tyane, a scientist and disciple of Pythagoras. During the long subterranean descent, the former is obliged (much like Verne's young Axel) to 'build up an entire arsenal of Science' by examining the geological history of the planet as shown in the successive strata of rock through which they pass."

But Verne's scheme doesn't owe a lot to either novel.

There are only three main characters: gruff but lovable Professor Lidenbrock; his orphaned nephew, Axel; and strong, stolid Hans, their Icelandic guide, who says about twenty words in the whole novel. The Professor has found an ancient manuscript written in old Icelandic that contains a coded parchment that says, "Descend into the crater of Yocul of Sneffels . . . audacious traveler, and you will reach the center of the earth. I did it. ARNE SAKNUSSEMM." They travel to Iceland, gather supplies (including a few handy Verne inventions, such as an electric-powered gaslight and "a voltaic battery on the newest principle"), and hire Hans, an eider hunter, as their guide. Proceeding to Mount Sneffels, they find the right opening and head down into it. After a torturous descent, they finally arrive in the vault of the inner world—more than a third of the way into the novel. There they encounter a prehistoric realm that seems a succession of *tableaux vivant* of all the

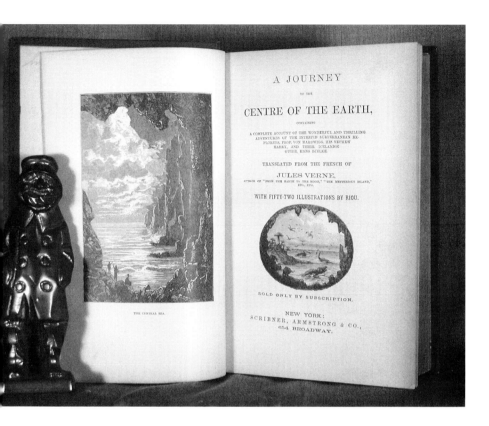

earth's geological periods. They have a variety of adventures, including being blown across the Central Sea on a raft they construct, witnessing an epic battle between two huge prehistoric sea monsters, and encountering a giant tending a herd of mastodons, before trying to head for home. They find Arne's rusty dagger and a stone-carved message amounting to "This way out." A massive boulder blocks the passage, so they blow it up, using fifty pounds of gunpowder they somehow still have with them. It blows a hole in this layer of the inner earth, and suddenly they're back on the raft, riding a torrent as the Central Sea rushes down the hole. Luckily, they're thrown into a passage that proves to be a volcano's chimney, so it's then up

(above) Title page from the 1874 American deluxe edition of *A Journey to the Center of the Earth* showing two examples of the fifty-two engravings by Edouard Riou (1838–1900) appearing throughout the volume. (Courtesy of Sumner & Stillman, Booksellers)

up and away, riding an erupting lava flow that pops them, alive and intact, onto a Mediterranean landscape—the island of Stromboli, near Sicily.

Verne uses the framework of an adventure into a world below to instruct his readers about geological science—which, along with Africa and the North Pole, was also a hot topic at the time. The novel might have as easily been called *A Journey to the Center of Geology*. Verne revised the 1867 edition, adding three new chapters, all of them introducing incidents—and creatures—drawn from recent advances in paleontology. Dinosaurs and pterodactyls and ape men had captured the popular imagination, and Verne was opportunely tapping into it.

Geology as a true science was barely seventy-five years old when Verne was writing his novel. The revolution had begun with James Hutton (1726–1797), a Scotsman whose ideas of "deep time" and "uniformitarianism" in the late eighteenth century had amounted to thinking the unthinkable. According to the Bible the world was less than 6,000 years old and had been created by God in six days. Hutton (and Sir Charles Lyell after him) argued that time beyond measure had gone into the making of the earth as we found it, that no miraculous acts of creation were needed to account for the way it is, and that processes observable today would do the trick. Against this uniformitarianism stood the "catastrophists," who believed changes in the earth occurred through a series of catastrophes—such as The Flood. They continued to have strong proponents well into the nineteenth century. Hutton also believed (correctly) that interior heat was the principle behind major geological processes, a theory that came to be called "Plutonist"—as distinguished from the more popular ideas of the "Neptunists," led by German geologist Abraham Warner (1749–1817), who conceived of the earth much as Burnet had in the late seventeenth century, as a watery sphere with a crust gradually forming as it cooled, with rocks precipitating out of the liquid, and major landscape features caused by disruptions in this unstable crust.

Two other related concepts also played a part in mid-nineteenth-century geological controversies: progressivism and directionalism. Progressivism meant what it suggests, that there is an observable *progress* in the geologic record, an upward march of creatures from lower to higher, culminating with man at the pinnacle. This was both in keeping with the spirit of the times—all sorts of progressive social measures were afoot—as well as being in harmony with religious ideas of a Divine Plan. Progressivism found metaphysical purpose in geological events. Directionalism was a scientific expression of the biblical idea, going back to the work of Burnet and others, that the earth is in a state of decline from an earlier perfection; it held that the major geologic processes were weakening over time, an attenuation caused by the continued cooling of the earth. Both these ideas were embraced by the catastrophists but dismissed by Lyell and his uniformitarian followers, Darwin among them.

Understanding of geology was proceeding by leaps, but even in the 1860s when Verne was writing, deep disagreements continued regarding basic ideas, with neptunists, plutonists, catastrophists, uniformitarians, nonevolutionists, evolutionists, scriptural geologists, and atheists all slugging it out. So where did Verne fit into all of this?

His take on these issues is a little surprising.

Early on in the novel he establishes Professor Lidenbrock as a world-class scientist, hobnobbing with the great and the near great: "Humphrey Davy, Humboldt, Captain Franklin, and General Sabine never failed to call on him when passing through Hamburg; and Becquerel, Ebelman, Brewster, Dumas, Milne-Edwards, and Sainte-Claire Deville frequently consulted him about the most difficult problems in chemistry."

Some of these savants we've encountered before. The first two—Davy and Humboldt—were both invoked by Symmes to be his "protectors" in his 1818 circular. Davy (1778–1829) was a British chemist who first suggested that chemical compounds are held together by an electrical force, becoming the first to isolate pure potassium and sodium from their compounds by zapping them with electricity. Also interested in geology, he was a founder in 1807 of the Geological Society of London.

Alexander von Humboldt (1769–1859) was a German explorer and geographer who had roamed much of Central and South America and then turned his attention to questions of the earth's magnetism and worked on his monumental *Kosmos,* his attempt at a *summa* of all known science. Captain Franklin (1786–1847) was the famous polar explorer whose disappearance caused such a scuffle. The others are less remembered today. Sir Edward Sabine (1788–1883), part of the Ross/Parry arctic expedition of 1818–1820, made notable studies of the earth's magnetic field. The Becquerel family produced several generations of prominent physicists. Jacques-Joseph Ebelman (1814–1852) was a French chemist, Sir David Brewster (1781–1868) a Scottish physicist who studied optics and invented the kaleidoscope, Jean-Baptiste Andre Dumas (1800–1884) a pioneering French organic chemist, Henri Milne-Edwards (1800–1885) a French naturalist who was a professor at the Museum of Natural History in Paris when Verne was writing, and Sainte-Claire Deville (1818–1881) a French chemist who developed the first commercially viable process for producing aluminum—a lightweight metal Verne would find many inventive uses for in his novels.

Listing this heavyweight crowd as the Professor's friends really amounts to Verne showing off a bit, establishing his scientific chops. Sir Humphrey Davy is the scientist most important to the geological ideas found in the novel. Verne has the Professor relate an anecdote to young Axel about a visit Davy paid him in 1825, when Davy was president of the Royal Society. Axel, ever the worrier—making him a convenient foil for the Professor's ideas—is fretting that they'll fry if they venture down into the earth, saying "it is generally recognized that the temperature rises about one degree for every seventy feet below the surface . . . if we were to go only twenty-five miles down . . . the temperature there is over 1,300 degrees." The Professor replies, sensibly, that no one really knows what is going on down there. He then asks Axel, "Isn't it a fact that the number of volcanoes has greatly diminished since the beginning of the world, and may we not conclude that if there is heat in the centre it is decreasing?"

This tidbit of directionalist thought is followed by the anecdote of Davy's 1825 visit. If you do the math, the fifty-year-old Professor (his stated age in 1863 when the novel takes place) would have been *twelve* when this great meeting of the minds happened. It seems such a glaring glitch that Verne should have been aware of it; but it also reveals how vital this little meeting with Davy was to his scheme. "Among the questions," the Professor says, "we spent a long time discussing the hypothesis of the liquid nature of the terrestrial nucleus. We agreed that this liquidity could not exist . . . Because this liquid mass would be subject, like the sea, to the attraction of the moon, and consequently, twice a day, there would be internal tides which, pushing up the earth's crust, would cause periodical earthquakes." So he and Davy are not Neptunists. Axel counters saying, "Yet it is obvious that the surface of the globe has been subjected to the action of fire, and it is reasonable to suppose that the outer crust cooled down first, while the heat took refuge in the centre." To this the Professor offers,

> You are mistaken there. The earth was heated by the combustion of its surface and nothing else. Its surface was composed of a great number of metals, such as potassium and sodium, which have the peculiar property of igniting at the mere contact with air and water. These metals caught fire when the atmospheric vapours fell in the form of rain on the soil; and little by little, when the waters penetrated into the fissures of the earth's crust, they started fresh fires together with explosions and eruptions. Hence the large number of volcanoes in the early period of the earth.

This is a clear statement of ideas on the earth's heat presented by Davy in the series of lectures on geology he presented to the London Royal Institution for the first time in 1805 and many times thereafter. Davy the chemist couldn't imagine internal heat without something to *burn,* and so he denied the widespread central heat proposed by Hutton and the uniformitarians. As Davy argued in one of the

1805 geology lectures, "if a permanent fire had been acting for ages upon the interior of the crust of the globe, its effects must long ago have been perceived upon the whole surface, which would have exhibited not a few widely scattered volcanoes but one ignited and glowing mass."[4] This idea was crucial to Verne's story, since if there actually were great heat down there, he couldn't send his explorers on their subterranean adventure. Even in 1805 Davy's chemical explanation for vulcanism was something of an outlier, and by Verne's time almost no one believed in it. So here is an instance of Verne relying on outmoded science to serve his story's needs.

The novel draws on a melange of geological ideas.

On their way from Reykjavik to their entry point on the quiescent volcano, Axel notices an unusual basalt wall rising in a series of thirty-foot columns. Basalt was a key point of argument between the Neptunists and Plutonists. The Neptunists believed basalts were precipitated out of water, while the Plutonists said (correctly) that they were of an igneous nature. Axel says, "As is well known, basalt is a brown rock of igneous origin," putting him among the Plutonists on this one. But as they finally begin their descent into the interior and start encountering lower strata, the terminology is Neptunist:

> At noon a change occurred in the walls of the gallery . . . The coating of lava had given place to solid rock, arranged in sloping and often vertical strata. We were passing through rocks of the transitional period, the Silurian Period. 'It is all quite clear!' I exclaimed. 'In the second period the water deposits formed these schists, limestones, and shales. We are turning our backs on the granite mass!'[5]

This language is consistent with the Neptunist model of rock formation. Primary rocks were crystalline, precipitated out of the primeval ocean. The next

---

4. Humphrey Davy, *Humphrey Davy on Geology: The 1805 Lectures for the General Audience*, edited by Robert Siegfried and Robert H. Dott, Jr. (Madison, Wisconsin: University of Wisconsin Press, 1980).

5. The translation here is Robert Baldick's, for a 1965 Penguin edition of the novel.

oldest transitional rocks were sedimentary but lacking in fossils. These were followed by secondary rocks, sedimentary and containing fossils, and then the newest tertiary rocks of an alluvial composition, the only ones formed according to present processes. This too is an antiquated scheme of classification, which equated rock type with age, not corresponding to the current categories of igneous, metamorphic, and sedimentary rocks, so designated by the processes creating them and unrelated to how old they are. In this passage Axel believes schist, limestone, and shale result from water deposits, and while he's batting two out of three, schist is a metamorphic rock not so formed.

The trio next find themselves in a passageway that seems to lead up, at least from the fossil evidence they encounter. "We have come to the rocks of the period when the first plants and animals appeared," observes Axel. "In the Silurian epoch," he continues, "the seas contained over fifteen hundred vegetable and animal species." And there are "distinct impressions of rock weeds and club mosses" and then "a perfectly preserved shell which had belonged to an animal rather similar to the present-day woodlouse"—a trilobite. They spend the next day walking through this gallery, passing arch after arch. "The schist, limestone, and old red sandstone sparkled magnificently in the electric light." Axel says,

> Most of the marbles bore impressions of primitive organisms. Creation had obviously made considerable progress since the previous day. Instead of the rudimentary trilobites, I noticed remains of a more advanced order of creatures, including ganoid fishes and some of those saurians in which palaeontologists have detected the earliest reptile forms. The Devonian seas were inhabited by a vast number of creatures of this species, and deposited them in thousands on the newly formed rocks. It was becoming obvious that we were climbing the ladder of animal life on which man occupies the highest rung.

Here Verne is expressing a divine plan progressivism. Like most French children, he was brought up Catholic, but he was never particularly religious. Various biographers have pointed out that his publisher, Hetzel, an atheist, routinely urged Verne to insert more family values–style Christianity into his stories to make them more commercially viable among mainstream readers. Here, and throughout the novel, the take on paleontology is decidedly progressivist: man is at the top of the heap of creatures, and all was brought about by the Creator. Whatever his own views, Verne was doing his best to be a popular author, and the Lyell/Darwin *non*-progressive view was, well, too progressive for most people at the time.

Moments later the rocks change dramatically, and they are surrounded by coal. Its formation was another of the great mysteries back then. Fossil evidence in coal revealed it chiefly to be the remains of tropical vegetation—but how could these plants, apparently needing a hot equatorial climate to thrive, have grown in all these currently frigid regions of the world? Before plate tectonics—the idea that the continents break up and move around like vast, slow puzzle pieces—accounting for this led to all sorts of convoluted theories. "The whole history of the coal period was written on these dark walls," Axel says, "and a geologist could easily follow all its various phases." The theory Verne/Axel proposes is so wonderfully cockeyed I can't resist quoting it at length:

> At that age of the world which preceded the Secondary Period, the earth was covered with vast stretches of vegetation, the product of the dual action of tropical heat and constant moisture. A misty atmosphere enveloped the earth, screening it from the rays of the sun.
>
> Hence the conclusion that the high temperature then prevailing was not due to the sun, which may not even have been ready yet to play the brilliant part it now acts. There were no "climates," as yet, and a torrid heat, equal at the equator and at both poles, was spread over the whole surface of the globe. This heat came from the interior of the earth.

Despite Professor Lidenbrock's theories, a violent fire was blazing in the bowels of the sphere, and its action extended as far as the outer layers of the earth's crust. The plants, deprived of the beneficent rays of the sun, produced neither flowers nor scent, but their roots drew vigorous life from the burning soil of this early period. There were few trees, only herbaceous plants—tall grasses, ferns, lycopods, sigillarias, and asterophyllites, belonging to families which are now rare but at that time contained thousands of species.

Now it is to this exuberant vegetation that the coal measures owe their origin. The as yet elastic crust of the earth obeyed the movements of the liquid mass underneath. Countless fissures and depressions resulted, and the plants, sinking beneath the surface of the waters, gradually formed huge accumulations.

Then natural chemistry came into action; in the depths of the seas, the vegetable masses were turned into peat to begin with, and then, under the influence of the gases and the heat of fermentation, were completely mineralized.

Thus were formed those huge beds of coal which, despite their size, the industrial nations will exhaust within three centuries unless they limit their consumption.

This explanation for the origin of coal sounds today more whimsically poetic than scientific: formed during a hot, misty primeval time when the sun may not have been properly lit up yet, and plants drew their energizing animus from the fires down below. A lingering Burnet/Werner Neptunism/catastrophism creates cracks and fissures sucking all this plant matter below the surface—the thinking being that the liquid earth shrank as it cooled, causing all sorts of disruptions in the newly forming crust—where it stews until it becomes coal. And then the forward-thinking little note at the end, about its rapacious use by industrial nations.

Verne's chief source for the geology in the novel appears to have been a prolific French popular science writer named Louis Figuier (1819–1894). This indebtedness went unnoticed for over a century, only recently brought to light by William Butcher, a Verne scholar who translated the Folio Society's illustrated edition of *A Journey to the Center of the Earth.* In a long article coauthored with John Breyer for the journal *Earth Sciences History,* he demonstrates that Verne leaned heavily on an 1863 book about earth history by Figuier titled *La terre avant le déluge,* which went into four editions and sold over 25,000 copies in two years.[6] As Butcher and Breyer note, the correspondences are so great and so numerous that Figuier, a fellow Parisian, might have been expected to cry *Zut alors!* when Verne's novel came out and, if not sue him for plagiarism, at least give him a good biff on the nose. It's hard to imagine that no one noticed, but apparently no one cared—an instance of literary laissez-faire that wouldn't happen today. Here's just one of many examples they cite:

From Verne:

> I hadn't gone a hundred yards further before incontrovertible proof appeared in front of my eyes. It was to be expected, for during the Silurian Period there were more than 1,500 species of vegetables and animals in the seas . . . On the walls could be clearly seen the outlines of seaweeds and Lycopodia . . . I picked up a perfectly-preserved shell, one that had belonged to an animal more or less like the present-day woodlouse. Then I caught up with my uncle and said to him:
>
> > "See!"
> >
> > "Well," he replied calmly, "it is the shell of a crustacean of the extinct order of trilobites. Nothing else."

Compare this passage with Figuier:

---

6. This article, "Nothing New Under the Earth: The Geology of Verne's *Journey to the Centre of the Earth,*" first published in 2003, is available at http://home.netvigator.com/~wbutcher/articles/nothing%20new.htm. His annotated *JTCOE* text is also online at http://home.netvigator.com/~wbutcher/books/journey_to_the_centre_of_the_earth.htm.

> Most trilobites . . . were able to roll themselves into a ball, like our wood-louse, doubtless to escape the attack of an enemy . . . The seas were already abundantly inhabited at the end of the Upper Silurian period, for naturalists today know more than 1,500 species, animal and vegetable, belonging to the Silurian period.

Similarly, the account of coal formation I quoted above is almost exactly as Figuier has it in *La terre avant le déluge.* Clearly Verne cribbed heavily from Figuier, and not only from his text. Butcher and Breyer also point out that Figuier's book was illustrated, and a number of the descriptions of plants and animals in *A Journey to the Center of the Earth* are taken from these illustrations. "The third edition of Figuier's *La terre avant le déluge*," they write, "published in 1864, contained 'twenty-five ideal views of landscapes of the ancient world' drawn by Edouard Riou (1833–1900) . . . Riou also provided 56 illustrations for *Journey to the Centre of the Earth* in 1864." Chummy of them, no? Butcher and Bryer summarize Figuier's views—and by default Verne's—thus: "Figuier advocated a directionalist view of earth history and progressionism in the organic realm. He thus fits squarely in the catastrophist camp. Moreover, like other members of this school, Figuier openly proclaimed his strong religious beliefs in his text, interpreting earth history and the progress of life as the visible working of the will of the Creator."

As was true of Poe and Melville (not to mention Shakespeare), however, plagiarism can become inspired borrowing, genius transforming theft. Verne may not rise to this level, being more clever than truly brilliant, but he does infuse Figuier's mundane science with a certain lyrical beauty, at least in places.

Probably the most stirring passage in the book owes its ideas almost entirely to Figuier, but it achieves a poetic quality found nowhere in the source. I refer to Axel's waking dream while they're scudding across the Central Sea on a raft of partially fossilized wood, in which Axel has the entire history of the earth flash before his eyes—backward—in a sort of cosmogony-recapitulates-phylogeny rapture:

I fancied I could see floating on the water some huge *chersites*, antediluvian tortoises like floating islands. Along the dark shore there passed the great mammals of early times, the *leptotherium*, found in the caves of Brazil, and the *merycotherium*, found in the icy regions of Siberia. Farther on, the *pachydermatous lophiodon*, a gigantic tapir, was hiding behind the rocks, ready to dispute its prey with the *anoplotherium*, a strange animal which looked like an amalgam of rhinoceros, horse, hippopotamus and camel, as if the Creator, in too much of a hurry during the first hours of the world, had combined several animals in one. The giant mastodon waved its trunk and pounded the rocks on the shore with its tusks, while the megatherium, buttressed on its enormous legs, burrowed in the earth, rousing the echoes of the granite rocks with its roars. Higher up, the *protopitheca*, the first monkey to appear on earth, was climbing on the steep peaks. Higher still, the pterodactyl, with its winged claws, glided like a huge bat through the dense air. And finally, in the upper strata of the atmosphere, some enormous birds, more powerful than the cassowary and bigger than the ostrich, spread their vast wings and soared upwards to touch with their heads the ceiling of the granite vault.

The whole of this fossil world came to life again in my imagination. I went back to the scriptural periods of creation, long before the birth of man, when the unfinished world was not yet ready for him. Then my dream took me even farther back into the ages before the appearance of living creatures. The mammals disappeared, then the birds, then the reptiles of the Secondary Period, and finally the fishes, crustaceans, mollusks, and articulated creatures. The zoophytes of the transitional period returned to nothingness in their turn. The whole of life was concentrated in me, and my heart was the only one beating in that depopulated world. There were no more seasons or climates; the heat of the globe steadily increased and neutralized that of the sun. The vegetation grew to gigantic proportions, and I passed like a ghost among arborescent ferns, treading uncertainly on iridescent marl and mottled stone; I leaned against the trunks of huge conifers; I lay down in the shade of *sphenophyllas*, *asterophyllas*, and *lycopods* a hundred feet high.

Centuries passed by like days. I went back through the long series of terrestrial changes. The plants disappeared; the granite rocks softened; solid matter turned to liquid under the action of intense heat; water covered the surface of the globe, boiling and volatizing; steam enveloped the earth, which gradually turned into a gaseous mass, white-hot, as big and bright as the sun.

In the centre of this nebula, which was fourteen hundred thousand times as large as the globe it would one day form, I was carried through interplanetary space. My body was volatized in its turn and mingled like an imponderable atom with these vast vapours tracing their flaming orbits through infinity.

What a dream this was!

A rhapsody of geology! It doesn't really matter that the substance was lifted from Figuier; Verne has found the silver in the ore. And not too much farther along, he does something else quite wonderful and historic: he gives us the very first battle in literature between two dinosaurs.

Dinosaurs were a fairly new invention when Verne was writing. Not the fossils and skeletons themselves, of course, but the *idea*. The word "dinosaur" was coined in 1841 by British anatomist Sir Richard Owen (1804–1892), sometime physician, tutor to Queen Victoria's children, head of the natural history department at the British Museum from 1856 to 1884, and longtime friend of Darwin until the younger man's rising star seemed to eclipse his own, transforming Owen into a bitter enemy both of Darwin and evolutionism.

One of the earliest specimens was unearthed in the United States in 1818 by Solomon Ellsworth Jr. while he was digging a well on his farm east of the Connecticut River. But discoveries in the 1820s in southern England by minister and geologist William Buckland (among the most famous of the antievolutionary "scriptural geologists") and physician Gideon Mantell gained more notice. Owen, something of a showman, collaborated with sculptor Benjamin Waterhouse Hawkins to create the first of the dinosaur reconstructions that are now a staple of natural history museums everywhere, making life-sized models of *Iguanodon* and *Hylaeosaurus* (two of the first three dinosaurs to be named) that were put on display in the Crystal Palace of London's Great Exhibition of 1851, setting off a dinosaur mania that cheerfully continues today.

It was in its first blush when Verne cannily pitted his two sea monsters against each other in mortal combat. Again, Becker and Breyer point out that one of the Riou illustrations in the third edition of Figuier's book showed "an ichthyosaurus emerging from the depths to confront a plesiosaur on the surface with its neck arched preparing to strike." The very same pair Verne picked to go at it in his novel.

As the trio zip along over the Central Sea, they decide to take a sounding to determine its depth. They tie a pickax to a cord and drop it overboard but fail to strike bottom at two hundred fathoms; and when they haul it up, they find tooth marks on the ax head! Worrywart Axel starts to sweat about what might be down there. He remembers that "the antediluvian monsters of the Secondary Period . . . held absolute sway over the Jurassic seas." And further observes:

> Nature had endowed them with a perfect constitution, gigantic proportions, and prodigious strength. The saurians of our days, the biggest and most terrible alligators and crocodiles, are only feeble, reduced copies of their ancestors of primitive times.

This not only sets the stage nicely, it's another bit of progressivism/

directionalism, which holds that things are falling from a former more intense state; not only were geologic forces stronger in the past, but plants and creatures tended to degenerate from an initial perfection at their first appearance. Two days later Axel's fears are realized. With a terrific *thwack!* the raft is lifted "up above the water with indescribable force and hurled a hundred feet or more." They see what they think is "a colossal porpoise," "an enormous sea-lizard," "a monstrous crocodile," and "a whale!"

"We stood there surprised, stupefied, horrified by this herd of marine monsters. They were of supernatural dimensions . . . a turtle forty feet long, and a serpent thirty feet long, darting its enormous head to and fro above the waves." Suddenly two of them "hurled themselves on one another with a fury which prevented them from seeing us. The battle began two hundred yards away." The Professor and Axel realize they hadn't seen a herd of terrible creatures but different parts of these two. "The first of those monsters has the snout of a porpoise, the head of a lizard and the teeth of a crocodile . . . it's the most formidable of the antediluvian reptiles, the ichthyosaurus! . . . The other is a serpent with a turtle's shell, the mortal enemy of the first—the plesiosaurus!" Butcher and Breyer point out that the detail here too is drawn from Figuier, "who describes his ichthyosaur as having 'the head of a lizard, the teeth of a crocodile, the vertebrae of a fish . . . and the fins of a whale.'" Verne also describes it as having a blood-red eye the size of a human head, another specific found in Figuier. But the latter never wrote this:

> Those two animals attacked each other with indescribable fury. They raised mountainous waves which rolled as far as the raft, so that a score of times we were on the point of capsizing. Hissing noises of tremendous intensity reached our ears. The two monsters were locked together, and could no longer be distinguished from one another. We realized we had everything to fear from the victor's rage. One hour, two hours went by, and the fight went on with unabated fury . . . Suddenly the ichthyosaurus

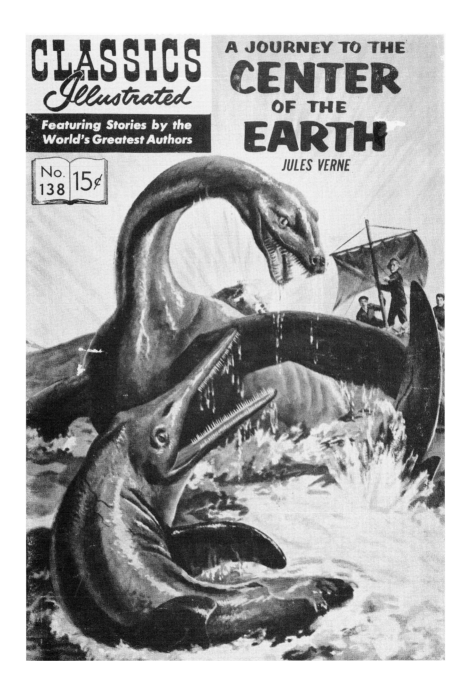

(above and opposite) Classics Comics edition of Verne's *Journey to the Center of the Earth,* first published in May 1957. (© Gilberton Company, Inc.)

WE STROLLED ALONG THE SHORE.

WHAT ARE THOSE STRANGE TREES?

THEY ARE NOT TREES, BUT MUSHROOMS. THEY HAVE GROWN SO TALL BECAUSE OF THE WARMTH AND DAMPNESS DOWN HERE.

THE SAME THING HAS HAPPENED TO THESE. THEY ARE HUMBLE SHRUBS IN THE UPPER WORLD, BUT LOOK AT THEM HERE!

AND SEE WHAT ELSE WE FIND. THE BONES OF PREHISTORIC ANIMALS ARE SCATTERED OVER THE GROUND.

YES. HUGE, TERRIBLE MONSTERS ONCE LIVED ON THESE SHORES.

PERHAPS ONE OF THEM IS STILL WANDERING ABOUT.

and the plesiosaurus disappeared, creating a positive whirlpool in the water. Several minutes passed. Was the fight going to end in the depths of the sea?

All of a sudden an enormous head shot out of the water, the head of the plesiosaurus. The monster was mortally wounded. I could no longer see its huge shell, but just its long neck rising, falling, coiling, and uncoiling. Lashing the waves like a gigantic whip and writhing like a worm cut in two. The water spurted all around and almost blinded us. But soon the reptile's death-agony drew to an end. Its movements grew less violent, its contortions became feebler, and the long serpentine form stretched out in an inert mass on the calm waves.

As for the ichthyosaurus, has it returned to its submarine cave, or will it reappear on the surface of the sea?

Thus ends the very first dinosaur battle in literature. The source of Steven Spielberg's fortune! Passages like this one have kept the novel in print for nearly 150 years, despite the obsolete geological pedagogy threaded throughout.

The geology/paleontology gets increasingly whimsical as the novel progresses, possibly as Verne veered away from the pop science magazine writing he'd done and began warming to the imaginative opportunities his story offered. He still tries to anchor things on a scientific basis, but he can't resist having some fun. This is especially the case in chapters 37–39, which follow almost immediately after the sea monster battle and were added to the 1867 edition. All three dramatize further developments in paleontology and evolution, but they are played more for their theatrical possibilities than the didactic moments they might provide. Evidently readers really liked the battle of sea monsters, and Verne decided to provide more of the same, whether or not it corresponded to current scientific thinking. Over time, he developed an ability to seamlessly intertwine fact and fantasy.

After the sea monster battle ends, a storm kicks up that sends them flying over the Central Sea for five days. The Professor is delighted; it means major headway. But when the storm abates, they are plopped on the shore right back where they started from. This is where the new material in chapter 37 begins. They decide to explore a bit to get their bearings and come across a "plain, covered with bones. It looked like a huge cemetery . . . great mounds of bones were piled up row after row, stretching away to the horizon, where they disappeared into the mist. There, within perhaps three square miles, was accumulated the entire history of animal life." In this welter of remains from all periods—a dreamlike comingling that goes unexplained—the Professor finds a human head. His first reaction is to lord it over the competition stuck on the surface above: "'Oh, Mr. Milne-Edwards! Oh, Monsieur de Quatrefages! If only you could be standing where I, Otto Lidenbrock, am standing now!" (Both Milne-Edwards and Quatrefages were distinguished professors at the Paris Natural History Museum at the time.) This ends chapter 37.

In chapter 38, Professor Lidenbrock goes a little batso and commences delivering a lecture to the sea of bones, thinking he is addressing a class back in Hamburg. Axel provides a bit of background regarding a discovery ("an event of the highest importance from the paleontological point of view") near Abbeville, France, on March 28, 1863, of "a human jaw-bone fourteen feet below the surface. It was the first fossil of this sort that had ever been brought to light." The aforementioned Milne-Edwards and Quatrefages had "demonstrated the incontestable authenticity of the bone in question," proving it a true human fossil from the Quaternary period. Axel then summarizes the debate that followed, mentioning additional human fossil finds in conclusive strata: "Thus, at one bound, man leapt a long way up the ladder of time; he was shown to be a predecessor of the mastodon . . . 100,000 years old, since that was the age attributed by the most famous geologists to the Pliocene terrain."

Amid all the other bones they see "an absolutely recognizable human body, perfectly preserved down the ages." This is where the Professor flips into lecture mode. "Gentlemen," he begins, "I have the honor to introduce you to a man of the

Quaternary Period." For the next several pages, he gives a rundown of fossil finds, real and fake, from antiquity down to the present. He next describes the specimen itself—less than six feet tall and "incontestably Caucasian, the white race, our own. This specimen of humanity belongs to the Japhetic race, which is to be found from the Indies to the Atlantic. Don't smile, gentlemen." Japhetic is a racial term derived from Japheth, one of Noah's sons, usually designating the nations of Europe and northern Asia. The phrase "Indies to the Atlantic" is obscure, but then he's lecturing to an endless boneyard. Given the prevailing racism of the time, it is hardly surprising that this Quaternary Man is a bona fide Caucasian. Verne dodges questions of evolution by making his specimen a modern man. How did he get down there? Once again the Professor relies on the catastrophist principle of a cooling, shrinking earth riddled with "chasms, fissures, and faults." So maybe the stratum he was buried in just fell through. Or had such people lived here? The chapter ends: "Might not some human being, some native of the abyss, still be roaming these desolate shores?"

In chapter 39, "Man Alive," Verne tosses in every paleontological element he can think of for a big finish. The three continue walking until they come to "the edge of a huge forest" that turns out to be a botanical garden of trees and plants from all habitats and climates, "the vegetation of the Tertiary Period in all its splendor." But "there was no colour in all these trees, shrubs, and plants, deprived as they were of the vivifying heat of the sun." Axel says, "I saw trees from very different countries on the surface of the globe, the oak growing near to the palm, the Australian eucalyptus leaning against the Norwegian fir, the northern birch tree mingling its branches with those of the Dutch Kauris. It was enough to drive to distraction the most ingenious classifiers of terrestrial botany." As well as the reader, since these trees couldn't possibly coexist in the same habitat. Verne is trying too hard in these added chapters, straining for effect in a way the original material seldom does.

Out of the blue, they come on a living man—a huge shepherd tending a flock of mastodons. This "Proteus of those subterranean regions, a new son of Neptune," is twelve feet tall and has a head "as big as a buffalo's . . . half hidden in the tangled growth of his unkempt hair . . . In his hand he was brandishing an enormous bough, a crook worthy of this antediluvian shepherd." A giant prehistoric hippie! For once the Professor agrees that they should run for it, and they take off so quickly that Axel later questions whether they really saw the apparition. The appearance of the giant shepherd goes unexplained, a brief tableau Verne felt moved to include as a further nod to the interest in ape men, for its sensational quality and not as an integral part of the plot. We glimpse him and he's gone.

I'm one in a long line of readers who has trouble with the way Verne gets Axel, the Professor, and taciturn Hans back up to the surface. While using their remaining "gun-cotton" (another item they drag along with them and produce at the right moment) to blow up a boulder lodged in their exit passageway, they accidentally use too much force:

> The shape of the rocks suddenly changed before my eyes; they opened like a curtain. I caught sight of a bottomless pit which appeared in the very shore. The sea, seized with a fit of giddiness, turned into a single enormous wave, on the ridge of which the raft stood up perpendicularly.

And the roller-coaster ride is on. They've blown a hole in this level of the inner earth and the sea goes rushing down into the abyss, carrying them along on the raft. An hour, two hours go by, and still they plunge. "We were moving faster than the fastest of express trains." Resourceful Hans manages to light a lantern, so they can see what's happening. They are in a wide gallery, and "the water was falling at an angle steeper than that of the swiftest rapids in America." Their speed increases and then "a water-spout, a huge liquid column, struck its surface [the raft's]"—and then they are being propelled upward. The Professor naturally has an explanation: "The water has reached the bottom of the abyss and is now rising to find its own level, taking us with it." The hydraulics here are murky at best. An hour goes by and then two as they ride the rising water toward the surface. The Professor calmly notes the passing strata. "Eruptive granite. We are still in the Primitive Period . . . Soon we shall come to the terrain of the Transition Period, and then" . . . The temperature rises precipitously. The water column is boiling hot. The compass "had gone mad." The following chapter title says it: "Shot Out of a Volcano." "Loud explosions could be heard with increasing frequency . . . Before long this noise had become a continuous roll of thunder." The Professor, pleased at this, is the first to realize they're riding an eruption. Axel is scared witless. Their ascent goes on through a night and into morning, though it's hard to know how they can tell.

> Soon lurid lights began to appear in the vertical gallery, which was grow-
> ing wider; on both right and left I noticed deep corridors like huge tunnels
> from which thick clouds of vapour were pouring, while cracking tongues
> of flame were licking their walls.
>
> "Look, look, Uncle!" I cried.
>
> "Those are just sulphurous flames. Nothing could be more natu-
> ral in an eruption."

Nothing ruffles the unflappable Professor. Axel asks if they won't be suffocated. Not a chance, says the Professor. What about the rising water? "There's no water left, Axel," he answers, "but a sort of lava paste which is carrying us up with it to the mouth of the crater." This is such an exciting close-up look at the innards of a volcano that I shouldn't carp, admittedly, but how does the raft keep from burning up if it's riding on molten lava? Picky, picky. At last the volcano spits them out. Narrator Axel conveniently has "no clear recollection of what happened." He comes to lying on a mountain slope and at first can't figure out where they are. He sees olive groves and "an exquisite sea"—"this enchanted land appeared to be an island barely a few miles wide." After a time walking through lovely countryside they encounter a little boy. Addressing him in various languages, finally they ask in Italian where they are. "Stromboli," he replies. It's a fitting choice. Stromboli even now has more or less regular volcanic eruptions, and they're distinctive, intermittent blasts, not a continual flow, a type known as Strombolian. This hearkens back to good old Athanasius Kircher, whose ideas of volcanic systems are echoed here, and who stuck his own curious nose down into an Italian volcano two hundred years earlier.

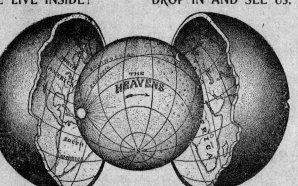

THE
HEAVENS

KOST 1. 18. 19.1

5

CYRUS TEED AND KORESHANITY

AROUND MIDNIGHT, EARLY AUTUMN 1869. Yellow wavering kerosene light dances off jars of colorful compounds, retorts, odd electrical devices, and other singular equipment in a little "electro-alchemical" laboratory near Utica, New York. Thirty-year-old Cyrus Teed has been working here all day and into the night, with great result.

As he later wrote in *The Illumination of Koresh*, he had discovered "the secret law and beheld the precipitation of golden radiations, and eagerly watched the transformation of forces to the minute molecules of golden dust as they fell in showers through the lucid electro-alchemical fluid . . . I had succeeded in transforming matter of one kind to its equivalent energy, and in reducing this energy, through polaric influence, to matter of another kind . . . The 'philosopher's stone' had been discovered, and I was the humble instrument for the exploiter of so magnitudinous a result."

Discovering the philosopher's stone—figuring out the age-old mystery of turning base metal into gold—would seem to be enough for one day's work. But

(opposite) Photo of Cyrus Reed Teed ("Koresh") on the grounds of his utopian community in Estero, Florida, along with a Koreshan promotional card. (Koreshan State Historic Site)

Teed wasn't done for the night. "I had compelled Nature to yield her secret so far as it pertained to the domain of pure physics. Now I deliberately set myself to the undertaking, of victory over death . . . the key of which I knew to be in the mystic hand of the alchemico-vietist." Hard to say exactly what he meant by alchemico-vietist, but a likely deconstruction is an alchemist working on the mysteries of life forces. In any case Teed considered himself one. He next explains his view of the universe, which leads to his greater immediate goal:

> I believed in the universal unity of law. I regarded the universe as an infinitely (the word is here employed in its commonly accepted use) grand and composite structure, with every part so adjusted to every other part as to constitute an integrality, constantly regenerating itself from and in itself; its structural arrangement in one common center, and its forces and laws being projected from this center, and returning to the common origin and end of all. I had taken the outermost degree of physical and material substance, that in which was the lowest degree of organic force and form, for my experimental research. Having in this material sphere made the discovery of the law of transmutation, law being universally uniform, I knew, by the accurate application of correspondential analogy to anthropostic biology, that I could cause to appear before me in a material, tangible, and objective form, my highest ideal of creative beauty, my true conception of her who must constitute the environing form of the masculinity and Fatherhood of Being, who quickeneth.

Teed loves nine-dollar words and isn't shy about making up new ones. Whatever he might mean about applying correspondential analogy to anthropostic biology (anthroposophy was a current term for knowledge of the nature of man), it seems he's *trying* to say that what he had achieved in transforming material substances he now intended to apply to the spirit, to make manifest his "highest ideal of creative beauty," though saying that *she* would be the embodiment of the "Fatherhood of Being" seems a little foggy. He sits in a thoughtful attitude and concentrates with all his might.

> I bent myself to the task of projecting into tangibility the creative princi- ple. Suddenly, I experienced a relaxation at the occiput or back part of the brain, and a peculiar buzzing tension at the forehead or sinciput; suc- ceeding this was a sensation as of a Faradic battery of the softest tension, about the organs of the brain called the lyra, crura pinealis, and conarium. There gradually spread from the center of my brain to the extremities of my body, and, apparently to me, into the auric sphere of my being, miles outside of my body, a vibration so gentle, soft, and dulciferous that I was impressed to lay myself upon the bosom of this gently oscillating ocean of magnetic and spiritual ecstasy. I realized myself gently yielding to the impulse of reclining upon this vibratory sea of this, my newly-found de- light. My every thought but one had departed from the contemplation of earthly and material things. I had but a lingering, vague remembrance of natural consciousness and desire.[1]

It has been suggested that this illumination was nothing more than an accidental near-electrocution from the electricity he was so fond of fiddling with, a *zzzolt!* to the brain that, instead of killing him, produced this vision. Ye of little faith!

Suffused by this ocean of electro-magneto-spiritual energy, he lies back on it, as if on a mystical water bed, drifting away into an unknown ecstasy. He has lost his body. "I started in alarm, for I felt that I had departed from all material things, perhaps forever. 'Has my thirst for knowledge consumed my body?' was my ques- tion." A touch of Faust here. He can't feel his body. He opens his eyes but can't

---

1. *The Illumination of Koresh: Marvelous Experiences of the Great Alchemist Thirty Years Ago, at Utica, NY* (Chicago: Guiding Star, n.d.).

see anything at first. Then he hears "a sweet, soft murmur which sounded as if thousands of miles away." He tries to speak, but it is in a voice he has never heard before. "Yet it was my own effort, and I knew it came from me. I looked again; I was not there."

"Fear not, my son," he finds himself saying in this strange voice, "thou satisfactory offspring of my profoundest yearnings! I have nurtured thee through countless embodiments . . ." The voice continues its revelations, taking him on a journey through his many past lives, good, bad, and horrible. The voice then tells him to look and "see me as I am, for thou has desired it. Offspring of Osiris and Isis, behold the revailing [*sic*] of thy Mother."

He sees a "light of dazzling brilliancy" appear. A sphere of luminescent swirling purple and gold, and "near the upper portion of its perpendicular axis, an effulgent prismatic bow like the rainbow, with surpassing brilliancy. Set in this corona or crown were twelve magnificent diamonds." This acid trip light show gradually resolves into human form—a beautiful woman. A *very* beautiful woman. Standing on a silvery crescent, holding a winged staff with entwined serpents—a caduceus, symbol of the medical profession—she wears a royal purple and gold gown, has "golden tresses of profusely luxuriant growth over her shoulders," and "exquisite" features. It is God herself! She reveals that she is the Father, the Son, and the Mother, all in one. "I have brought thee to this birth," she says, "to sacrifice thee upon the altar of all human hopes, that through thy quickening of me, thy Mother and Bride, the Sons of God shall spring into visible creation." And she has a lot more to tell him.

At last the vision ends and Teed finds himself lying on the couch in his laboratory. He closes the *Illumination* by recounting his achievement in demonstrating the "law of transmutation":

> I had . . . demonstrated the correlation of force and matter. I had formu-
> lated the axiom that matter and energy are two qualities or states of the

same substance, and that they are each transposable to the other . . . In this I knew was held the key that would unlock all mysteries, even the mystery of Life itself.

What's eerie about this is that through the most occult, electro-alchemical path, Teed has arrived at an idea—matter is energy, energy matter, simply different forms of the same thing—that would shortly become an essential scientific truth.

But then he says he made this transmutation spiritually as well:

I had transformed myself to spirituous essence, and through it had made myself the quickener and vivifier of the supreme feminine potency . . . While thus inherent and clothed upon with the femininity of my being, how vividly was awakened in my mind the memory of the passage of Scripture found in Jeremiah xxxi: 22: "How long wilt thou go about, O thou backsliding daughter? For the Lord hath created a new thing in the Earth, a woman shall compass a man."

Through force of will Teed not only summoned God to appear to him, but he *really* got in touch with his feminine side! The main points of Teed's *Illumination* are summarized in Sara Weber Rea's *The Koreshan Story* (1994):

- *The universe is a cell, a hollow globe*, eternally and perpetually renewing itself by virtue of involution and evolution, and *all life exists on its inner concave surface.*
- God being perfect is both male and female—a biune being, and personal to every individual.
- Matter and energy are inter-convertible. Matter is destructible resulting in transmutation of its form to energy and conversely, from energy to form.

- Reincarnation is the central law of life—one generation passing into another with all humanity flowing down the stream of life together.
- Heaven and hell constitute the spiritual world. That is, they are mental conditions and within mankind.
- The Bible is the best written expression of the Divine Mind but is written symbolically. The symbolism must be interpreted by a prophet who would appear in every age and in the context of that age.
- Man lives best by communal principles to correspond with the primitive Christian church. The Koreshan form of socialism would be the expression of the natural laws of order, to include the elimination of money power and wage slavery.
- Equity, not equality, is a natural law for women as for men. There is no equality, and to say any two people are equal is merely trying to enforce uniformity.

Amazing that Teed got all this down without taking notes. And that wasn't all. Rea adds, "Dr. Teed indicated there was a great deal more knowledge that had been imparted to his mental consciousness, but he felt the ordinary minds of mortals could not immediately comprehend or evaluate it. It would be presented to the world in time."

So: the earth is hollow and we all live inside. Teed is the second coming of Christ. God is male and female. Matter and energy are interchangeable. Reincarnation is a fact of existence. Heaven and hell are within us. The Bible should be read symbolically, not literally. People should live according to communal socialist principles—no money. Equity for men and women.

These ideas are part of a mainstream of American millenarian thinking that goes back to the Pilgrims and the Boston Puritans. Eschatological details varied, but the thread of the last days being upon us shines through the fabric of American history, with new messiahs practically a dime a dozen. What sets Teed

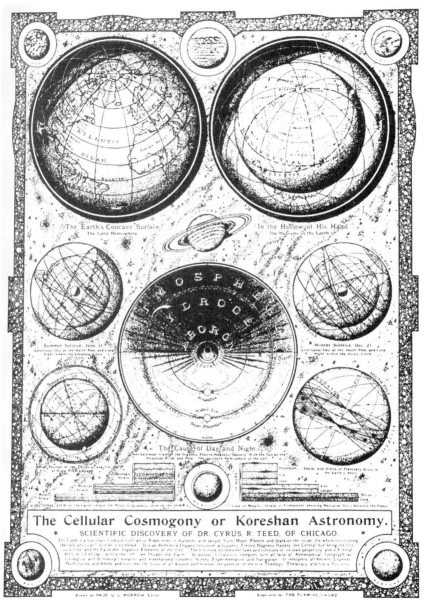

(above) Chart depicting Koreshan cosmogony from an 1880s edition
of the *Flaming Sword*. (Koreshan State Historic Site)

apart is his insistence that the earth is hollow and that we all live inside a "cosmic egg." Robert S. Fogarty briefly summarizes Teed's cosmology:

> He discovered that the universe is all one substance, limited, integral, balanced and emanating from one source, God. The Copernican theory of an illimitable universe was false because the earth had a limited form: it was concave . . . The sun is an invisible electro-magnetic battery revolving in the universe's center on a 24 year cycle. Our visible sun is only a reflection, as is the moon, with the stars reflecting off seven mercurial disks that float in the sphere's center. Inside the earth there are three separate atmospheres: the first composed of oxygen and nitrogen and closest to the earth; the second, a hydrogen atmosphere above it; third, an aboron[2] atmosphere at the center. The earth's shell is one hundred miles thick and has seventeen layers. The outer seven are metallic with a gold rind on the outermost layer, the middle five are mineral and the five inward layers are geologic strata. Inside the shell there is life, outside a void. One can then understand why the Koreshan group was reported to have sported badges which proclaimed "We live on the inside."[3]

These details were elaborated over time and remained central to Teed's theology, even though his insistence on the earth's hollowness and our interior living arrangements got him branded a crackpot and worse. Ready to take his lumps, he declared, "To know of the earth's concavity is to know God, while to believe in the earth's convexity is to deny Him and all His works." No ambiguity there.

Although Teed's conviction that the earth is hollow had antecedents in the work of Edmond Halley, Cotton Mather, John Cleves Symmes, and Jules Verne, he was the first to claim we're living in it.

------

2. Aboron would appear to be an element of Teed's own invention—or one God told him about that hasn't been revealed to the rest of us. The word doesn't appear in the *Oxford English Dictionary*, and a Google search turns up only a West African tribe of that name.

3. Robert S. Fogarty, introduction to a reprint of *The Cellular Cosmogony* by Cyrus Teed and Professor U. G. Morrow (Philadelphia: Porcupine Press, 1975). The original edition appeared in 1898.

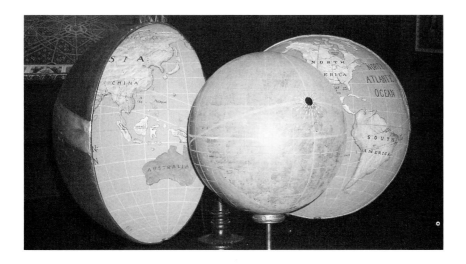

A "scientific" book supporting the earth's hollowness appeared in 1871 and went through several editions in the next few years. Whether Teed read it isn't known. But it contains notable parallels to his ideas, particularly in regard to their inspiration and electromagnetism. It had the slightly askew title *The Hollow Globe; or The World's Agitator and Reconciler.* The title page writing credits are revealing:

Presented through the Organism of
M. L. SHERMAN, M.D.,
And Written by
PROF. WM. F. LYON

As Professor Lyon humbly relates in the preface, he had little to do with the "original, natural and startling ideas, which seem to be entirely irrefutable," since they were channeled from the spirit world through Dr. Sherman, and Professor Lyon simply wrote them down. He says that in September 1868, he was sitting in his Sacramento office "when a strange gentleman made his appearance" and told Lyon

(above) Teed's hollow globe, on display in Art Hall at the Koreshan Historic Site in Estero, Florida. (Koreshan State Historic Site)

that he had repeatedly "been thrown into a semi-trance condition becoming partially unconscious of his earthly surroundings" (sound familiar?). During this trance spirits gave him scientific information about the nature of the world. Over the next months, Sherman conveyed these ideas "in broken fragments" to Lyon, who organized them. In some respects they are a further iteration of existing hollow earth ideas and in others represent a new departure.

Like many hollow earth theorists going back to Halley, the authors in chapter 1 insist on divine purpose but give it a peculiarly American manifest destiny twist. After charting the American movement westward and citing the human universality of this drive, they point out that America is filling up and people will soon have nowhere to go. (This is actually forward-looking, since historian Frederick Jackson Turner didn't declare the frontier a goner until 1893.) But an all-wise spirit wouldn't permit this thwarting of human need and so, voilà, the paradisiacal hollow earth awaits! Humanity not only needs it to be there, it would be a horrible waste of space if it weren't.[4] But how to get inside? Here the authors fall back on Symmes (without naming him): a vast opening at the pole. What about all that ice? Chapter 2 takes up another standby, the open polar sea. It definitely exists, and a passage will be found through the ice, probably through the Bering Straits. What about the burning heat that's supposed to be down there, per prevailing geological thinking? Chapter 3, "The Igneous Theory," demolishes that folly. Okay, then what about volcanoes and earthquakes? These occupy chapters 4 and 5. And here's where we see a new wrinkle in hollow earth thinking. Lyons goes to great pains, and into frightening detail, to show that what causes them—as well as what holds the fabric of the earth together—is a complex electromagnetic matrix that I won't even attempt to describe. This insistence on electromagnetism as the essential force at work is something new, and it's also essential in Teed's formulation.

Electromagnetism was a hot topic in science at the time. The nineteenth century could be designated the Electrical Century, starting in 1800 with the first electric battery developed by Alessandro Volta, followed by the discovery of electro-

---

4. This idea hearkens back to the notion of an "abundant creation" that was a commonplace in the seventeenth century, invoked by Halley in his hollow earth paper to suggest that there might be life down there, and used by Symmes as well to explain the paradise he expected to find inside.

magnetism by Hans Christian Oersted in 1820. Samuel F. B. Morse was granted a patent on the electromagnetic telegraph in 1837, and this heralded all the electric wonders to come before century's end: incandescent light, the telephone, phonograph records, movies, radio. So it makes sense that electromagnetism would also be incorporated into the most trendy and up-to-date metaphysics, both by Sherman/Lyon and Cyrus Teed.

Promulgating these ideas would be a large order for a young man whose life so far had been undistinguished at best. Teed had been born in 1839 in the village of Trout Creek, New York, one of two sons among eight children. The family moved north to the Utica area when he was just a year old. By an odd coincidence, he was a distant cousin to Joseph Smith, whose own vision (a pillar of fire that turned into God and Jesus) as a teenager in 1820, just three hundred miles from Utica, led to the founding of the Mormon Church.

As a child, Teed showed no particular spark. He quit school at age eleven to work on the Erie Canal, as a driver on the towpath of the canal, which had been completed twenty-five years earlier. At some point he started to study medicine with a physician uncle. At twenty-two he enlisted in the Union army as part of the medical corps; he had already married Delia M. Row, a distant cousin, and fathered a son, Douglas. After Teed was released from the army, he returned to New York to continue studying medicine at the Eclectic Medical College—an esoteric institution that emphasized what would be called alternative remedies today. As Fogarty characterizes it, "Eclectic practitioners were more poorly educated than regular physicians, combined a variety of methods derived from regular and homeopathic medicine and, in the main, had their practices in smaller communities. Some eclectics were disreputable charlatans while others worked in the botanical drug tradition and served their communities as well as the other sects."

After graduating in 1868, Teed moved to Deerfield, New York, to join his uncle in practice. According to Peter Hicks, they hung out a sign saying, "He who deals out poison, deals out death." Hicks explains: "They were referring to drugs—

a very busy pharmacy . . . an half block away shows no record of the Teeds ever writing a prescription. However, below the doctors' office was a tavern, and people found this reference to poison very humorous."[5] Teed called his approach to medicine "electro-alchemy," blending "modernized" alchemy with strategically placed zaps of electric current and doses of polar magnetism, a mixture of science (of a sort) and mysticism that would continue in his religious efforts. During his illumination, the lovely manifestation of God had also told him, as Hicks puts it, "that he would interpret the symbols of the Bible for the scientific age."

After this profound spiritual experience, Teed couldn't resist adding his metaphysical insights to the other restoratives he offered his patients. But most didn't want to hear about how we're living inside the hollow earth and that Copernicus had it all wrong from someone they were trusting to take care of their ailments. His practice, barely a year old when his illumination occurred, began to suffer, and the Teed family made the first of many moves in hopes of doing better somewhere else. He next tried his peculiar amalgam of doctoring and cosmic revelation in Binghamton, New York.

In 1873 he and Dr. A.W.K. Andrews—a close friend and one of his first true believers—visited the Harmony Society in Economy, Pennsylvania, a few miles above Pittsburgh. It was his first close-up look at a utopian religious community, and the experience put a gleam in his eye. As it happened, Harmonist founder George Rapp had been a fellow alchemist.

In their time, the Harmonists were among the more successful of the communal religious societies that sprouted like wildflowers all over the Northeast and Midwest during the nineteenth century. There were so many in New York alone that a swath through the center of the state was known as the "burned-out area" for the fervent religiosity and communal experiments it had seen. Teed's spiritual revelation, leading him to create his own religious sect and utopian community, was not some isolated sport. His ideas about living inside the hollow earth were novel, but he was hardly alone in cooking up a new religion and establishing a community

---

5. Hicks was a ranger at the Koreshan State Historic Site in Estero, Florida, at the time of writing this unpublished article, which is available online at http://koreshan.mwweb.org/teed.htm.

based on his ideas. It was going around. As Emerson famously wrote in a letter to Carlyle in 1840:

> We are all a little wild here with numberless projects of social reform. Not a reading man but has a draft of a new community in his waistcoat pocket ... One man renounces the use of animal food; and another of coin; and another of domestic hired service; and another of the State.

The Harmonists had gathered to lead lives that would prepare them for the Second Coming of Christ, which they were certain was right around the corner. The society was communist, with no privately held property, and all worked for the common good. They felt they were following the model of the primitive Christian church—"united to the community of property adopted in the days of the apostles," said their Articles of Association. They also practiced celibacy, believing it to be a higher state than marriage. Both these ideas would turn up in Teed's program.

Teed continued, reluctantly, to stay on the move, trying various towns in New York and Pennsylvania. Around the time he visited the Harmonists, his wife's health took a bad turn, and she went with their son, Douglas, to live with her sister in Binghamton, where she remained until her death in 1885. Teed seems to have largely put them behind him to become the new hollow earth messiah. After his wife's death, Douglas was taken in by a Mrs. Streeter, who supported him emotionally and financially and also provided the means for him to study art in Italy. Teed had other things on his mind.

In 1878, he visited another successful utopian community, the Shaker enclave at Mount Lebanon, New York, near the Massachusetts border just west of Pittsfield. According to Peter Hicks he was admitted as a member in the North Family there. This was the first formal Shaker community, consisting then of almost four hundred people, and one of fifty-eight such Shaker groups scattered as far west as Kentucky.

The Shakers had come together around Ann Lee, an Englishwoman born in 1736. At twenty-three she joined a Quaker society of a spirited sort that earned them the nickname "Shaking Quakers" because of the way they shook, whirled, and trembled to be rid of evil. They suffered persecution, and in 1770 Ann Lee had her illumination in jail. "By a special manifestation of divine light the present testimony of salvation and eternal life was fully revealed to her," as a Shaker history from 1859 puts it. Ann Lee learned that she was the Second Coming of Christ, and in 1773 "she was by a direct revelation instructed to repair to America" to establish "the second Christian Church." (It was also revealed that the colonies would win the coming war and that "liberty of conscience would be secured to all people.") With seven followers (including her soon to be ex-husband and brother), Mother Ann, as she was now known, came to New York in 1774 and eventually settled in the wilderness a few miles northwest of Albany. Their numbers swelled in 1780 when seekers from a Baptist religious revival in nearby New Lebanon found them and then brought others to hear Ann Lee speak, and then to remain as part of the community. But their troubles weren't over. Accused of being "unfriendly to the patriotic cause," several of their number, including Mother Ann, were jailed in Albany until December 1780, when they were finally pardoned by Governor George Clinton. Mother Ann died at Watervliet in 1784 at forty-nine, on the land she had first settled, but the society she began continued to thrive.

Teed would have found much to admire and ponder about the Shakers at Mount Lebanon. Like him, Ann Lee had been the Second Coming of Christ. She had received no special instruction about the earth being hollow and people living inside the cosmic egg, but she too believed God has a dual male and female nature. Like the Harmonists, the Shakers practiced communalism as it seemed to derive from the primitive church, were celibate, and believed in equality of the sexes—all ideas that Teed incorporated into his Koreshan community. Like the Quakers, the Shakers were pacifist nonresisters. Two things chiefly set them apart. One was their spiritualism. "We are thoroughly convinced," wrote Shaker Elder George Lomas in

1873, "of spirit communication and interpositions, spirit guidance and obsession. Our spiritualism has permitted us to converse, face to face, with individuals once mortals, some of whom we well knew, with others born before the flood."[6] The other was their exuberance when this spirit struck them. In the main, their services were sober and restrained. But when the spirit moved—shaking, quaking, talking in tongues, ecstatic screaming, foaming at the mouth, jerking with convulsions, rolling about the floor, and swooning weren't unheard of. Teed didn't incorporate such flamboyance into his church. But he did take inspiration from the Shakers' orderly prosperity. Like the Harmonists, the Shakers had created a self-contained, self-sustaining community. Unlike the Perfectionists led by John Humphrey Noyes at Oneida, New York, whose economic success lay primarily in manufacturing—Oneida was built on a better bear trap of their invention and handsome flatware—the Shakers did it mainly through agriculture, plus a few small cottage industries. Teed duly noted this profitable mixture.

Around this time Teed's parents had relocated to Moravia at the southern tip of one of the lesser Finger Lakes, where they had started a mop-making venture, and invited him to work at it with them, probably hoping to distract him from the arcane religious notions his Baptist father didn't accept. Teed joined them but continued to pursue his interest in religion. With a small number of followers he established the first of his celibate Koreshan communities. He adopted the name Koreshanity for his beliefs and renamed himself Koresh (Cyrus in Hebrew). Both the mop business and the communal venture in Moravia failed after two years. "He alienated the residents of the town," according to Howard D. Fine, "and moved his community to Syracuse. There he established the Syracuse Institute of Progressive Medicine. In circumstances similar to those of his earlier move, he and his followers left Syracuse for New York City in the mid-1880s,"[7] ahead of charges by Mrs. Charles Cobb that Teed had defrauded her (and her mother) out of a sum of money

6. From *Plain Talks upon Practical Religion* by George Albert Lomas (Watervliet, NY, 1873), quoted in Charles Nordhoff's *The Communistic Societies of the United States* (London: John Murray, 1875; New York: Harper & Brothers, 1875).

7. Howard D. Fine, "The Koreshan Unity: The Chicago Years of a Utopian Community," *Journal of the Illinois State Historical Society* 68 (1975).

by claiming he was the new messiah. It seems to have been a case of heated religious enthusiasm burned to cold ashes, but the publicity was enough to force Teed to pack up and leave town, in such pinched financial circumstances that he had to ask his friend Dr. Andrews for a loan to do so. A *New York Times* account of the Cobb business also said that while in Moravia Teed had encouraged the wife of a liveryman to run off with him, and that *that* small scandal had made moving to Syracuse seem like a very good idea to him.

In New York City Teed established another modest commune, this time in a third-floor walkup apartment on 135TH Street near Eighth Avenue, where he was living with four women (two being his sister and his cousin). He was forty-six years old and had been the new messiah of the hollow earth for sixteen years, but he was unable to sustain even this little enclave.

Everything changed in 1886. The National Association of Mental Science was holding a convention in Chicago in September, and Teed got an offer to give an address. Once again, an enthusiastic woman was involved. Mrs. Thankful H.

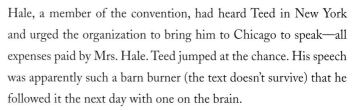

Hale, a member of the convention, had heard Teed in New York and urged the organization to bring him to Chicago to speak—all expenses paid by Mrs. Hale. Teed jumped at the chance. His speech was apparently such a barn burner (the text doesn't survive) that he followed it the next day with one on the brain.

The brain lecture concluded with faith healing, and a woman so fat she could hardly walk made it home on foot. Teed was a hit. He soon moved to Chicago, using the association as a springboard for his many plans and schemes. Soon he had established a metaphysical school called the World College of Life. Its first graduates in June 1887 were fourteen women, who had earned Psychic and Pneumic Therapeutic Doctorates, making them, it seems, Ph.D.s in brain and soul therapy. He also set up the Guiding Star Publishing House to get the word out, beginning the first of a long torrent of Koreshan publi-

(above) Mrs. Annie G. Ordway, Teed's alter ego and coleader of the Koreshans. (Koreshan State Historic Site)

cations. The monthly *Guiding Star* ("a magazine devoted to the science of being") commenced in December 1886. It became the more kinetic *Flaming Sword* in November 1889. And, of course, he started a church, the Assembly of the Covenant (Church Triumphant). Chief among the church leaders, theoretically coequal with Teed, Mrs. Annie G. Ordway (yet another *Mrs.*) was named Dual Associate, and later rechristened Victoria Gratia. Teed had been promised a feminine counterpart during his illumination, and Mrs. Ordway filled the bill. She remained a close associate to Teed until his death—*too* close, some thought, as she was persistently rumored to be his mistress as well.

He had at last begun to attract more followers, most of them women, educated, middle-class, married. It is hard to understand at this distance how he gained any converts to the idea that we're all living inside the concavity of a hollow earth. Indeed, it is hard to understand why the hollow earth business was such an important part of Teed's creed in the first place. Possibly the women just thought it an incidental quirk, forgiving this further evidence of male weirdness, focusing instead on his belief in a male/female God, his insistence on equality of the sexes, and a peaceful life of chastity outside the dungeon of marriage. By this time he had also added another appealing promise—his followers would enjoy personal immortality. Possibly, too, it was a certain sexy charisma on Teed's part. He wasn't big, about 5'6" and 165 pounds, but he had square-jawed good looks, a deep resonant voice, and an unwavering focus to his eyes usually described as "forceful" and "penetrating."

By 1888 the number of believers had so grown that he signed a lease on "a large double brick house on the corner of 33rd Place and College [Cottage] Grove Avenue," where he set up his largest celibate community to date.[8] The numbers continued to increase in a modest way, and four years later the core group moved into expanded quarters. By then Teed counted 126 followers in Chicago, nearly three-quarters of them women, almost all living in or near a South Side Washington Heights enclave of eight and a half acres containing a mansion, cottages, beautiful gardens and shady walks, and two ponds big enough for ice skating in the

---

8. *The Koreshan Story* by Sara Weber Rea (Estero, Florida: Guiding Star Publishing House, 1994).

winter. They called the compound Beth-Ophra. An 1894 article in the *Chicago Herald* described it as "a fine property . . . surrounded by broad, shady verandas and magnificent grounds thickly studded with old trees and made attractive by grass plats and flower beds. With . . . [Teed] in the same fine building live some of the prominent angels [of his church]. There are seven cottages besides in which other members of the Koreshan community live, and an office building—formerly a huge barn—in which is the printing office."[9] Today this once peaceful spot lies beneath the Dan Ryan Expressway, thundered over nonstop by trucks pounding along, except during rush hour gridlock.

Eventually Teed began looking around for an unspoiled pastoral place to build a new community from scratch, where his New Jerusalem might arise. And how would he recognize the right place? It would be at "the point where the vitellus of the alchemico-organic cosmos specifically determines," another of those recondite locutions Teed was so fond of. He also called this special spot "the vitellus of the cosmogenic egg." By cosmogenic egg he meant the earth, and the more common word for vitellus is yolk—though here he was probably using it in the sense of "embryo." The yolk is inside the egg, of course, its center. In other words, in Koreshan cosmology, they were seeking to locate their magnificent city at the center of the center, *inside* the earth.

Teed set off from Chicago in 1893 with an entourage of three women—Mrs. Annie G. Ordway, Mrs. Berthaldine Boomer, and Mrs. Mary C. Mills. They followed an itinerary set by prayer. Robert Lynn Rainard says that "each night the group sought in devotions guidance for the following day's journey. Spiritual direction 'guided' them into Florida and to their ultimate destination."[10] In January 1894, they found themselves in Punta Rassa on the southwest coast, a few miles west of Fort Myers at the mouth of the Caloosahatchee River. Today the peninsula is occupied by the Sanibel Harbour Resort and Spa near the causeway to toney Sanibel Island. Punta Rassa was a former cattle shipping town that had died after the Civil

---

9. Quoted by Howard D. Fine.

10. Robert Lynn Rainard, unpublished 1974 master's thesis, "In The Name of Humanity: The Koreshan Unity," for the University of South Florida, Tampa.

War, reborn in the 1880s as a sportfishing resort for the wealthy, complete with its own fancy hotel, the Tarpon House Inn. Teed and his attractive spiritual helpmeets were stopping there when they had a momentous encounter. Rainard says:

> At Punta Rassa the Koreshans met an elderly German named Gustav Damkohler, and his son Elwin, who were on their way back from their Christmas visit to Fort Myers. Teed engaged Damkohler in conversation which led to the Koreshans being invited to visit Damkohler's homestead at the Estero River, twenty miles down the coast from Punta Rassa. Damkohler, who had been a Florida pioneer since the early 1880s, had lost his wife in child-birth, and all but one child to the treacheries of pioneer life. A man in need of companionship, Damkohler was receptive to the fellowship of the Koreshans and the pampering of their women. At Estero Dr. Teed came to the realization that he had been directed to the remote Florida wilderness by the Divine Being.

The Koreshan Story, a more "official" account, though not necessarily a more accurate one, has this fortuitous meeting taking place differently. According to it, a prospective seller had sent Teed train tickets to inspect a property on Pine Island, Florida, just north of Punta Rassa, and in December 1893 he and the three women went to check it out. It proved prohibitively expensive, but while in Punta Gorda, Teed had taken the opportunity to give a few lectures and distribute a few pounds of Koreshan pamphlets, and some of this literature found its way to Damkohler, who wrote a letter to Teed—in German, sent in a Watch Tower Society envelope covered with biblical quotes. *The Koreshan Story* has it, "as Victoria Gratia (Annie

(above) This early view of the Estero River facing east reveals the wild tranquility of the setting Teed selected for his New Jerusalem. The roof in the middle distance belongs to Damkohler's original cottage. (Koreshan State Historic Site)

Ordway) held the letter (unopened) she seemed to know that it would lead them back to Florida that winter to the right place to begin." Back in Florida in January 1894, the momentous meeting took place in Punta Rassa. Teed lit right into expounding his doctrines, and Damkohler soaked it all in like a sponge: "Tears of joy rolled down the man's cheek, and he exclaimed repeatedly, 'Master! Master! The Lord is in it!' He then besought them to come with him and see the land he had held for the Master."

Except for their mutual religious fervor, Damkohler and Teed were a study in contrasts. Teed, sleek, meticulously groomed, given to custom-tailored suits, cultured, sophisticated, silver-tongued. And Damkohler, an aging swamp rat, though a handsome one, with forceful features, silvery hair, and an abundant white beard, lacking sight in one eye, more at home speaking German than his halting English.

Damkohler wanted them to see his land right away. They set out down the coast in a borrowed sailboat. At Mound Key they stopped for supper around a fire. Navigating through coastal mangrove thickets, they used two rowboats to make their way up the small sinuous Estero River, captivated by the wild serene beauty of the place, its solemn stillness, sand pines and cabbage palms rising more than forty feet above the placid coffee-colored river, alligators snoozing on the banks, the occasional bright chirp and chatter of tropical birds. They reached Damkohler's little landing around ten o'clock at night on New Year's Day 1894. The circumstances were rather more spartan than Teed was accustomed to. The only building was Damkohler's one-room board cabin, where all camped out. As *The Koreshan Story* describes their arrangements,

> The cabin also had a front and back porch, but furnishings were scant. They sat on boxes to eat their meals from a broad shelf built into the back porch. The chief bed was in the cabin's living room and was assigned to the three sisters. The ladies lay cross-wise with the tall Victoria's feet resting on boxes along side the bed. Dr. Teed, Mr. Damkohler and the boy

slept on cots and piles of old sails on the floor of the attic. This old cabin still stands in Estero today. . . . Dr. Teed busied himself grubbing and clearing land, while the women were occupied with improving the cabin, preparing meals and other activities about the place. For food and supplies they were obliged to row and sail to Pine Island. The river provided fish and Damkohler's beehives produced excellent honey.

It sounds like a pleasant idyll. Teed remained three weeks before returning to Chicago, possibly because Damkohler needed additional convincing when it came to turning over the land. Damkohler seems to have been ready to give the Koreshans half his 320 acres, but Teed was urging him to deed over the other half as well—for a token price of one dollar. Thrifty German Damkohler wasn't so sure about that, but in the end he gave in. The deal they finally struck was $200 for three hundred acres, with Damkohler holding on to twenty for himself. He would later have second thoughts.

The women stayed on—their company no doubt added inducement to Damkohler—while Teed took the train back to Chicago to put together a group of recruits. A few weeks later twenty-four Koreshans arrived from Chicago and began constructing a two-story L-shaped log building with a thatched roof (known as the Brothers House) as a temporary shelter while they built the first of the community's permanent buildings. They also put up white canvas "tent-houses" beneath groves of live oaks, with overhangs to create shady front porches with raised wooden floors and decorated with cheery trailers of flowering plants; they were big enough for a few wicker rockers and canvas deck chairs—quite inviting looking in the surviving photographs.

Over the next years they gradually turned Damkohler's wilderness (he had cleared only one of his 320 acres) into a charming tidy community consisting of over thirty buildings, extensive gardens, and pleasing walkways laid out in a radial pattern from the community's center. Estero never became the mighty megalopolis of

Teed's dreams. It was to be, he wrote, "like a thousand world's fair cities. Estero will manifest one great panorama of architectural beauty . . . Here is to exist the climax, the crowning glory, of civilization's greatest cosmopolitan center and capital . . .

which shall loudly call to all the world for millions of progressive minds and hearts to leave the turmoil of the great time of trouble, and make their homes in the Guiding Star City." Estero would be the primary city on earth—or rather *in* it—with a population of 10 million. His plan called for a star-shaped radial geometry reminiscent of Pierre L'Enfant's graceful design for Washington, DC, boasting grand avenues four hundred feet across, "with parks of fruit and nut trees extending the entire length of these streets," as an 1895 Koreshan publication describes it. It continues:

The construction of the city will be of such a character as to provide for a combination of street elevation, placing various kinds of traffic upon different surfaces; as for instance, heavy team traffic upon the ground surface, light driving upon a plane distinct from either, and all railroad travel upon distinct planes, dividing even the freight and passenger traffic by separate elevations. There will be no dumping of sewage into the streams, bay or Gulf. A moveable and continuous earth closet will carry the 'debris' and offal of the city to a place thirty or more miles distant, where it will be transformed to fertilization

(top) Brothers House, one of the first structures the Koreshans built on the tangled Florida wilderness they bought from Gustav Damkohler. (Koreshan State Historic Site)

(bottom) Koreshan manicured grounds, with walkways meandering through beautiful plantings and the occasional stone urn overflowing with flowers in bloom—truly a garden in the wilderness. (Koreshan State Historic Site)

and restored to the land surface to be absorbed by vegetable growth. There will be no smudge or smoke. Power by which machinery will be moved will be by the utilization of the electromagnetic currents of the earth and air, independently of steam application to so called 'dyanmos.' Motors will take the place of motion derived from steam pressure. The city will be constructed on the most magnificent scale, without the use of so called money. These things can be done easily once the people know the force of co-operation and united life, and understand the great principles of utilization and economy.[11]

Futurama! The multiple divisions of the roadway seem unduly complicated, but the ecological concern shown here is definitely enlightened for the time, even if it's hard to envision the continuously moving "earth closet." Not dumping sewage into waterways and recycling for fertilizer were practically unheard of then. And proclaiming "no smudge or smoke" is definitely utopian, as is the plan to achieve it by using a new Koreshan form of clean energy—"the electromagnetic currents of the earth and air." Ditto accomplishing all of this "without the use of so called money"!

Estero never quite got that far, but in its prime it was pretty nice, if decidedly smaller and more homey than it appeared in Teed's fertile imagination. As a visiting Shaker described it around 1904:

The buildings are mostly set in a park along the right bank of the Estero River for about a mile. This park contains sunken gardens filled with flowers, banana trees loaded with fruit, paw-paw trees in fruit, palm trees of many varieties, the tall and stately eucalyptus, the bamboo waving its beautiful foliage, and many flowering trees and shrubs. Mounds are cast up, and crowned with large urns or vases for flowering plants. Steps lead down into the sunken gardens and to the water's edge at the river. This

11. *Koreshan Unity: Communistic and Co-operative Gathering of the People* by Frank D. Jackson and Mary Everts Daniels (Chicago: Guiding Star Publishing House, 1895). Quoted in *The Koreshan Unity in Florida*, unpublished 1971 master's thesis by Elliott J. Mackle Jr. for the University of Miami.

land, where the park and the buildings are located, was at times swallowed with water before the Koreshans came. They expended $3,000 or more in dredging the river, besides making a deep ravine to carry off the surplus water into the river. The ravine is now beautified with Para and Guinea grasses, both native of Cuba, and is crossed by several artistic foot-bridges made of bamboo and other woods. Almost every kind of tropical fruit possible to grow in Florida can be found in this delightful garden, flowering vines cover the verandas of the houses and the foot-bridges in the park. Steps leading down to the boat landing, made of concrete colored with red clay, are quite grand, and were made and designed by the brethren. In fact, all the work in this magnificent garden is the product of home brains and industry. Koresh says he intends parking the river on both sides down to the bay, a distance of five miles.[12]

Shortly after 1900, at its height, Estero had a population of about two hundred people, who engaged in all sorts of self-sustaining enterprises. Among the first of these was a Fort Myers sawmill they bought in 1895 and moved to nearby Estero Island, where they produced lumber both for their own construction purposes and for sale to others. Members working the mill also built houses on the island, and soon there was a small satellite colony there. A substantial three-story dining hall went up in 1896, with a large eating area on the first floor (where seating arrangements were sexually segregated), while the floors above served as dormitories for the "sisters." Next came the Master's House, a snazzy residence for their visionary leader, along with structures to serve their many cottage industries. They also had their own post office, and the general store they opened where the Estero River crossed the trail that would become Route 41 did a brisk business. (The old frame building is still standing, just off the highway, seeming to cringe from the traffic roaring by.) The Koreshans were a busy, productive bunch.

---

12. From *American Communities and Co-operative Colonies* by William A. Hinds, 2ND edition (Chicago: C. H. Kerr, 1908). Quoted by James E. Landing in *America's Communal Utopias* (Chapel Hill: University of North Carolina Press, 1997).

One of the most ambitious Koreshan buildings at Estero was Art Hall, which included an expansive stage where plays, concerts, and musicales were regularly performed. Music and art were important to the Koreshans, as were aesthetics of every sort. Those ornamental urns set on mounds around the property, aglow with flowering plants, were emblematic. Nearly everyone was musical in some way. The Koreshan orchestra gave weekly concerts at Art Hall, and the brass band took

first prize at the state fair one year—an expensive pair of well-bred horses. "Victor concerts" were another musical diversion. One of the female members had a collection of two hundred or so records, and getting together 'round the old Victrola was a popular pastime. "Picnics were frequently organized and held in the woods around Estero, or on one of the islands in the bay," writes Elliott Mackle Jr. "These were 'enlivened with music by the band, speeches, jokes, and the playing of various games' . . . Pleasure boating added to the enjoyment of life at Estero, and moonlight cruises were often organized. Assembling the brass band in one boat, the Koreshans would follow in others, music filling the night as the little flotilla cruised up the river and around the bay. There were, in addition, fishing and hunting expeditions, classes, rehearsals, and trips to various points of interest in the area."[13]

(above) Koreshan children dressed in costumes, standing in front of the Tea House. (Koreshan State Historic Site)

---

13. *The Koreshan Unity in Florida* by Elliott J. Mackle Jr., an unpublished 1971 master's thesis for the University of Miami. He is quoting the Koreshan newspaper, *The American Eagle,* February 14, 1907.

They also had a little riverside outdoor theater. As Carl Carmer, a *New Yorker* writer who visited Estero in 1948, describes it in *Dark Trees to the Wind*,

> They built a floating stage at a bend where the river had made from its banks a natural amphitheater and there they played dramas by Lord Dunsany and other modern playwrights . . . Some evenings their string and wood-wind orchestra gave programs of classical music on the stage of their raft theater and the audience, sitting under the palms beside the star-reflecting river, found life as good as they had thought it would be when they left their northern homes to follow Koresh.[14]

Sounds pleasant, doesn't it? Almost utopian. The peaceful scenes Mackle and Carmer depict go a long way toward explaining why these two hundred or so people were willing to leave Chicago and follow Teed into the Florida wilderness— even given his peculiar messianic hollow earth theology. Koreshanity, and Estero as its physical incarnation, provided sanctuary. Teed's belief that we are living inside the earth, beyond which there is *nothing,* can be seen as a sort of ultimate metaphysical retreat to the womb—the entire universe as a small enclosed protective egg, finite, comprehensible, safe. And in the later innings of the nineteenth century, there was a lot to retreat from.

Teed's illumination had come in October 1869, just four years after the Civil War ended. Teed had seen its horrors firsthand as a member of the medical corps. Reconstruction and the fate of freed slaves was not a pretty picture, and President Grant's administration set new standards for incompetence and corruption. The transcontinental railroad, completed in May 1869, seemed a tangible symbol of the way things were racing along. That it had been "financed by a group of crooked promoters who hired Congressmen to do their bidding" was a sign of the times as well.[15] America had been largely rural in 1860, and businesses were mainly farms

---

14. Carl Carmer, *Dark Trees to the Wind* (New York: William Sloane Associates, 1949).

15. *A Short History of the United States* by Allan Nevins and Henry Steele Commager (New York: The Modern Library, 1945).

and small private enterprises. But in the 1870s and 1880s, greed, materialism, and the application of Darwinism to the social fabric inspired the first of the robber barons to suit up and begin constructing the vast impersonal corporate trusts that would dominate the American economy by 1900, amassing profits in the multimillions while their factory workers living in grimy cities grubbed along at sixteen-hour days for crummy wages. Darwinism itself seemed the second hit of a one-two punch after Copernicus had eighty-sixed the formerly supreme earth and its solar system to an obscure corner of an obscure galaxy; now in 1871 Darwin announced that we were all descended from monkeys. Teed's theology repudiated both these assaults on human self-esteem.

The primarily Anglo ethnic makeup of the United States was being altered as Germans, Italians, and Eastern Europeans poured in—nearly 12 million between 1870 and 1900, and this out of a total population in 1900 of 76 million. Overcrowded Italy alone provided over 650,000 immigrants, two-thirds of them men, between 1890 and 1900. These new arrivals sent cultural jolts through the formerly homogeneous communities where they settled, as well as giving unwanted competition for jobs. Most landed in cities; between 1880 and 1900 urban populations grew by 16 million. The cities became noisy, overcrowded rats-warrens, darkened by smoke, painted black by coal dust. The Koreshans knew about this firsthand, having lived in Chicago for ten years before moving to Estero. It was also a period of political upheaval, bracketed by the assassination in 1865 of Lincoln and President McKinley's 1901 shooting at the Buffalo Pan-American Exposition by anarchist Leon Czolgosz, with the assassination in 1881 of President Garfield by that infamous Disappointed Office Seeker in between. Garfield himself had commented on "the general tendency to fast living, increased nervousness, and the general spirit of rush that seems to pervade life and thought in our times." Much of the upheaval during this time was fueled by economic problems, the two largest manifestations being the Panic of 1873, which dragged into a prolonged depression, and the worse Panic of 1893, whose effects were being felt even as Teed negotiated with

Damkohler for his remote Florida land. Nearly a fourth of the country's railroads went bankrupt, and in some cities, unemployment hit 25 percent. The so-called Coxey's Army of disgruntled unemployed workers marched on Washington, arriving on April 30, 1894, and briefly camped out under the Washington Monument before the leaders were arrested and the others dispersed. Not two weeks later, workers for the Pullman railroad car works in Chicago—only a few miles from Teed's South Side headquarters—went on strike and were soon joined by 50,000 sympathetic rail workers who refused to handle Pullman cars, which promised to shut down the nation's rail system. Federal troops were called in to keep the trains moving, as rioting, bloodshed, and looting broke out in Chicago. On July 6, several thousand rioters destroyed seven hundred railcars, to the tune of $340,000 damage, and the next day a fire demolished seven buildings at the Columbian Exposition. National Guardsmen were assaulted and fired into the crowd, killing or wounding dozens. And all of this practically in Teed's backyard.

So to Teed's adherents, sitting about on a soft warm evening listening to a string quartet down by the riverside beneath the palms probably seemed like the best place to be. It was a peaceful existence, far from the turmoil of what passed for modern life elsewhere. "They saw a world in chaos," writes Robert S. Fogarty in his introduction to a 1975 reprint of Teed's *The Cellular Cosmogony,* "with force and greed central elements in that universe; therefore, they constructed a static world that closed in on itself, denied progress and affirmed man's place in that world. Cyrus Reed Teed may have been a lunatic, a fraud, and a swindler; however, to his followers he was Koresh, the prophet whose philosophy was a divine mandate to cultivate the earth and save it for future generations."

Teed hadn't forgotten about the hollow earth. Starting in 1896, after his little colony was well established in Florida, he began orchestrating a series of experiments to prove scientifically his contention that we are living inside—that the earth around us is concave, not convex, as most people believed in their delusion.

In 1898 he produced, in collaboration with Professor Ulysses Grant Morrow, a definitive volume combining a long section by himself about Koreshan cosmology with a detailed account by Morrow of their "geodesic" experiments. It's revealing to reproduce the entire title page from the 1905 edition:

THE

CELLULAR COSMOGONY

...OR...

THE EARTH A CONCAVE SPHERE

CYRUS. R. TEED

PART I

The Universology of Koreshanity

(WITH ADDENDUM: "ASTRONOMY'S FALSE FOUNDATION.")

BY KORESH

THE FOUNDER OF THE KORESHAN SYSTEM OF RELIGIO-SCIENCE; AUTHOR
OF VOLUMES OF KORESHAN LITERATURE

PART II

The New Geodesy

BY PROFESSOR U. G. MORROW

ASTRONOMER AND GEODESIST FOR THE KORESHAN UNITY,
AND EDITOR OFTHE FLAMING SWORD

Judging from the defensive tone of his introduction, it would appear that one common question asked of Teed was, Well, if we're inside the earth like you say, and from that perspective it's concave, why does it *look* convex, curving downward in the distance? And what about all those stars and galaxies that sure seem like they're millions of miles away? Huh, Koresh?

He leaps right into refuting "that dangerous fallacy, the Copernican system":

> Deity, if this be the term employed to designate the Supreme Source of being and activity, cannot be comprehended until the structure and function of the universe are absolutely known; hence mankind is ignorant of God until his handiwork is accurately deciphered. Yet to know God, who, though unknown by the world is not 'unknowable,' is the supreme demand of all intellectual research and development.
>
> If we accept the logical deduction of the fallacious Copernican system of astronomy, we conclude the universe to be illimitable and incomprehensible, and its cause equally so; therefore, not only would the universe be forever beyond the reach of the intellectual perspective of human aspiration and effort, but God himself would be beyond the pale of our conception, and therefore beyond our adoration.
>
> The Koreshan Cosmogony reduces the universe to proportionate limits, and its cause within the comprehension of the human mind. It demonstrates the possibility of the attainment of man to his supreme inheritance, the ultimate dominion of the universe, thus restoring him to the acme of exaltation—the throne of the Eternal, whence he had his origin.

This is sweet, really. Copernicus can't be true because his theories produce an unfathomable, limitless universe we humans cannot understand; God wouldn't do that to us because then we couldn't understand him. Koreshan cosmogony restores us to our true and rightful place—the center of the universe, sitting on the throne of the Eternal, right where we belong. The demotion we all suffered thanks to Copernicus regarding our importance, locationwise, continues to sting. Teed rectified that by returning us to the center of things, albeit inside them. In this regard and others, Koreshanity was deeply conservative.

Next he says that he established the "cosmogonic form" of the universe, which he "declared to be cellular," determining that the surface of the earth is concave, with an upward curvature of about eight inches to the mile. Even though he ascertained all this with theoretical rigor, still people scoffed. What else for this avatar of "religio-science" to do but conduct experiments proving his theory true? He says, "The suggestion urged itself that we transpose, from the domain of optical science to that of mechanical principles, the effort to enlighten the world as to cosmic form." The idea was simple. If the earth's curvature were convex, a straight line extended for any distance would touch at only one point; but if it were concave and the line long enough, it would eventually bump into the upcurving surface. So Professor Morrow invented the Rectilineator. As he described it in *The Cellular Cosmogony:*

> The Rectilineator consists of a number of sections in the form of double T squares [|––––|], each 12 feet in length, which braced and tensioned cross-arms is to the length of the section, as 1 is to 3. The material of which the sections of the Rectilineator are constructed of inch mahogany, seasoned for twelve years in the shops of the Pullman Palace Co., Pullman, Ill.

Visitors to the Koreshan State Historic Site can still see a section of it inside Art Hall, sun-bleached and dusty, leaning against the back of the stage. Morrow and some fellow religio-scientists had tried a few tests in Illinois, along the

(above) Koreshan experiment involving the Rectilineator. (Koreshan State Historic Site)

shore of Lake Michigan on the grounds of the Columbian Exposition and on the Illinois & Michigan Canal between the Chicago and Illinois rivers, but neither provided the requisite uninterrupted spaces needed. The plan was to construct a perfectly straight line . . . four miles long.

This experiment was another reason Estero attracted Teed. Florida's Gulf Coast then offered endless empty beaches stretching for miles. In January 1897 they began the undertaking near Naples because the coast there offered the needed distance. They set up shop in Naples at a beachfront enclave belonging to Colonel W. N. Haldeman, owner/publisher of the Louisville *Courier Journal,* which says something about Teed's connections. The Rectilineator sections were transported from Estero in the *Ada,* a small sloop Teed had acquired in 1894. Work on the experiment continued until May. After an "air line" was established, segments of the Rectilineator were meticulously aligned and connected, the trailing section then removed and carefully attached to the front, the lengthy double T square apparatus laboriously hopscotching along the beach while measurements were constantly made. By April 1 they'd gone one mile and by April 16 two, but they took until May 5 to make it another half mile. Elliott Mackle Jr. describes the progress from there:

> On May 5, another half mile had been covered and the line's distance from the fixed water line was 54 inches closer than at the beginning, a difference of 4 inches from calculation. At this point, however, the beach curved away and, in any case, the vertical bar of the double T square was within seven inches of the ground, and so it was necessary to employ another method of survey. Using telescopes, poles in the water, and the sloop *Ada,* the line was projected another mile and five-eighths on May 5 and repeated on May 8. Return surveys were performed on May 6 and 11. This projected line met the water four and one-eighth miles from the starting point, indicating to Morrow that the earth's surface had curved upward 128 inches . . . the earth had, according to the terms of his experiment, curved upward, proving the validity of the cellular theory.

The care and precise exertion involved were prodigious, although surviving pictures suggest they had fun while they were at it. Needless to say, their efforts were rewarded—as Professor Morrow attests for a dense 140 pages or so in *The Cellular Cosmogony.* They determined the earth's concavity to their complete—and scientific—satisfaction.

Things at Estero sailed along serenely for the next few years except for a couple of blips. The first came from Gustav Damkohler. In 1897 he sued to get his land back. The reasons are a little obscure. He may have believed that Teed promised him a fine house in the community's center that never materialized. If so, he probably got increasingly peeved as he watched the impressive residence for Teed and Mrs. Ordway (where they would presumably live together in cozy chastity) going up. Damkohler got fed up with Teed and his grandiose plans and took him to court. He found a clever lawyer who used an ingenious gambit—placing the Koreshans' unconventional beliefs into evidence, essentially trying to get a judgment against them for their odd views.

But Teed understood public relations and from the start had gone out of his way to be sure his Estero community was both friendly and accommodating to its neighbors, especially people in growing Fort Myers, fourteen miles to the north. It paid off. The lengthy trial commenced in April 1897 but was eventually settled out

(above) Koreshan leadership at Estero, probably in the late 1890s, with Cyrus Teed and Mrs. Annie G. Ordway front and center. Note the ceremonial faux medieval halberd bearers on either side.

of court. Damkohler got half of his original 320 acres back, but none that affected the Koreshan community.

A considerably more flamboyant attack came the next year, swooping down on them in the form of Editha Lolita, one of the many names and titles she trailed behind her like a long feather boa. According to Rainard, "She claimed to be the Countess Landsfeld, and Baroness Rosenthal, daughter of Ludwig I of Bavaria, and Lola Montez, god child of Pius IX, divorced wife of General Diss Debar, widow of two other men, bride of James Dutton Jackson, and the self-proclaimed successor to the priestess of occultism, Madame Blavatsky."[16] She showed up in southwestern Florida with current hubby Jackson, whom she'd married in New Orleans on November 13, 1898, her maiden name listed on the official marriage record as Princess Editha Lolita Ludwig. Knowing nothing about him, we would have to suppose James Dutton Jackson a brave man. Editha had come to Florida to establish her own backwoods utopia, the Order of the Crystal Sea, on several thousand acres Jackson apparently owned in Lee County—where they would all live on fruits and nuts (appropriately, Rainard notes), while kicking back to await the millennium. But this was near the Koreshan community, and Editha Lolita decided there wasn't room for two utopias in one county. She launched into attack mode against Teed and his followers, adroitly using the *Fort Myers Press* as her chief outlet for innuendo and abuse, expressing her shock that a "scoundrel" like Teed could be permitted to live among the decent folk of Fort Myers. "Day after day," says

---

16. Can't resist deconstructing this just a bit. Lola Montez (1821–1861) was born in Ireland as Marie Gilbert, but debuted on the London stage in 1843 as "Lola Montez, the Spanish Dancer," famous for her "Spider Dance" and inspiration for the phrase, "Whatever Lola wants, Lola gets." She married at least three men, not always bothering to get divorced first. On first seeing her, Ludwig I of Bavaria was so struck by her beauty he offered her a castle, which she accepted. She became his mistress in 1846 (making Editha putatively a daughter from this illicit union), and he bestowed the titles Baroness Rosenthal and Countess of Landsfeld on her the following year. In between fooling around, she helped him govern the country until he was dethroned in 1848. She also had reported dalliances with Franz Liszt and Alexandre Dumas and found herself in 1853 doing her Spider Dance for gold miners in San Francisco. I can find no information about General Diss Debar or James Dutton Jackson. Madame Blavatsky, born in the Ukraine in 1831, claimed to have studied for years under Hindu and Tibetan masters before arriving in New York in 1873 and soon founding the Theosophical Society, a "philosophico-religious" organization giving the occult scientific trappings. Like Teed's, her writing was both voluminous and opaque, her principal work being *The Secret Doctrine*, published in 1888. Still a name to conjure with in occult circles, she died in London in 1891 after years of chronic illness. While living in New York, she kept on display in her flat a stuffed baboon, fully dressed and wearing spectacles, holding a copy of Darwin's *Origin of Species*.

Rainard, "she reported to the *Fort Myers Press* stories of Teed's allegedly sordid past." This went on for months. When the Koreshans decided enough was enough, they revealed to the Fort Myers paper that Editha had been a Koreshan in Chicago but left and then tried to break up the community in ways that had drawn the attention of the police and the Chicago newspapers. In a follow-up story Editha Lolita admitted belonging to the Chicago enclave but had only joined them, as Rainard says, quoting her, "after she had been 'released by the Jesuit priest' who had 'kidnapped her.'" Not long after these revelations, Editha Lolita and her husband faded out of the picture, heading on to greener delusional pastures elsewhere.

Estero was calm as the new century began. Its population dropped to twenty-eight at one point, in part because Teed had returned to Chicago to begin closing out the operation there, while his esteemed counterpart, Victoria Gratia, was in Washington, DC, helping set up a new Koreshan colony in the heart of the beast. The last of the Chicago crowd moved lock, stock, and fifteen railway cars full of stuff to Florida in 1903, raising the population to around two hundred—hardly 10 million, but not bad. Everything was peachy at Estero until 1904 or so. Their various enterprises were humming along, and all was going so well that Teed decided to incorporate as a town, mainly because it would qualify them for tax money to improve the roads. This first step into the local political realm proved to be the beginning of the end. Non-Koreshans in the lightly populated county were understandably apprehensive about the influence of this relatively large group of people, all of whom were pledged to vote in a bloc. Pronouncements such as "I am going to bring thousands to Florida . . . and make every vote count in Florida and Lee County," reported in the increasingly hostile *Fort Myers Press,* didn't help. Also, Fort Myers—or at least the newspaper—began feeling it might have more to lose after the railroad was extended there in 1904, and dream balloons of great growth and prosperity began inflating. They didn't want a bunch of crazy hollow earthers spoiling their prospects.

The editor of the *Fort Myers Press,* Philip Isaacs, played a major part in what followed. He had political ambitions and offered Koreshans a weekly news column (written by Rectilineator inventor U. G. Morrow) in exchange for a pledge to vote for him for county judge in the 1904 Democratic primary and general election. They kept their end of the bargain, and he was elected. This was back in the heyday of the "solid South," meaning solidly Democratic. But the election of 1906 proved more troublesome. It became known that in 1904 the Koreshans had defected from the Democratic party and voted as a group for Teddy Roosevelt, though he was the only Republican they voted for. This peeved local Democrats, who came up with a scam to bar them from voting in the 1906 Democratic primary—a pledge each voter was required to sign affirming that he had supported all Democratic candidates in 1904. The Koreshans, not easily scared off, simply amended the pledge before signing it and voted anyway.

The Democratic Committee, chaired by Philip Isaacs, then proceeded to toss out all votes from the Estero precinct. Okay, said the Koreshans, watch this. They announced they would support non-Democratic candidates in November and set about putting together their own new Progressive Liberty party, in which, Elliott Mackle Jr. says, "Koreshans, Socialists, Republicans, dissatisfied Democrats, and other dissidents (but, notably, not Negroes) could band together in opposition to the Democratic organization." Since they couldn't hope to get fair coverage from Isaacs' paper and since they had the equipment handy anyway, they started their own weekly newspaper, the *American Eagle*, in June 1906. The first issues were almost entirely devoted to politics, both stumping for the candidates they were endorsing and pounding on the incompetence and corruption of their opponents. A main target, not surprisingly, was Philip Isaacs. Naturally the *Fort Myers Press* blasted right back. The Progressive Liberty party began staging political rallies in various towns around Lee County, bringing along the Koreshan brass band to churn up enthusiasm and get everybody in the mood for the speechifying.

By October tempers on both sides were getting frazzled, and a disputed telephone call triggered an ugly encounter like something out of the Old West orchestrated by Monty Python.[17] It began when W. W. Pilling arrived in Fort Meyers on his way to join the Koreshan community. Finding no one there to pick him up, he sent a note to Estero and repaired for the night to a hotel belonging to a Colonel Sellers and his wife. The next morning someone called from Estero asking for him but was apparently told by Mrs. Sellers, "He is not here." What she meant by that wasn't made clear to the caller—whether he was still upstairs, or out, or what. She definitely did *not* mean that he wasn't registered there, a point that didn't get through to the Estero caller. During a second call later in the day, when Mrs. Sellers said she would get Pilling, the caller said, "I thought you told me no one by that name was stopping there." Pilling later said that Mrs. Sellers didn't seem upset by this exchange.

Two weeks later, W. Ross Wallace, a Koreshan, and the only one running for office in the election, was accosted by Colonel Sellers on a Fort Meyers street. Sellers accused Wallace of calling Mrs. Sellers a liar, and, without waiting for a reply, began beating on him. Wallace tried to defend himself and begged the mayor of Fort Myers, who was standing nearby impassively watching this, for help, which wasn't forthcoming. Wallace prudently fled. One week later, on October 13, Cyrus Teed, dressed as always in a spiffy black suit, was in town to meet a group of new Koreshans arriving by train from Baltimore. As he was walking down the street toward the station, he encountered Wallace, Sellers, and town marshal S. W. Sanchez in front of R. W. Gilliam's grocery store. They'd gotten together to discuss Sellers' attack—though why they were doing so on the street is a good question. Wallace was explaining that he was out of town campaigning on the day in question and couldn't have been the caller. Sellers was saying that wasn't what *he* had heard when Teed walked up to them and jumped into the discussion, offering that people often misunderstand telephone conversations but then repeating what people in Estero had overheard their caller saying.

"Don't you call me a liar!" exclaimed Sellers, slugging Teed three times in the face, *whap! whap! whap!* Like the mayor before him, the town marshal stood

17. I am indebted to Elliott Mackle, Jr. for the details that follow, pieced together by him in *The Koreshan Unity in Florida,* his unpublished 1971 master's thesis for the University of Miami.

there watching, making no move to stop it. Teed raised his hands to protect his face without fighting back. Sellers pulled a knife, but someone grabbed his arm and persuaded him to put it away.

Any good fight draws a crowd. Meanwhile, the train had arrived, and the Koreshans, including several young men, came upon this scene. Estero resident Richard Jentsch, seeing Teed being pummeled, slugged Sellers and was knocked down by the crowd for his trouble. Then the boys jumped in, fighting until they were bloody and their luggage dumped into the gutter.

Marshal Sanchez at last leaped into action, grabbing Teed by the lapel and shouting, "You struck him and called him a liar!"

"I did not strike him, nor call him a liar," said Teed.

"Don't tell me you did not strike him," said Sanchez, slapping Teed across the face and knocking off his glasses.

Sanchez then grabbed Teed and one of the Baltimore Koreshans, telling them they were under arrest. At this moment irrepressible Jentsch, somehow shaking loose from the crowd, threw himself at Sanchez and landed a good punch. Taking his nightstick to Jentsch, Sanchez hissed, "You hit me again and I will kill you!" clubbing him repeatedly until he fell to the ground. Placing Teed, Jentsch, and Wallace under arrest, Sanchez hauled them off to jail, where each had to post a $10 bond for a court appearance the next Monday—an appearance none of them, sensibly, ever showed up for.

Fort Myers politics, circa 1906.

Teed never recovered fully from this beating. His Progressive Liberty party didn't win a single office, but some candidates drew over 30 percent of the vote—a respectable showing given that in previous elections Democratic candidates had a virtual lock on winning. The PLP vowed they'd get 'em next time but didn't. Teed withdrew from public view and spent the winter of 1906–1907 writing a *novel*. Its title was *The Great Red Dragon, or, The Flaming Devil of the Orient*, a book at once millenarian (no surprise there), anticapitalist, and apocalyptically racist (the bad guys are an invading Oriental army). Elliott Mackle Jr. summarizes the plot as follows:

> The leaders of capitalism and of western governments unite in agreement to enslave the masses, thus ensuring higher profits for themselves. The masses within the United States are organized by a partially-messianic general to meet this threat, and the forces of the capitalist-dominated United States government and its allies are eventually brought to terms. Japan, in the meantime, at the head of a Chinese horde, has begun a conquest of the world. Rome and Russia have been laid waste, and the Oriental forces, threatening to encircle the world, have gathered off all the coasts of the United States. The American navy is defeated, America begins to fall to the invaders, and the army of the masses—the only bulwark between Western civilization and Oriental savagery—withdraws to northern Florida. The Orientals are eventually defeated by an aerial navy of "anti-gravic" platforms which fire ball bearings upon the invaders. By the use of the platforms, which were manufactured at Estero, together with high ideals and truth, the forces of righteousness conquer the world. Assisted by a beautiful young woman, the triumphant leader of the masses ushers in a new dispensation. The Divine Motherhood rules over this dispensation—she is the duality of the miraculously unified leader and his assistant. Peace and tranquillity reign in the perfected New Jerusalem. And the world follows principles identical to Koreshan Universology.

By 1908 Teed had returned to his usual busy schedule, although he was in constant pain; the beating he suffered in 1906 caused lasting nerve damage that made his left arm ache, sometimes excruciatingly so. In May he and Mrs. Ordway went to Washington, DC, and spent the summer helping the new colony there, probably in part because even muggy Washington was more comfortable than summertime in pre-air-conditioning Florida. The Koreshans participated in the political activity leading up to the fall elections, but in a subdued way. When Teed and Mrs. Ordway returned to Estero in early October, he was clearly in decline. For the first time Mrs. Ordway prayed for him before the gathered assembly; there was no longer an attempt to keep his condition secret. Gustav Faber, a Koreshan living in Washington State who was a nurse during the Spanish-American War, came all the way to Estero to care for him. Teed was moved to La Partita, a house the Koreshans had built on the southern tip of Estero Island, and there Faber gave Teed saltwater baths and tried to cure him with an "electrotherapeutic machine" he had invented.[18] During these last days, Teed was heard to exclaim, "O Jerusalem, take me!"

He died at this island cottage on December 22, 1908.

Teed had preached reincarnation and, beyond that, physical immortality for himself. He claimed to be capable of what he called theocrasis, "the incorruptible dissolution of the physical body by electro-magnetic combustion." This is yet another of his opaque coinages and definitions, but it seems to mean that through this mysterious electromagnetic combustion, his body would renew itself. He would come back!

His more devout believers were certain this was true—and wouldn't Christmas, three days later, be perfectly apt? They refused to bury him, and his body was returned to Estero, where it was placed in state and the vigil began. Christmas came and went, and Teed's body was showing no signs of reviving. To the contrary, it was beginning to get pretty ripe in the unseasonably hot weather. Health officials from Fort Myers showed up, took one look, pronounced him dead, and insisted that he be buried immediately. A simple concrete tomb was prepared on Estero Island, and Teed was interred there. Some of the more fanatical believers, however, were unsatisfied with this outcome, and one dark night tried to break into the tomb to get a look, convinced he wasn't really gone for good. A watchman was put on nightly duty. As Carl Carmer relates it:

---

18. Carl Carmer, *Dark Trees to the Wind*

Night after night, among the wild mangroves and the coconuts and mango trees, Carl Luettich stared into the blackness that surrounded the circle of light in which he sat. Once, just before dawn, he fell asleep and the fanatics came again and opened a side of the tomb before sunlight frightened them away. Carl Luettich was more alert after that, but watching the tomb was not necessary much longer.

This was because a hurricane and tidal wave hit the island on October 23, 1921, washing both the mausoleum and the cottage out to sea. Only the headstone was recovered, which is now on display in the auditorium of the Koreshan Unity Headquarters Building. It says simply:

CYRUS

Shepherd Stone of Israel

The aftermath of Teed's death was a predictable scramble for power with certain black humor flourishes. Nurse Gustav Faber claimed to be Teed's successor, saying Teed had named him the new leader with his final breaths and transferred authority through "theocrasis." But the Estero Koreshans weren't having it, and Faber departed early in 1909. Strangely, Teed's longtime spiritual companion, Mrs. Ordway, had been off in Washington during Teed's final days and didn't make it back to Estero until December 27. She would seem his natural successor, but this was resisted, possibly by sexist elements who wouldn't abide a woman leader, possibly because a Koreshan furniture works in Bristol, Tennessee, named for her, was going under, and the debt weighed on the community. In any case, she rather rapidly packed up and left with a few of her more dedicated followers to start up her own Koreshan commune in Seffner, Florida. It soon failed, and she married Charles A. Graves, recently mayor of Estero. They eventually settled in St. Petersburg, where she remained until her death in 1923.

The Estero community continued in diminishing circumstances for many years, until the land was finally given to the state by the last four members in 1961. The grounds are now the Koreshan Historic Site, which opened to the public in 1967. Across Highway 41 from the Koreshan Historic Site, in a modest building, the Koreshan Unity Foundation is still engaged in keeping Cyrus Teed's legacy and ideas alive.

(above) Teed's tomb on Estero Island. (Koreshan State Historic Site)

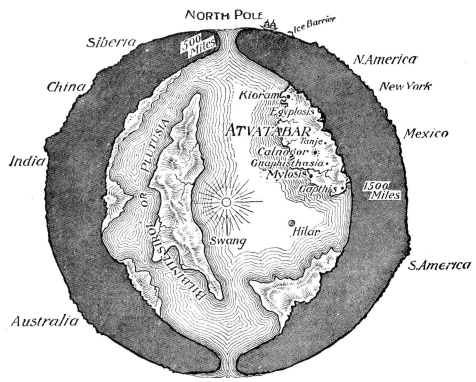

NORTH POLE

Ice Barrier

Siberia

500 Miles

N. America

China

New York

Kioram

Egyplosis

ATVATABAR

Mexico

Tanje

Calnogor

Gnaphisthasia

India

Mylosis

Gapthis

1500 Miles

Hilar

Swang

S. America

Australia

SOUTH POLE

MAP of the Interior World.

6

HOLLOW UTOPIAS, ROMANCES, AND A LITTLE KIDDIE LIT

Toward the end of the nineteenth century, the hollow earth began turning up regularly in fiction. Symmes' famous holes were well-known, if widely ridiculed, and Verne's *A Journey to the Center of the Earth* became a perennial best seller that moved the idea from the esoteric fringe into mainstream culture. Writers found it had many uses—as a handy place to set utopias, or their dark or satiric mirror opposite, dystopias; as somewhere to set improbable romances now that formerly remote, unknown corners of the earth were becoming less believable as settings the more they were explored and reported upon; and as a convenient fairyland where magical adventures could take place to amuse younger readers. Some used it for several of these ends at once.

The period between the Civil War and the beginning of the twentieth century saw the scribbling of more utopian fiction than any other time before or since. Jean Pfaelzer, in *The Utopian Novel in America, 1886–1896*, says that more than one hundred such fictions were written in the United States in that ten years alone.

(opposite) *The Goddess of Atvatabar* (1892) by William R. Bradshaw was one of many hollow earth novels that appeared toward the end of the nineteenth century. This is a map of that interior world, reached by explorer Lexington White through a convenient Symmes' Hole at the North Pole.

There were only a few before the Civil War—*Symzonia* comes to mind—because the culture hadn't needed utopian literary productions before then. From the beginning America was seen as its own meta-utopia, one coming into actual existence. European settlers, dating back to the Pilgrims, had thought of it that way, and generations of new arrivals after them carried on the belief. If one forgot about those inconvenient Indians (and most tried to), North America's bounteous landscape and democratic vistas were an empty canvas on which to paint actual utopian experiments. It was a perfect society aborning—the City on the Hill, a moral beacon to the world—no need to create literary counterparts.

Before the Civil War America seemed bright with this promise of perfectability, of a utopia being realized. But in the years following the war, for many, that promise shattered in bewildering, demoralizing ways. The industrialization of the United States, begun in earnest during the Civil War, went roaring on, bringing with it huge change, for better and worse. A grid of shining steel rails was being laid on the country, making movement easy in unprecedented ways. The Gilded Age (so named by Mark Twain) saw the rise of the first cyclopean corporations and the multimillionaire robber barons who headed them. Monopolies and trusts, new mutant financial creatures, ran roughshod over economic life. With all that money, corruption was inevitable, and it reached the inner sanctums of the White House. Factories multiplied like mushrooms after rain, and people poured out of the countryside to work in them, creating a huge urban laboring class that hadn't existed before. Most worked long hours for little pay—another source of social difficulty. This population shift gave rise to big cities, with all their attendant pleasures and problems.[1] It was a qualitative change, from tranquil, uneventful village life where everyone knew everyone else, to the anonymous, crowded, uncaring, fast-paced metropolis. Waves of new immigrants were also rolling into the cities looking for work.

And the stuff these factory workers were turning out! It was a period of galloping materialism fueled by almost overwhelming technological change—telegraph, telephone, electric lights, automobiles, movies, even air conditioning—and

---

1. Chicago in 1850 had a population of about 30,000; by 1900, despite an 1871 fire that burned down most of the city, that number was 1,698,575. Cleveland jumped from 17,034 to 381,768 in that same time, and Detroit went from 21,019 to 285,704.

everyone seemed to be out to get his share (or more), using whatever methods came to mind. Darwinism, chiefly as interpreted by Herbert Spencer, was being applied to the social organism, and survival of the fittest became the ringing slogan of the day (it helped the robber barons sleep peacefully at night). Forget milquetoast Sunday school lessons about loving thy neighbor and treating him as you would yourself. It was a ruthless, bloodthirsty world, and only the strong survived. Poverty simply meant you were inferior.

All of this was a long way from the America of Jeffersonian dreams. It added up to major-league culture shock on a national scale. But social upheaval, disruption, disillusionment, and confusion weren't confined to the United States. The shock wave was worldwide. And one response writers had was to create literary utopias offering solutions to the rampant social problems they saw all around them. They began constructing ideal, alternate societies and/or dystopic satires on the evils they saw proliferating in their own. Most of these are forgotten, or nearly so, and for good reason—they were generally pretty bad. But some have lasted, most notably Samuel Butler's *Erewhon* (1872) and Edward Bellamy's *Looking Backward* (1888). Mark Twain's *A Connecticut Yankee in King Arthur's Court* (1889) can arguably be tossed in here as well, as could H. G. Wells' still nicely creepy *The Time Machine* (1895). Others that haven't quite fallen off the cultural charts into oblivion include William Morris's *News from Nowhere* (1890), William Dean Howells' *A Traveler from Altruria* (1894), and Wells' *When the Sleeper Wakes* (1899). The list of novels that only academic utopian specialists remember would run to many pages.

It was a dark and stormy night . . . inside the hollow earth.

Well, it wasn't *really* dark and stormy down there. But the writer who kicked off this thirty-year fling with utopias and dystopias inside the hollow earth with *The Coming Race* (1871) is best remembered for those timelessly dopey opening words to his 1830 novel, *Paul Clifford,* made famous by Snoopy at his typewriter atop his doghouse.[2]

---

2. The full opening line is: "It was a dark and stormy night; the rain fell in torrents—except at occasional intervals, when it was checked by a violent gust of wind which swept up the streets (for it is in London that our scene lies), rattling along the housetops, and fiercely agitating the scanty flame of the lamps that struggled against the darkness."

Edward Bulwer-Lytton (1803–1873) was a prolific, popular author in his lifetime. Of his many books, only *The Last Days of Pompeii* (1834) is remembered, largely because it was filmed in 1908, 1913, 1935 (Basil Rathbone as Pontius Pilate), and 1960 (Steve Reeves as Marcus), and made into a miniseries in 1984 (Ernest Borgnine as Marcus). He was born in London as just plain Edward Bulwer and added the hyphenate Lytton, his mother's surname, after inheriting her ancestral family manse.

Compared to the pace in Verne, the narrator in *The Coming Race,* an American, gets below in nothing flat. Once he is out in the well-lit, carefully groomed landscape of the inner earth, he is discovered by members of a serene, advanced civilization. They take him home and commence teaching him about their society—in fairly alarming detail.

They are the descendants of surface dwellers who fled from prehistoric floods by descending into caverns. In this *The Coming Race* is only a semi–hollow earth novel, in that the interior space, while vast, is a cavern system further enlarged by vril, to which they owe everything from their living space to their social perfection. It's a versatile source of energy, both physical and mental, created from focused willpower and directed by wands that the An-ya carry—the essence of Nietzsche turned into an all-purpose laser zapper.

You name it, vril can do it: "It can destroy like the flash of lightning yet, differently applied, it can replenish or invigorate life . . . by this agency they rend their way through the most solid substances, and open valleys for culture through the rocks of their subterranean wilderness. From it they extract the light which supplies their lamps."

Bulwer-Lytton was a politician who started out as a liberal member of Parliament in 1831 but resigned in 1841 over the government's Corn Law policies. He returned in 1852 as a conservative Tory, and *The Coming Race* reflects both his political interests and his somewhat conflicted views on social ideals.

Vril has created a society of perfect harmony. No competition or ego-driven striving for power or fame. No poverty—robots do all the work. No crime. No lawyers. All worship the same Creator—there are no pointless theological disputes and religious services are short. They have flying boats and detachable vril-powered wings they use to flit from place to place. Like the Symzonians, they're all handsome and beautiful, strict vegetarians and teetotalers, most living well beyond one hundred years. Everyone's kind to everyone else and nobody's rude—not even the kids (*truly* utopian!). The economy is a sort of laissez-faire socialism. They've moved beyond base, lowest-common-denominator democracy, which they consider a barbaric social structure. You can be rich and have vast estates if you feel like it. But most don't bother, preferring to live modestly, kick back, and smell the roses. Working as an obscure artisan is as valued as being a muckety-muck, and not working at all is just fine. "They rank repose among the chief blessings of life."

Women down here have equal rights—and then some. The beautiful Gy, as the women are called, are bigger and stronger than the men ("an important element in the consideration and maintenance of female rights") and generally smarter, exercising a better control of vril, "her will being more resolute than his, and will being essential to the direction of the vril force." Most work is performed by children as a form of training. One job generally given to the little girls is "the destruction of animals irreclaimably hostile" because the girls are "by constitution more ruthless under the influence of fear or hate." The Gys initiate courtship, which leads to most of the narrator's troubles while he's there. One Gy named Zee falls in love with him, pursuing him so avidly it scares the hell out of him, largely because her important father doesn't like this inferior creature from above and has plans to vaporize him with vril to eliminate the problem. At the end she selflessly helps him escape back to the surface world. He writes this book to warn people about the An-ya's plans to come to the surface and kill humans and start over—*The Coming Race* of the title.

The Coming Race draws on two important ideas of the time: evolution and the emerging machine age. The An-ya are an evolutionary step ahead of surface people and have solved the problems of the nineteenth century. But their superior, rational society comes at a price, and is ultimately seen as a threat. They're coming to get us! So is evolution, even if true, a good thing or not? Maybe not so good if you happen to be the Neanderthals and the brainy Cro-Magnons are coming. As regards the machine age, the novel suggests that science, and the technology it produces, will eliminate all difficulties. As J. O. Bailey puts it in *Pilgrims Through Space and Time,* "By gaining control over such forces as electricity . . . man will establish a civilization in which there will be no toil, struggle, or poverty." Again and again, science will be the savior, and electricity the chief instrument of salvation. It's presented as a virtual religion in many of these novels.[3]

One such is Mary Bradley Lane's *Mizora: A Prophecy.* When the visitor-narrator voices shock that the inhabitants of Mizora have no religion, a resident replies, "Oh, daughter of the dark ages, turn to the benevolent and ever-willing Science. She is the goddess who has led *us* out of ignorance and superstition; out of degradation and disease, and every other wretchedness that superstitious degraded humanity has known. She . . . has placed us in a broad, free, independent, noble, useful and grandly happy life."

The goddess Science has worked wonders in Mizora, but She had a little help. The critical factor in making their perfect society possible has been the total elimination of *men.* Mizora is all-female. Men have been extinct for 2,000 years, and with their disappearance all social ills have disappeared as well.

Mizora seems to have been the first feminist utopia—certainly the first set in the hollow earth. Originally published under a pseudonym as "The Narrative of Vera Zarovitch" in the *Cincinnati Commercial* between November 6, 1880, and

---

3. There were a few curmudgeonly counterexamples. One such was Samuel Butler's *Erewhon* from 1872, which early readers supposed was written directly in response to *The Coming Race*—an idea that Butler is at pains to dispel in the preface to the second edition. Both deal with evolution and machines, but in Butler's utopia (set on the surface, in a remote part of the world suspiciously like New Zealand), people evolved to produce marvelous machines, and then evolved a little more and *got rid of them all* when they began to fear that the machines themselves might evolve into monstrous mechanical creatures that would somehow do away with mere fleshy humanity. This fear of a mechanical takeover became a staple of science fiction thereafter.

February 5, 1881, it didn't appear in book form until 1890.[4] Its author was a Cincinnati housewife. The story takes its geography directly from John Cleves Symmes. The Cincinnati area was his old stomping ground, and his devoted son Americus had just written a summary defense of his father's ideas. *The Symmes Theory of Concentric Spheres* appeared in 1878, two years before Lane's story began serialization.

As the novel opens, Vera, an aristocratic Russian, has been sentenced to life in the Siberian mines for her revolutionary opinions. Bribing her way free, she escapes northward in disguise on a whaling ship, which crashes into an ice floe and sinks in Arctic waters. She and other survivors make their way to an Eskimo encampment, but she wakes up one day to find the others in her party gone. She overwinters with the Eskimos and accompanies them in the spring as they head north to hunt. At about eighty-five degrees latitude, they come upon the open polar sea. Vera feels an overpowering desire to sail farther north on it. The accommodating Eskimos build her a boat on the spot, and she sets off.

Soon she drifts right into the closing pages of *Arthur Gordon Pym:* her boat is caught in a fast current and travels in an accelerating circle, while before her rises "a column of mist," spreading into "a curtain that appeared to be suspended in midair . . . while sparks of fire, like countless swarms of fire-flies, darted through it and blazed out into a thousand brilliant hues"—as if she's sailing through the aurora borealis itself. Not inconveniently, "a semi-stupor, born of exhaustion and terror, seized me in its merciful embrace." She later awakes along a broad river flowing through paradise:

> The sky appeared bluer, and the air balmier than even that of Italy's favored clime. The turf that covered the banks was smooth and fine, like a carpet of rich green velvet. The fragrance of tempting fruit was wafted by the zephyrs from numerous orchards. Birds of bright plumage flitted

---

4. *Mizora: A Prophecy* by Mary E. Bradley Lane (Syracuse, NY: Syracuse University Press, 2000), edited and with a Critical Introduction by Jean Pfaelzer. The cover provides an additional subhead: AN 1880s RADICAL FEMINIST UTOPIA.

among the branches, anon breaking forth into wild and exultant melody, as if they rejoiced to be in so favored a clime. And truly it seemed a land of enchantment.

Some hollow earth novels are practically Cook's tours, devoting considerable space to imaginative geographical descriptions, but Lane gives only token sketches of the landscape, brushstrokes of physical detail, little more. Mizora seems to be a large continent surrounded by a forbidding ocean; it is populated enough to have a few large cities and many towns, but these, too, are given only glancing mention. The only real indication that we're inside the hollow earth comes early on, when Vera observes, "The horizon was bounded by a chain of mountains, that plainly showed their bases above the glowing orchards and verdant landscapes. It impressed me as peculiar, that everything appeared to rise as it gained in distance."

Lane's interest lies in elaborating her utopian program. Action is virtually nonexistent. Once Vera gets to Mizora, virtually nothing happens. Drama, conflict, romance, and adventure are elbowed off the stage by an endless examination of the Mizorans' social mores and technical achievements. The only real plot question pulling a reader through the narrative is, What happened to the men? and the closely related mystery, How do you reproduce without them?

Vera encounters a boat shaped like a fish carrying Mizorans, all of whom are young, female, beautiful, and blond. Brunette Vera soon discovers that dark hair and complexions don't exist in Mizora. Late in the novel Vera finds that just as Mizora formerly had men, some people had swarthy complexions as well. She presses her guide, the Preceptress, about this, who replies first with a policy statement: "We believe that the highest excellence of moral and mental character is alone attainable by a fair race. The elements of evil belong to the dark race." Are these utopian Nazis? Vera asks what happened to the dark complexions. The terse reply, not elaborated on, is: "We eliminated them."

Lane presumably does not endorse this solution, but it's revealing that a feminist society got rid of men to achieve a state of perfection and did away with troublesome dark-skinned types as well. This was written in a time when race was arguably even more troublesome than it is today. Millions of former slaves were technically free, but Radical Reconstruction had collapsed, Jim Crow laws were created to keep blacks in "their place," and they were facing a future filled with difficulty and hardship as second-class citizens. American Indians were being shooed west to reservations on land deemed worthless (though not without a fight—the Battle of Little Big Horn took place just four years before *Mizora* appeared). Millions of European immigrants were causing cultural upheaval of yet another sort. Color difference, then as now, was a huge social problem. Eliminating it entirely was a magic-wand solution, though hardly utopian. Vera's take is that the Mizorans' "admirable system of government, social and political, and their encouragement and provision for universal culture of so high an order, had more to do with the formation of superlative character than the elimination of the dark complexion."

How did they achieve this social paragon?

Thousands of years ago, men ran everything and women were regarded as inferior. A revolution toppled the original aristocracy, but the new republic had one fatal flaw: a portion were slaveholders, and a civil war soon followed. Sound familiar? The war should have ended quickly, but the corrupt government prolonged it for profit. At war's end the slaveholders collapsed and the former commander in chief of the free government, "a man of mediocre intellect and boundless self-conceit," was made president. Could this be a parallel universe U. S. Grant? In Mizora he became a despot, assuming all the prerogatives of royalty he could manage, elevating "his obscure and numerous relatives to responsible offices." When in a rigged election he is proclaimed President for life, all hell breaks loose. Soldiers called out to protect the government refuse to do so, chaos and faction reign.

Now, up until this point, women had been kept out of government. But in this anarchic time, "they organized for mutual protection from the lawlessness that prevailed. The organizations grew, united and developed into military power. They used their power wisely, discreetly, and effectively. With consummate skill and energy they gathered the reins of Government in their own hands." And threw all the men out. The new Constitution, the Preceptress tells Vera, "provided for the exclusion of the male sex from all affairs and privileges for a period of one hundred years. *At the end of that time not a representative of the sex was in existence.*" Italics courtesy of the Preceptress. The men aren't killed off. Instead, when they can no longer run things, spend their time and energy wheeling and dealing and being important, they simply wither away!

With them out of the picture, Mizoran society soars toward perfection.

And the key to it all, indeed, the key to the novel's purpose, is female education.

Prior to their takeover of Mizora's government, "colleges and all avenues to higher intellectual development had been rigorously closed against them. The professional pursuits of life were denied them"—just as they were in the United States at the time.

Women in 1880 were largely still supposed to be only mothers and homemakers. But things were changing in small ways. One effect all those new factories popping up had, for better or worse, was to give women jobs working in them, taking them out of the home in previously unthought-of numbers. Emancipation of former slaves by constitutional amendment added impetus for women's suffrage as well, and such leaders as Elizabeth Cady Stanton (who had organized the first women's rights convention in 1848), and Susan B. Anthony had started the National Woman Suffrage Association (NWSA) in 1869 and repeatedly petitioned Congress to give women the vote. Higher education was still primarily male. Oberlin College had been one of the first to admit women in the 1830s. The first all-women's college opened in 1836 as Georgia Female College (now Wesleyan College), and Mount Holyoke had begun as a female seminary in 1837. Vassar didn't come along until 1861, Hunter College in 1870, and Smith and Wellesley in 1875, making them brand-new institutions when Lane was writing. But most women were stuck at home, doing housework and raising kids, stuck, too, up on that pedestal, where sentimental worship, far from elevating them, kept them from acting on any professional aspirations they might entertain. Educated, accomplished women were in the main regarded as "unnatural." Anything beyond a little schoolmarming was suspect, and that was regarded as the province of unfortunate spinsters unable to perform women's "true calling"—childbearing and housekeeping. The pressures to restrict women to their "special province"—the home—were still tremendous in 1880.

Lane envisioned a life for women with none of these restrictions.

Vera is ensconced in the National College to learn their musical language and soon finds that universal education is of the highest importance to the Mizorans—and that *teachers* are not only the highest-paid profession of all, they represent the pinnacle of Mizora's intellectual aristocracy. Dream on, Mary Bradley. "The idea of a Government assuming the responsibility of education, like a parent securing the interest of its children, was all so new to me," Vera thinks, "and yet, I confessed to myself, the system might prove beneficial to other countries than Mizora." She reflects that in her world, "education was the privilege only of the rich. And in no country, however enlightened, was there a system of education that would reach all."

The rest of the novel details the fabulous rewards of Mizora's education policy.

One has been to provide a terrific standard of living for all. The Preceptress admonishes Vera regarding the potential benefits of universal education for her world: "The bright and eager intellects of poverty will turn to Chemistry to solve the problems of cheap Light, cheap Fuel and cheap Food. When you can clothe yourselves from the fibre of the trees, and warm and light your dwellings from the water of your rivers." They've figured out how to create cheap energy by reducing water to its two separate elements by zapping it with electricity, then burning the result. "Eat of the stones of the earth, Poverty and Disease will be as unknown to your people as it is to mine."

Better living through chemistry.

Lane does come up with a number of nifty sci-fi devices. The preferred conveyance is a low carriage "propelled by compressed air or electricity." They also have airplanes—this nearly twenty-five years before successful heavier-than-air flight, though many at the time were working on it. More predictive is the Mizorans' "elastic glass" (plastic by any other name) "as pliable as rubber." Almost indestructible, among its many uses, "all cooking utensils were made of it" and "all underground pipes were made of it." It's also spun into "the frailest lace," which "had the advantage of never soiling, never tearing, and never wearing out," sort of a precursor of that old Alec Guinness movie, *The Man in the White Suit.* Other gizmos anticipate television, e-mail, and holography. The key to most of these advances is electricity, and naturally all of the living spaces and city streets in Mizora are bathed in bright artificial lighting. This was more a sign of the times than some visionary stroke, since even as Lane was writing, tireless Thomas Alva Edison was slaving away in his lab looking for the perfect filament for his revolutionary incandescent lightbulb, and in 1879 the first electric streetlights in the United States were turned on around Public Square in Cleveland, Ohio.

Such gadgets are a commonplace in the futuristic hollow earth novels from this time. What sets *Mizora* apart is its vision of an ultimate matriarchy, where women have done away with men entirely. Here mothers produce only daughters and live with them in harmony until the daughters in turn become mothers. Lane is vague about how this asexual procreation is achieved. She says they have discovered "the secret of life" and suggests something like in vitro conception.

Like the narrator of *The Coming Race,* Vera at last decides to go back home with her friend Wauna, the Preceptress's daughter, to show her world a shining example of Mizoran society and to proselytize for universal free education. But it doesn't work. Vera finds that her husband and son, who had migrated to the United States, are both dead. The brutality of the surface world overwhelms Wauna, and she dies attempting to return to Mizora. Nearly her last words are: "The Great

Mother of us all will soon receive me in her bosom. And oh! my friend, promise me that her dust shall cover me from the sight of men." True to her school to the very end.

In 1882, just a year after Lane's story was serialized, a novel titled *Pantaletta* appeared. It described a comic dystopia written with broad-stroke vaudeville flourishes that reads like a send-up of the serious feminism in *Mizora*. The author was Mrs. J. Wood, likely the pseudonym of a man unappreciative of efforts toward women's rights.[5]

The narrator is an American named Icarus Byron Gullible. After demolishing the family fortune starting a newspaper but fortuitously marrying a wealthy young woman, he devotes his time after serving in the Civil War to invention, and the result is an aircraft he calls the American Eagle.

Gullible's goal? The North Pole. He wants to get there "to stop the further sacrifice of heroic lives by polar expeditions." With success he plans to "patent my invention and organize a company" to manufacture his Eagle airships, these to "carry all kinds of passengers to the new American possessions, at remunerative rates." His Eagle flies, but not very fast, so the trip to the pole takes days. He passes "leagues of glistening ice" and then "below me, apparently boundless in diameter, rolled the gulf of gulfs," a combination of the open polar sea and the great polar abyss. He flies on, the temperature rises, he sights land unknown on maps, and comes to earth at last, of course, in some Edenic country—"a spot which rivalled the garden of our first parents in beauty." He is immediately nabbed by a group of martial women wearing strange garb and taken prisoner. His chief captor is the Pantaletta of the title, a half-mad virago given to loony, disjointed Lady Macbeth soliloquies who's also captain of the army. Gullible is drugged and dragged off to meet the president of the Republic of Petticotia, a topsy-turvy land where women have assumed power as well as men's clothing, while the remaining men (millions have fled) are forced to wear what were formerly women's clothes and perform all

---

5. The book is listed thusly in one bibliography of feminist utopian novels: Wood, Mrs. J. (pseud.) *Pantaletta: A Romance of Hesheland* (1882: American News Co., New York). A full listing of feminist science fiction, fantasy, and utopian fiction can be found at http://www.feministsf.org/femsf/.

the duties formerly relegated to women. Petticotia is a cross-dresser's paradise, where transvestitism has the rule of law. The word "man" has been banned as well. Former "men" are now called "heshes," while women are "shehes." The absurdity of this is a clear indication of the writer's attitude toward women's equality.

The novel ends with Gullible popping up out of the interior world at the North Pole and winging his way south toward Greenland, eager to report that "the North Pole is discovered and is ours." Filled with emotion, he rhapsodizes, "Oh, my native land, my soul goes out to thee . . . Long seems the time since I stretched me under thy umbrageous trees and felt the gentle influence of thy emerald face."

After *The Coming Race, Mizora,* and *Pantaletta,* novels of the 1880s and 1890s set in the hollow earth both multiplied and took on a certain sameness. It would be tedious to consider every one in detail. Indeed, it would be impossible, since several of them, while continuing to exist on various bibliographical lists, have proved impossible to turn up despite considerable searching. But the number of hollow earth novels produced between 1880 and 1915 is remarkable. The list includes:

Mizora by Mary Bradley Lane (1880).

Pantaletta: A Romance of Sheheland by Mrs. J. Wood (1882).

Interior World, A Romance Illustrating a New Hypothesis of Terrestrial Organization &c by Washington L. Tower (1885).

A Strange Manuscript Found in a Copper Cylinder by Anonymous [James DeMille] (1888).

Under the Auroras, A Marvelous Tale of the Interior World by Anonymous [William Jenkins Shaw] (1888).

Al-Modad; or Life Scenes Beyond the Polar Circumlfex. A Religio-Scientific Solution of the Problems of Present and Future Life by Anonymous [M. Louise Moore and M. Beauchamp] (1892).

The Goddess of Atvatabar by William R. Bradshaw (1892).

Baron Trump's Marvellous Underground Journey by Ingersoll Lockwood (1893).

Swallowed by an Earthquake by Edward Douglas Fawcett (1894).

The Land of the Changing Sun by Will N. Harben (1894).

From Earth's Center, A Polar Gateway Message by S. Byron Welcome (1894).

Forty Years with the Damned; or, Life Inside the Earth by Charlies Aikin (1895).

The Third World, A Tale of Love & Strange Adventure by Henry Clay Fairman (1895).

Etidorhpa by John Uri Lloyd (1895).

Through the Earth by Clement Fezandie (1898).

Under Pike's Peak; or Mahalma, Child of the Fire Father by Charles McKesson (1898).

The Sovereign Guide: A Tale of Eden by William Amos Miller (1898).

The Last Lemurian: A Westralian Romance by G. Firth Scott (1898).

Through the Earth; or, Jack Nelson's Invention by Fred Thorpe (1898).

The Secret of the Earth by Charles W. Beale (1899).

Nequa; or, The Problem of the Ages by Jack Adams [pseud. of Alcanoan O. Grigsby and Mary P. Lowe] (1900).

Thyra, A Romance of the Polar Pit by Robert Ames Bennet (1901).

Intermere by William Alexander Taylor (1901–1902)

The Land of the Central Sun by Park Winthrop (1902).

The Daughter of the Dawn by William Reginald Hodder (1903).

My Bride from Another World: A Weird Romance Recounting Many Strange Adventures in an Unknown World by Rev. E. C. Atkins (1904).

Mr. Oseba's Last Discovery by George W. Bell (1904).

Under the World by John DeMorgan (1906).

The Land of Nison by C. Regnus [pseud. of Charles Sanger] (1906).

Dorothy and the Wizard in Oz by L. Frank Baum (1908).

The Smoky God by Willis George Emerson (1908).

Five Thousand Miles Underground, or The Mystery of the Centre of the Earth by Roy Rockwood [pseud. of Howard Garis] (1908).

Upsidonia by Archibald Marshall (1915).

Let's look at a small sample of the titles.

The opening sections of *A Strange Manuscript Found in a Copper Cylinder*, published anonymously in 1888, exemplify the creeping sameness. Various amounts

of Symmes, Poe, and Verne are stirred together to concoct a warmed-over hollow earth stew. Adam More (Adam Seaborn was Symmes' hero, you will remember; and More wrote the first *Utopia*), shipwrecked with a companion in the Southern Ocean, lands on an island peopled by ferocious black cannibals who promptly eat his pal. More escapes on a small boat, drawn ever southward by a strong current until his craft is sucked downward into a black tunnel and pops up in a calm, warm sea lapping against a paradisiacal countryside. Here the author reaches even farther back in his ransacking, giving us a turned-on-its-head society that seems inspired by those in *Niels Klim*. As Steve Trussel summarizes the action,

Upon landing, he finds a strange race very much resembling Arabs. They take him to their underground city, where he is taught a language similar to Arabic by the beautiful Almah, and discovers that the cultural and

(above) Published anonymously in 1888, *A Strange Manuscript Found in a Copper Cylinder* is an example of a creeping sameness in hollow earth novels of the time. Various amounts of Symmes, Poe, and Verne are stirred together to concoct warmed-over hollow earth stew, including the requisite sea monster shown here on the cover of a pirated British edition.

moral values of this peculiar race are weirdly inverted. These pseudo-Arabs see better in the dark than in daylight. They seek poverty, giving their possessions to whomever will take them; they long for death as the highest blessing of their lives; and, although peaceful, they practice human sacrifice on hundreds of willing victims. Adam and Almah fall in love, and find that they are destined to be given the honor of dying for her people. At the last moment, More kills several of the populace with his rifle, and the multitudes, awe-stricken, fall down and worship him as a god who can bring the greatest good—death—instantly.[6]

This novel is at best an orientally embroidered celebration of life over death, an exotic romance without much redeeming value. Perhaps most interesting is that this story appeared serially in nineteen installments in one of the most popular American magazines of the time—*Harper's Weekly* (which billed itself as "A Journal of Civilization")—an indicator of how mainstream the idea of the hollow earth had become. The anonymous author turned out to be a Canadian college professor named James de Mille (1833–1880), a prolific and popular novelist in his day. He's pretty much forgotten now, though he lives on in Ph.D. dissertations and academic criticism, and a surprising number of his novels are available online as e-texts. *A Strange Manuscript Found in a Copper Cylinder*, published posthumously, is considered the first Canadian science fiction novel and was reprinted by Insomniac Press in 2001.

William R. Bradshaw (1851–1927) wrote *The Goddess of Atvatabar*, first published in 1892. This hollow earth novel has an almost overwhelming sumptuousness and richness of detail. An Irish immigrant who settled in Flushing, New York, Bradshaw was a regular contributor to magazines, edited *Literary Life* and *Decorator and Furnisher*, and was associated with *Field and Stream* as well. At his death in 1927

---

6. This summary is part of a section about Prehistoric Fiction on Trossel's extensive and wide-ranging website, EclectiCity, http:/.trussel.com.

he was a Republican district captain in Flushing and president of the New York Anti-Vivisection Society.

A number of new elements show themselves here. One is revealed in the full title:

THE

GODDESS OF ATVATABAR

BEING THE

HISTORY OF THE DISCOVERY

OF THE

INTERIOR WORLD

AND

CONQUEST OF ATVATABAR

Earlier hollow earth novels such as *Symzonia* had land-grabbing imperialism as a subtext, but here it is announced blazing right in the title. This novel came at a time when America was running out of open land and the easy promise (seldom realized) of riches on the frontier. What had been called Seward's Folly—the vast tract of Alaska purchased from Russia in 1867—was looking visionary by the end of the century. And 1892 was just a few years before American policy changed to engage in a little empire building in the form of the Spanish-American War, which on slim excuse not only kicked Spain out of the New World but occupied the Philippines as well. So the conquest of Atvatabar is imaginatively predictive of geopolitical forces starting to simmer in the real world.

And wouldn't you know it? The name of the narrator/hero/chief conqueror is Commander Lexington *White*. The story opens aboard the *Polar King*, with White and his crew on a mission to discover the North Pole—something very much in the news at the time. Even as Bradshaw was writing, Admiral Robert Peary was making his second expedition to Greenland, a prelude to the one that would take him successfully to the pole on April 6, 1909—or so he believed and claimed. Toward the end of the nineteenth century and in the early years of the twentieth, the idea of reaching the pole became a sort of frenzy, with explorer after explorer obsessed with gaining the dubious "glory" of being the first to do so. Just as Poe had tried to cash in on a polar mania fifty years earlier, Bradshaw's polar framing for his hollow earth novel was quite timely.

On the *Polar King,* frustrated at trying to find an opening in the ring of polar ice, they fire one of their powerful guns containing shells of "terrorite" at it— a supergunpowder of White's invention—cleaving the mountain of ice and creating a narrow passage to, yes, the open polar sea lying beyond. As they sail into it, White reflects, "I was romantic, idealistic. I loved the marvelous, the magnificent, and the mysterious . . . I wished to discover all that was weird and wonderful on the earth." And does his wish ever come true.

White says he became absorbed in this polar quest after learning about the failure of a recent expedition whose ship was frozen in at Smith's Sound in Baffin Bay, but had tried for the pole in a "monster balloon," failing when the balloon's car smashed into an iceberg. This reminded him of "the ill-fated Sir John Franklin and *Jeannette* expeditions," which in turn led him to read "almost every narrative of polar discovery" and to converse "with Arctic navigators both in England and the United States." His polar homework fits neatly into a tradition of hollow earth novels going back to Symmes and Poe. He says he found it strange that modern sailors "could only get three degrees nearer the pole than Henry Hudson did nearly three hundred years ago," and when his father opportunely dies and leaves him a huge fortune, he decides to try for the pole. He builds the *Polar King* according to his own advanced specs, one being a handy device also of his own invention, an "apparatus that both heated the ship and condensed the sea water for consumption on board ship and for feeding the boilers." As he's listing the other provisioning details, the first hint of the novel's deep eccentricity appears. Along with "the usual Arctic outfit to withstand the terrible climate of high latitudes," White has a special item of clothing made for all:

> Believing in the absolute certainty of discovering the pole and our consequent fame, I had included in the ship's stores a special triumphal outfit for both officers and sailors. This consisted of a Viking helmet of polished brass surmounted by the figure of a silver-plated polar bear, to be worn by both officers and sailors. Each officer and sailor was armed with a cutlass having the figure of a polar bear in silver-plated brass surmounting the hilt.

White sets out with his ace crew, not via Greenland and Baffin Bay as so many had before him, but through the Bering Straits, despite the *Jeannette* expedition's horrific experiences while attempting the same route.[7] They encounter the open polar sea and the usual abundance of wildlife up there, and at last Professor Starbottle, the chief scientist aboard, proclaims, "I am afraid, Commander, we will never reach the pole . . . we are falling into the interior of the earth!" After predictable shouts of "Turn back the ship!" the pilot observes that they are still sailing along nicely. "If the earth is a hollow shell having a subterranean ocean, we can sail thereon bottom upward and masts downward, just as easily as we sail on the surface of the ocean here." Here, as in other hollow earth novels, ideas of gravity are conveniently cockeyed. They press on into the polar opening. "The prow of the *Polar King* was pointed directly toward the darkness before us, toward the centre of the earth."

---

7. Lasting between 1879 and 1881, the so-called "*Jeannette* expedition," led by Lieutenant Commander George Washington De Long of the U.S. Navy, went in search of the North Pole via the Bering Straits with the goal of verifying Augustus Petermann's "open polar sea" theory. Funded by newspaper publisher James Gordon Bennett (whose *New York Herald* had also financed Stanley's 1871 effort to find Livingstone in Africa) and popularly named for the small steamship bearing them, the *Jeannette* expedition spent two winters trapped in ice before the ship was crushed and sank. The diminishing number of survivors suffered horribly, crossing the Siberian arctic islands dragging boats and supplies for hundreds of miles—one of those expeditions rightly known as "ill-fated."

A dozen of the more fearful sailors are permitted to take a boat and head back where they came from.

About 250 miles down into the abyss they begin to experience lessened gravity, while getting their first glimpse of "an orb of rosy flame"—Swang, the inner earth sun. Professor Starbottle exclaims, surveying the scene with his telescope, "The whole interior planet is covered with continents and oceans just like the outer sphere!"

"'We have discovered El Dorado,' said the Captain."

"'The heaviest elements fall to the centre of all spheres,' said Professor Goldrock. 'I am certain we shall discover mountains of gold ere we return.'" Ideas of profit never lag far behind the excitement of discovery.

A storm comes up after a week's subterranean sailing, providing the first real taste of the sensuous detail to come:

> The sun grew dark and appeared like a disc of sombre gold. The ocean was lashed by a furious hurricane into incredible mountains of water. Every crest of the waves seemed a mass of yellow flame. The internal heavens were rent open with gulfs of sulphur-colored fire . . . a golden-yellow phosphorescence covered the ocean. The water boiled in maddening eddies of lemon-colored seas, while from the hurricane decks streamed cataracts of saffron fire. The lightning, like streaks of molten gold, hurled its burning darts into the sea. Everything bore the glow of amber-colored fire.

There is a sumptuous, painterly quality to the writing throughout the book. This is a hollow earth paradise of exquisite detail described in exquisite detail, literally reveling in it, though after a while it almost becomes overwhelming, like one too many bites of a thirteen-layer German chocolate cake. This hyperestheticism is part of *Atvatabar's* larger purpose—to show a society as devoted to art and spirituality as most are to profit and power. It's as if Bradshaw is straining to take the visual ideas and aesthetics of newly developing art nouveau—a style that had just come along in the 1880s, breaking with classicism, emphasizing rich organic qualities—and render them in prose. One goal of art nouveau (which had its origins in the 1860s with William Morris's Arts and Crafts movement) was to integrate beauty into everyday life, to make people's lives better by greater exposure to it, and this is a main pillar of the civilization White & Co. encounter—before they begin crashing around in it ruining everything, anyway.

Nathaniel Hawthorne's son, Julian, wrote the introduction to *The Goddess of Atvatabar,* in which he raves about the novel as a fine example of portraying the "ideal" in fiction, taking the opportunity to beat such "realists" as Zola and Tolstoy about the head and shoulders and claiming that their day has come and gone—a singularly wrongheaded judgment that served his own writerly purposes. Like Bradshaw's novel, Julian Hawthorne's fiction chiefly dealt with the fantastic and the supernatural. After citing Symmes, Verne, and Bulwer-Lytton's *The Coming Race*— proof he's done his hollow earth homework—Hawthorne declares that Bradshaw "has not fallen below the highest standard that has been erected by previous writers," and in fact "has achieved a work of art which may rightfully be termed great." It's actually superior to Verne, who, "in composing a similar story, would stop short with a description of mere physical adventure." Bradshaw goes beyond this, creating "in conjunction therewith an interior world of the soul, illuminated with the still more dazzling sun of ideal love in all its passion and beauty." This world of the soul lies at *Atvatabar's* core:

> The religion of the new race is based upon the worship of the human soul, whose powers have been developed to a height unthought of by our section of mankind, although on lines the commencement of which are already within our view. The magical achievements of theosophy and occultism, as well as the ultimate achievements of orthodox science, are

revealed in their most amazing manifestations, and with a sobriety and minuteness of treatment that fully satisfies what may be called the transcendental reader.

While it strives for a certain high-mindedness, *The Goddess of Atvatabar* is shot through with elements of Gilbert and Sullivan–style comic opera. The *Polar King's* first encounter with the people down here comes when the crew sees several flying soldiers, hovering above the ship like large bumblebees, wearing strange uniforms and flapping mechanical wings. Flathootley, the resident buffoon, makes a leap at one, who flits out of the way, leaving Flathootley to plop into the ocean, from which he is rescued by one of the flying soldiers, who deposits him back on deck—and is promptly captured as a reward for his kindness. Examining the captive's wings, they discover that a small "dynamo" powers them, consisting "of a central wheel made to revolve by the attraction of a vast occult force evolved from the contact of two metals . . . a colossal current of mysterious magnetism made the wheel revolve." Here again electromagnetism appears as the occult force that propels all sorts of ingenious gadgets down here in Plutusia, as the realm is known.

They learn Atvatabarese from the two flying soldiers, who direct the *Polar King* to Atvatabar's principal port and fill them in on the basics of the geography and social structure. The layout of the interior world is analogous to the known surface world—its map is reproduced here on page 186. The government is an elective monarchy, with a king and nobles elected for life. "The largest building in Calnogor was the Bormidophia, or pantheon, where the worship of the gods was held. The only living object of worship was the Lady Lyone,

(above) Lyone, the goddess of Atvatabar, in all her over-the-top splendor.

the Supreme Goddess of Atvatabar. There were different kinds of golden gods worshipped, or symbols that represented the inventive forces, art, and spiritual power." The summary continues: "The Atvatabarese were very wealthy, gold being as common as iron in the outer world." As always, luxury beyond imagination is the rule down here. Things are really up-to-date in Atvatabar:

> There were plenty of newspapers, and the most wonderful inventions had been in use for ages. Railroads, pneumatic tubes, telegraphs, telephones, phonographs, electric lights, rain makers, seaboots, marine railroads, flying machines, megaphones, velocipedes without wheels, aërophers, etc., were quite common, not to speak of such inventions as sowing, reaping, sewing, bootblacking and knitting machines. Of course printing, weaving, and such like machines had been in use since the dawn of history. Strange to say they had no steam engines, and terrorite and gunpowder were unknown. Their great source of power was magnicity, generated by the two powerful metals terrelium and aquelium, and compressed air their explosive force.

(above) The bockhockids, shown here towering above the crowd, are "immense walking machines" reminiscent of ostriches. These are the ungainly mounts of the Atvatabarese cavalry and police force.

"They were a peaceful people, and Atvatabar being itself an immense island continent, lying far from any other land, there had been no wars with any external nation, nor even civil war, for over a hundred years." As soon as virile Commander White lays eyes on Lyone, not only fetching but a goddess to boot, Atvatabar's comfortable tranquillity is doomed.

The *Polar King* pulls up to the wharf—constructed of white marble—to a huge festive greeting by the governor and welcoming throngs that include regiments of cavalry mounted on mechanical ostriches. "They were forty feet in height from toe to head . . . The iron muscles of legs and body, moved by a powerful magnic motor inside the body of the monster, acted on bones of hollow steel." As the sailors scurry up the legs to mount them, "a military band composed of fifty musicians, each mounted on a bockhockid, played the March of Atvatabar in soul-stirring strains . . . A brigade of five thousand bockhockids fell into line as an escort of honor," and it's off in procession through the beautiful all-marble city. These ungainly, not to say wildly unlikely, bockhockids would suggest this is satire, but given all the other oddball stuff in the book, I'd have to say it's not. Rather it seems to be evidence that Bradshaw was letting his imagination sprout any strange fruit it might—and may have had a little help from his chemical friends as well. There's a distinctly *druggy* cast to the whole business. Another such example from a little farther on is a little botanical garden containing specimens merging the plant and animal kingdoms, flowers blooming kitten heads, flitting birds trailing aerial roots. A spoof on Darwin? Or just trippy flashes? My vote goes to the latter. There's a hypersensuous quality, a reveling in minute

(above) The lilliputum, shown here, "was another wonderful creature, half-plant, half-bird."

physical detail and description practically for its own sake—along with these stoner ideas—that suggests Bradshaw may have been indulging in some writer's little helpers.

Boarding the Sacred Locomotive, after appropriate preparatory prayers ("Glorious annihilator of time and space, lord of distance, imperial courier"), White and a few officers are whisked five hundred miles inland to Calnogor for a reception with the king and queen. Between heady glasses of squang, the king explains

(above) Lyone's Aerial Yacht (left) and The Sacred Locomotive (right).
Note too Atvatabar's dramatic, picturesque landscape.

Atvatabar's religion to White. "We worship the human soul," he says, "under a thousand forms, arranged in three great circles of deities." These are the gods of invention, the gods of art, and a third group containing "the spiritual gods of sorcery, magic and love." Together "this universal human soul forms the one supreme god Harikar, whom we worship in the person of a living woman, the Supreme Goddess Lyone."

The king drones on, detailing the various religious divisions. After the obligatory tour of religious temples, they're taken to meet the living goddess Lyone, who is lovely, with bright blue hair and "firm and splendid" breasts. "I was entranced with the appearance of the divine girl . . . All at once she gazed at me! I felt filled with a fever of delicious delight, of intoxicating adoration."

"Our religion is a state of ecstatic joy," Lyone says, "chiefly found in the cultured friendship of counterpart souls, who form complete circles with each other." They are known as "twin-souls," and there are twenty thousand in Egyplosis, where Lyone and these devotees live.

When Lyone is called to Egyplosis to oversee the installation of a twin-soul, White is invited to go along on her aerial yacht, another ornate contraption powered by magnicity. This seat of worship is a city consisting of a great temple carved from a single block of pale green marble, with "one hundred subterranean temples and labyrinths" beneath it, having "the enchanted charm of Hindoo and Greek architecture, together with the thrilling ecstasy of Gothic shrines." Bradshaw can't resist voluptuous descriptions that amount to aesthetic heavy breathing:

> The chief temple at Egyplosis was interiorly of semi-circular shape, like a Greek theatre, five hundred feet in width. It was covered like the

(above) The Living Battery consists of hundreds of twin-souls.

pantheon with a sculptured roof and dome of many-colored glass. The roof was one hundred and thirty feet above the lowest tier of seats beneath. The walls were laboriously sculptured dado and field and frieze, with bas-reliefs of the same character as the golden throne of the gods that stood at the centre of the semi-circle.

The dado was thirty-two feet in height, on which were carved the emblems of every possible machine, implement or invention that conferred supremacy over nature in idealized grandeur. Battles of flying wayleals [soldiers] and races of bockhockids were carved in great confusion. It was a splendid reunion of science and art . . .

Above all rose the dome whose lights were fadeless. The pavement of the temple had been chiselled in the form of a longitudinal hollow basin, containing a series of wide terraces of polished stone, whereon were placed divans of the richest upholstery. In each divan sat a winged twin-soul, priest and priestess, the devotees of hopeless love. On the throne itself sat Lyone, the supreme goddess, in the semi-nude splendor of the pantheon, arranged with tiara and jewelled belt and flowing skirt of sea-green aquelium lace. She made a picture divinely entrancing and noble. Supporting the throne was an immense pedestal of polished marble, fully one hundred feet in diameter and twenty feet in height, which stood upon a wide and elevated pavement of solid silver, whereon the priests and priestesses officiated in the services to the goddess. On crimson couches sat their majesties the king and queen of Atvatabar, together with the great officers of the realm. Next to the royal group myself and the officers and seamen of the *Polar King* occupied seats of honor. Behind, around and above us, filling the immense temple, rose the concave mass of twin-souls numbering ten thousand individuals, each seated with a counterpart soul. The garments of both priests and priestesses were fashioned in a style somewhat resembling the decorative dresses seen on Greek and Japanese vases, yet wholly original in design. In many cases the priestesses were swathed in transparent tissues that revealed figures like pale olive gold within.

Stop him before he describes more!

Afterward, in a private audience, Lyone and White at last get down to it. "The pleasure we aspire to is superior to any physical delight," she insists. "It is the quintessence of existence. We are willing to pay the price of hopelessness to taste such nectar." She explains that at one time in its past, Atvatabar experimented with a form of free love, but the result was disastrous: "unbridled license devastated the country." So the lawmakers reestablished marriage as "the only law suitable to mankind." But some of these married couples chose to remain celibate, and "for these Egyplosis was founded, for the study and practice of what is really a higher development of human nature and in itself an unquestionable good." This higher state of celibacy, of course, echoes the practices of many nineteenth-century utopian communities, from the Rappites to the Koreshans.

But White isn't convinced. "Hopeless love seems to me one of the most disquieting things in life. Its victims, happy and unhappy, resisting passion with regret or yielding with remorse, are ever on the rack of torture." Is everyone content with their celibate state here? he asks. Just then they hear a terrible commotion, shouts, a woman shrieking. Two twin-souls are brought before Lyone, and the woman of the pair is carrying a beautiful baby. Apparently not everyone. "Did you not think of your lifelong vows of celibacy?" asks Lyone. "We have," says the youth. "Such vows are a violation of nature. Everything here bids us love, but the artificial system under which we have lived arbitrarily draws a line and says, thus far and no further. Your system may suit disembodied spirits, if such exist, but not beings of flesh and blood. It is an outrage on nature. We desire to leave Egyplosis." And furthermore, he says, "There are thousands of twin-souls ready to cast off this yoke. They only await a leader to break out in open revolt."

The next day Lyone makes a confession to White. She came to Egyplosis a true believer in ideal love and found it in a chaste, loving connection with a twin-soul. But then he died. Heartbroken, she was elevated to the throne of goddess, but "I continually long for something sweeter yet . . . at times I know I could forgo even the throne of the gods itself for the pure and intimate love of a counterpart soul." What would be the punishment for this? White asks. "A shameful death by magnic-ity. No goddess can seek a lover and live." And yet, moments later, White can control himself no longer:

> I sprang forward with a cry of joy, falling at the feet of the goddess. I encir-cled her figure with my arms and held up my face to hers. Her kiss was a blinding whirlwind of flame and tears! Its silence was irresistible entreaty. It dissolved all other interests like fire melting stubborn steel. It was proclamation of war upon Atvatabar! It was the destruction of a unique civilization with all its appurtenances of hopeless love. It was love defying death. Thenceforward we became a new and formidable twin-soul!

But before they actually declare war, Lyone takes White below to the Infernal Palace to meet the Grand Sorcerer. Twenty thousand twin-souls appear, all carrying wands connected to "fine wires of terrelium." They commence a "strange dance" beneath a huge statue of a golden dragon, and "a shower of blazing jewels issued from its mouth. There were emeralds, diamonds, sapphires, and rubies flung upon the pavement." To impress White and amuse Lyone, the sorcerer sets these hard-dancing ecstatic souls to creating an entire *island,* whose existence can only be maintained "so long as the twin-souls support it by never-ceasing ecstasy." During this idyll their love grows, but on their return they find they've been spied on. But rather than give up White and send him packing back to the surface, Lyone tells the king that she's seen the light. The whole system they've been living by is wrong and rotten. "The true union of souls is not artificial restraint." When Lyone renounces her throne and calls for religious reform, the king proclaims that the penalty for this is "death on the magnetic scaffold." White is ordered out of Atvatabar. Not a chance. This means war!

Of the population of 50 million, 20 million are for Lyone and reform. Soon civil war rages, with casualties on both sides. Just as White's forces are losing a sea battle, two fighting ships under the flags of the United States and England show up and save the rebels. After a torturous trek through arctic wastes, those fearful sailors who left the ship had spread the word about the existence of the interior world. Bradshaw reproduces a headline from a New York newspaper:

AN ASTOUNDING DISCOVERY!
The North Pole Found To Be An Enormous Cavern,
Leading To A Subterranean World!
The Earth Proves To Be A Hollow Shell One Thou-
Sand Miles In Thickness, Lit By An Interior Sun!
Oceans And Continents, Islands And Cities Spread Upon
The Roof Of The Interior Sphere!

. . .

Tremendous Possibilities For Science And Commerce!
The Fabled Realms Of Pluto No Longer A Myth
Gold! Gold! Beyond The Dreams Of Madness!

The American and British ships that steam into view and save the day for White's forces are the first of many rushing to check out the interior world and claim a piece of the pie: "All civilized nations immediately fitted out vessels of discovery . . . for the benefit of their respective governments." The blithe imperialism in all of this couldn't be more blatant. The assumption is that Atvatabar is there to be exploited, no matter what the inhabitants might have to say about it. And there's a parallel attitude regarding its culture and religion. Lyone is ready to stop being a *goddess* because she's so attracted to White, and willing to let her country plunge into bloody civil war, the result of which is an utter wreckage of the value system that had been in place there for centuries. It's all presented as reform. Six years after *Atvatabar* was published, the United States marched into Cuba and the Philippines. Certainly the Spanish government in Cuba "had long been corrupt, tyrannical, and cruel," but intervention in the long Cuban civil war had as much to do with economic considerations and a national spirit of empire building as with altruism.[8]

John Uri Lloyd's *Etidorhpa*, published in 1895, is easily the weirdest hollow earth novel of all. "To say that it is one of the strangest books of the century is to put it mildly," wrote a contemporary reviewer in Lloyd's hometown *Cincinnati Enquirer.* Another for the *Chicago Medical Times* gushed that "It excels Bulwer-Lytton's *Coming Race* and Jules Verne's most extreme fancy. It equals Dante in vividness and eccentricity of plot . . ." The *Western Druggist,* also published in Chicago, called it "a book like to nothing ever before seen; a book in which are blended, in a harmonious whole, romance, exact science, alchemy, poetry, esoterism, metaphysics, moral teachings and bold speculation."

Lloyd's novel was reviewed in these medical papers because he was a pharmacist who'd made a reputation writing on pharmacological subjects before the publication of *Etidorhpa* (Aphrodite spelled backwards). "Psychedelics Lloyd must have had contact with include marijuana and opium poppies," wrote Neal Wilgus in the introduction to a 1976 reprint, "belladonna containing plants such as nightshade, henbane and jimsonweed . . . ergot, an LSD containing fungus . . . most likely of all perhaps are the *Psilocybe mexicana* and other psilocybin producing mushrooms of Mexico which act very much like LSD and mescaline in producing just the kind of 'head trip' which Lloyd calls Eternity without Time." Lloyd appears to have been the Carlos Castaneda of the hollow earth. As a more recent reviewer put it, "*Etidorhpa* recounts one of the earliest and most intensely evoked hallucinatory journeys in literature."

---

8. *A Short History of the United States* by Allan Nevins and Henry Steele Commager (New York: The Modern Library, 1945).

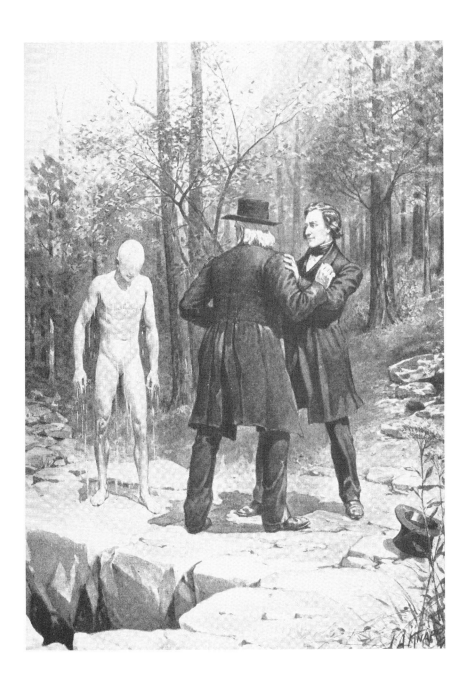

(above) John Uri Lloyd's *Etidorhpa* (1895) includes this eyeless humanoid creature that looks like a cross between E.T. and a cave fish.

The narrator appears at Lloyd's doorstep as an old bearded man and forces him to listen as he reads the manuscript he's written. He has violated an occult society's secret taboo, and his punishment is to be taken on a forced pilgrimage through a vast labyrinth leading down to the earth's hollow center. He's transported to a cave opening in Kentucky, where he is met by his guide—a gray-skinned eyeless humanoid creature who looks like a cross between E.T. and a cave fish. But the trip, while physical, is largely spiritual. He's on his way to personal enlightenment and he is scared—suggestive of a line from Herman Hesse's *Demian:* "Nothing in the world is more distasteful to a man than to take the path that leads to himself."

Deep in the cavern, they pass through a forest of giant mushrooms and then zoom across a vast lake at nine hundred miles an hour in a metal boat with no seeming means of propulsion. The guide tries to explain that it taps an invisible "energy fluid," but the narrator doesn't understand. The lake is contained by a stone wall, beyond which looms "an unfathomable abyss." Returning from this excursion, they continue downward. Gravity decreases to near zero, and his breathing slows until it stops; still he lives. The narrator is terrified and feels "an uncontrollable, inexpressible desire to flee." His guide explains that breathing is just a "waste of energy," that the closer you get to pure spirit it's not needed. They're in another mushroom forest. The guide breaks one open, and insists that he drink its "clear, green liquid."

As the guide delivers a short history of drunkenness worldwide from the earliest times, they enter a cavern "resonant with voices—shrieks, yells, and maniacal cries commingled."

"I stopped and recoiled, for at my very feet I beheld a huge, living human head. 'What is this?' I gasped. 'The fate of a drunkard,' my guide replied. 'This was once an intelligent man, but now he has lost his body, and enslaved his soul, in the den of drink.' Then the monster whispered, 'Back, back, go thou back!' . . . Now I perceived many such heads about us . . . I felt myself clutched by a powerful hand—a hand as large as that of a man fifty feet in height. I looked about expecting to see

(above) The subterranean pilgrim in *Etidorhpa* visits a mushroom forest (top); and tiny tormented people (bottom).

a gigantic being, but instead beheld a shrunken pygmy. The whole man seemed but a single hand. Then from about us, huge hands arose; on all sides they waved in the air. 'Back, back, go thou back.' . . . The amphitheater was fully a thousand feet in diameter, and the floor was literally alive with grotesque beings. Each abnormal part seemed to be created at the expense of the remainder of the body. Here a gigantic forehead rested on a shrunken face and body, and there a pair of enormous feet were walking, seemingly attached to the body of a child, and yet the face was that of a man." "This is the Drunkard's Den," his guide tells him. "These men are lost to themselves and to the world. You must cross this floor. No other passage is known." He adds, "Taste not their liquor by whatever form or creature presented." If they offer inducements, he must refuse to drink or he'll end up one of them.

Abruptly he's borne aloft by one of the huge hands and carried to a stone platform in the center of the cavern. Amid the grotesques, a handsome man appears to him, insisting he's a friend, a deliverer, saying that all the deformities he's seeing aren't real, are produced in his imagination by the influence of an evil spirit (his guide), they're really happy normal people. "They seek to save you from disaster. One hour of experience such as they enjoy is worth a hundred years of the pleasures known to you. After you have partaken of their exquisite joy, I will conduct you back to the earth's surface whenever you desire to leave us." Drink this! Tempted, the narrator begins to drink but then dashes the cup on a rock. Suddenly the twisted creatures and the handsome persuader vanish. Slowly they are replaced by beautiful vocal and instrumental music. And "by and by, from the corridors of the cavern, troops of bright female forms floated into view. Never before had I seen such loveliness in human mold."

The following scene could have been choreographed by Busby Berkeley on acid.

Carrying "curious musical instruments and beautiful wands, they produced a scenic effect of rare beauty that the most extravagant dream of fairyland could not surpass. The great hall was clothed in brilliant colors. Flags and streamers fluttered in breezes that also moved the garments of the angelic throng about me." They begin to dance around him to "music indescribable," group after group of them, each singing "sweeter songs, more beautiful, and richer in dress than those preceding." The narrator nearly swoons in ecstasy. "I was rapt, I became a thrill of joy. A single moment of existence such as I experienced, seemed worth an age of any other pleasure."

Can he get any higher? Yes. The music ceases and Etidorhpa herself appears. "She stood before me, slender, lithe, symmetrical, radiant. Her face paled the beauty of all who preceded her." She announces that "love rules the world, and I am the Soul of Love Supreme"—and that he can have her all to himself forever. She and her beautiful minions have appeared to him as a preview of things to come. But first he must undergo a few more trials. "You can not pass into the land of Etidorhpa until you have suffered as only the damned can suffer," she says, offering him a cup filled with green liquid. Again, he almost drinks but dashes that cup to the floor too. Etidorhpa disappears along with all the chorus girls. The narrator finds himself back on the surface, surrounded by endless desert sand. For days he struggles along in the fiery heat, without food or drink. He's dying of thirst when he encounters a caravan whose leader offers a lifesaving glass of clear green liquid. "No. I will not drink." The caravan abruptly vanishes, and a cool, refreshing breeze begins to blow. Soon he is nearly freezing, and days pass without number. He curses God and prays for death. He wishes he'd given in to one of the tempters—but then, no. "I have faith in Etidorhpa, and were it to do over again I would not drink."

The magic words! Suddenly he is once again back in the cavern with his guide. It's all been a brief hallucination, occurring in the moment after he sipped the magic mushroom cocktail. Their journey continues, literally downhill for them and for the reader as well. They get to the end of a shelf of rock overhanging an unfathomable abyss—the enormous hollow center of the earth—and his guide bids the narrator to jump. Are you crazy? he asks. The guide says that here lies Enlightenment, grabs him, and they leap into nothingness. Instead of falling, they seem to float, and after a time they reach the very center, "the Sphere of Rest." Here the narrator experiences a midair satori. "Perfect rest came over my troubled spirit. All thoughts of former times vanished. The cares of life faded; misery, distress, hatred, envy, jealousy, and unholy passions, were blotted from existence. I had reached the land of Etidorhpa—THE END OF THE EARTH."

He's achieved a moment of spiritual awakening. His guide tells him:

> It has been my duty to crush, to overcome by successive lessons your obedience to your dogmatic, materialistic earth philosophy, and bring your mind to comprehend that life on earth's surface is only a step towards a higher existence, which may, when selfishness is conquered, in a time to come, be gained by mortal man, and while he is in the flesh. The vicissitudes through which you have recently passed should be to you an impressive lesson, but the future holds for you a lesson far more important, the knowledge of spiritual, or mental evolution which men may yet approach; but that I would not presume to indicate now, even to you.

He stands on the edge of "The Unknown Country"—but cannot reveal what comes next. It would be too mind-blowing for mere mortals. And so ends the novel's action.

Etidorhpa is horribly flawed as novels go—I've left out the frequent long tedious asides in which Lloyd challenges the writer of the manuscript about seemingly impossible aspects of his story, which he then explains/defends at "scientific" and philosophical length. But it is certainly a landmark departure from the usual hollow earth novels, using the conceit not for mere adventure, or as the device for concocting some new sociopolitical utopia. The utopia it presents, if it can be called that, is purely spiritual—however deeply weird.

Arguably the most boring hollow earth novel ever, in a couple of respects, is Clement Fezandie's *Through the Earth* (1898). Fezandie (1865–1959) was a math teacher in New York City and eventually wrote science fiction for Hugo Gernsback (1884–1967), the pioneering editor who invented sci-fi magazines, starting with *Amazing Stories* in 1926. *Through the Earth* qualifies only marginally as a hollow earth novel. It tells of a project to bore a tunnel between New York City and Australia to carry goods and people between the two places, like the world's longest freight elevator. Most of the book is occupied by an account of the first test ride, essayed by a brave impoverished lad for the prize money of £100 (offered because no one was willing to try it for free). As he plunges through the tube, he relates scientific observations of gravity, temperature, and distance. At the end, the tunnel self-destructs, but the plucky volunteer lives through it, sells his story to a New York newspaper for $100,000, tours the country as a celebrated hero, and marries the inventor's pretty daughter. Horatio Alger meets the hollow earth. But it's another example of how writers of every period have used the notion for purposes appropriate to their time. The first attempts at building subways went back to the 1840s in London, where underground railways were first pioneered, but by the turn of the new century a certain mania for subway building was taking place in major cities worldwide. The first practical subway line in the United States was under construction in Boston while Fezandie was writing *Through the Earth,* as was New York's (which would officially open in 1904), and it seems likely that Fezandie simply used these as a jumping-off point. Why not a really *long* one?

The Secret of the Earth by Charles Beale (1899) features two characters who have invented an airplane that they fly to the North Pole and into a Symmes' Hole into the interior. They find a paradise that was mankind's first home and then fly out through the hole in the South Pole. Their airship beats the Wright Brothers by four years, of course, but in the 1890s, trying to come up with one was all the rage with inventors. It's often forgotten that the Wrights had serious competitors racing with them to develop a reliable design, and that one incentive was a large cash prize offered by France to the inventor of the first one that really worked—which is to say that the *idea* of airplanes was, well, in the air at the time Beale's *Secret of the Earth* appeared.

William Alexander Taylor's *Intermere* (1901) is like a bad rewrite of *Symzonia*. It too uses the hollow earth as a vehicle for current ideas. This otherworldly society has solved all earthly problems. It is a perfect democracy—almost. Women are supposedly equal, but their "chosen" role is generally that of housewife, and those who work don't make as much money as men. They receive five fewer years of education than men do, and they're not allowed to own real estate. But everybody's pretty and handsome, nobody's poor, there's a four-hour workday, the communities are lovely and idyllic, crops go from planting to harvest in ten days, all marriages are happy and harmonious, and the food is fabulous but nobody has to cook. They have Medocars, Aerocars, and Merocars—autos, airplanes, and ships—which zip silently about at "a rate of speed that makes our limited railway trains seem like lumbering farm wagons." They are powered by a force derived from electricity, which proves to be the secret behind their social and economic perfection.

The Intermerans also have a device that's rather like an online fax machine. When the displaced narrator asks for news from home, his host goes to a cabinet and opens it: "Soon his hands began to move with rhythmic rapidity over the curiously inlaid center of the flat surface of the open cabinets. At the end of ten or fifteen minutes his manipulations ceased, a compartment noiselessly opened, and eight beautifully printed pages, four by six inches, bound in the form of a booklet, fell upon the table. The pages before me comprised a compendium of yesterday's doings of the entire world." In their opinion, surface events, which they keep close track of, are really stupid. "Selfishness, oppression, slaughter, pride, conquest, greed, vanity, self-adulation and base passions make up ninety-nine one-hundredths of this record," sighs the host. This leads him into a tirade against surface world newspapers. He says this objective compendium "is to promote wisdom. The newspaper [exists] to feed vicious or depraved appetite, as well as to convey useful information.

This is the cold, colorless, passionless record of facts and information, from which knowledge and wisdom may be deduced to some extent. Your newspaper is the opposite, taken in its entirety. It consists of the inextricable mingling together of the good and the bad, of the useful and the useless, and the elevating and the degrading, the latter always in the ascendant."

Sounds like he's been reading the papers, all right. In fact, this critique comes from someone who spent much of his career *writing* them. Taylor was an Ohio lawyer born in 1837 who turned to newspaper work in 1858, and was associated with various papers (chiefly the *Cincinnati Enquirer*) until 1900. So he knew the failings of American newspapers from the inside.

Gabriel de Tarde's *Underground Man,* first published in 1896, appeared in English translation in 1905 with a preface by H. G. Wells. This hollow earth novel by a French sociologist set in the thirty-first century is a satire on prevailing sociological thinking. It tells the story of how a near-utopia had been created on the surface, until the sun began sputtering out and dying, killing nearly all of mankind. Those remaining are driven beneath the surface, where they establish yet another utopia, bristling with thoroughly modern machines and techniques: thermal power, electric trains, monocles, and other gizmos. But the main idea is that being driven underground has "produced, so to say, a purificaton of society." It has, in effect, changed human nature. He writes:

Secluded thus from every influence of the natural milieu into which it was hitherto plunged and confined, the social milieu was for the first time able to reveal and display its true virtues, and the real social bond appeared in all its vigor and purity. It might be said that destiny had desired to make in our case an extended sociological experiment for its own edification by placing us in such extraordinarily unique conditions.... The mental space left by the reduction of our needs is taken up by those talents—artistic, poetic, and scientific—which multiply and take deep root. They become the true needs of society. They spring from a necessity to produce and not from a necessity to consume.

Worth noting is that this perfect society has been produced by "the complete elimination of living nature, whether animal or vegetable, man only excepted." This idea of completely overcoming nature, subduing and totally dominating it, was one that had been growing during the nineteenth century. And how could it not, given the ceaseless succession of scientific and technical marvels that just kept unfolding? So in *Underground Man* de Tarde pushes such hubris to the limits, by getting rid of nature entirely!

The Smoky God (1908) by Willis George Emerson has a familiar structure but is more charming than many, thanks to the narrator's voice, as told to Emerson, the putative editor. Ninety-five-year-old Norwegian Olaf Janson had this adventure in 1829 when he was a teenager, so the telling combines the innocence of a young boy with an old man's nostalgia. Olaf and his father set off on a fishing voyage to the north in a small sloop and sail over the long gradual curve of a Symmes' Hole into the interior. There they encounter a beautiful, verdant land lit and warmed by a reddish central sun—the smoky god—and peopled by a race of gentle giants who live to be six hundred years old. They're twelve feet tall and dress like medieval Scandinavian peasants, with big gold buckles on their shoes—gold being common as beach pebbles there.

The argument for the existence of this inner paradise is the same one that Edmond Halley made over two hundred years earlier: it is demanded by God's purpose and parsimony regarding waste. It had to be there. *The Smoky God* goes farther. The inner earth is "the cradle of the human race," the original Eden. In fact, "God created the earth for the 'within'—that is to say, for its lands, seas, rivers, mountains, forests and valleys, and for its other internal conveniences, while the outside surface of the earth is merely the veranda, the porch . . . in the beginning this old world of ours was created solely for the 'within' world." It's not so far from the beliefs of

Cyrus Teed, except he thought we were all still inside.

Olaf and his father are treated to the standard tour, but the novel mercifully treads lightly on the details of the utopia, dealing more with the adventure of getting there and finally, after great hardship, getting home. But we do learn a few things. The smoky red sun is like a natural gro-lite for plants *and* animals—trees a thousand feet tall, herds of huge elephants, great soaring birds. They are an agricultural people, but they, too, have super fast ships and monorail bullet trains powered by a force suspiciously like electricity. And perhaps most civilized of all, "the people are exceedingly musical. Their cities are equipped with vast palaces of music, where not infrequently as many as twenty-five thousand lusty voices of this giant race swell forth in mighty choruses of the most sublime symphonies."

After two years there, Olaf and his father decide it's time to head for home. They try to return to the surface via the northern opening, but the strong prevailing winds beat against them, so they turn around and practically fly southward and through the opening there. In rough Antarctic seas their fishing boat overturns, Olaf's father is killed, and Olaf is rescued by a Scottish whaler—and promptly clapped in irons as a madman when he relates what's happened to him. On getting back to Norway, he tells his story again—and is put in an insane asylum for nearly thirty years. When he gets out, he becomes a successful fisherman, and finally retires to sunny Southern California—"living alone in an unpretentious bungalow out Glendale way, a short distance from the business district of Los Angeles"—where on his deathbed he tells his tale one final time to Emerson.

By 1908 the hollow earth had become enough of an established landmark on the literary landscape that it had been added to the map of children's books. In that year two were published, one by a celebrated writer, and another by a writer chiefly celebrated under many pseudonyms.

L. Frank Baum's career had been spotty before *The Wonderful Wizard of Oz* came out in 1900 and became the year's best-selling book, establishing a franchise for him for the rest of his life—whether he liked it or not. Born in 1856 near

Syracuse, New York, to an oil magnate father and a women's rights activist mother, Baum suffered a lifelong heart ailment that limited his physical activity and expanded his imagination. At fourteen his father gave him a little printing press, and the next year he was writing and publishing a paper, the *Rose Lawn Home Journal,* in which some of the local businesses even bought advertising. He had an early

passion for theater, encouraged by his father, who owned a string of theaters in New York and Pennsylvania—which Baum began managing while in his early twenties. In 1881 he wrote and starred in a musical called *The Maid of Arran,* which played to good reviews. He also began breeding prize Hamburg chickens, which led to his first book in 1886—*The Book of Hamburgs, A Brief Treatise upon the Mating, Rearing, and Management of the Different Varieties of Hamburgs*—a long way from Dorothy and her companions. About this time the family fortunes took a nosedive, and Baum moved his wife and children to the Dakota Territory, where he operated a general store in Aberdeen until it went under in 1890. He then got a job running the local paper. When the paper failed—like his store, victim of the hard times in the early 1890s—he moved to Chicago and took a reporting job on the *Evening Post.* In 1897 he teamed up with illustrator Maxfield Parrish to produce *Mother Goose in Prose,* which became a best seller. In 1900 *The Wonderful Wizard of Oz* quickly became a blockbuster, selling over 90,000 copies within two years.[9] Sequel followed sequel—he wrote thirteen Oz books before his death in 1919. The fourth, *Dorothy and the Wizard in Oz* (1908), took the Oz crowd down into the hollow earth.

The story opens with Dorothy and her kitten, Eureka, getting off a train from San Francisco at a little station stop town in California, where she's met by a

(above) *Dorothy and the Wizard in Oz* (1908), in which some of the Oz crowd visited the hollow earth. (© 1908 by L. Frank Baum)

---

9. Cautiously, however, he didn't give up his day job right away. In 1897, among his many stray professional interests—which is to say, attempts to stay afloat—he had started *The Show Window,* a trade magazine for window dressers, founding the National Association of Window Trimmers the following year, and continuing as editor of the magazine until 1902.

boy named Zeb. He puts them in a buggy drawn by Jim, his bony old horse, and they head off for her uncle's ranch. But moments later, the ground shakes and cracks open (this was being written just a year after the devastating San Francisco earthquake), and suddenly they're falling through darkness down into the hollow interior. Dorothy faints but revives as they continue slowly falling, realizing that she isn't going to die. "She had merely started upon another adventure, which promised to be just as queer and unusual as were those she had before encountered."

Good advertising for what's to come, but not quite true. *Dorothy and the Wizard in Oz* lacks the moral depth and resonance of the original, in which the characters seek spiritual qualities—wisdom, courage, and heart. In this one, after they land safely in the hollow earth, they pass through a number of fancifully peculiar kingdoms trying to find their way back to the surface; but while diverting, their adventures don't really add up to much more than that.

They first come to the Land of the Mangaboos, plant people who grow on bushes and live in glass houses. The Wizard shows up in a hot-air balloon that has also fallen through a crack and has a magic showdown with the resident Sorcerer, in which the Wiz chops the Sorcerer in half with a sword. But no problem— he can be replanted! The Mangaboos drive these Meat Creatures into a dark mountain cave and seal it with stones. The cave leads to the Valley of Voe, another beautiful land, this one inhabited by invisible people. They eat a special fruit to keep them that way, so that the fierce red bears also living there can't see them and devour them. One of the Voe people gives them directions to Pyramid

(above) Dorothy and her faithful pals—Zeb, the farm boy; Jim, the talking cab horse; and Eureka, the mischievous kitten—are plunged into the hollow earth during a California earthquake. (© 1908 by L. Frank Baum)

Mountain, beyond which lies the Land of the Gargoyles, whose inhabitants prove to be aggressive *wooden* people.

Finally, just as they seem hopelessly trapped in a cave full of Dragons, Dorothy remembers that Ozma has a magic picture hanging in her room in Oz, in which she can see whatever Dorothy's doing. By making a special sign to Ozma, she and her friends can instantly be transported to Oz. Of course, if she had thought of this handy solution earlier, the novel would have been a lot shorter. Soon they are safely back in the Emerald City. After some adventures there, it's time to use the Magic Belt and go home.

The other hollow earth novel for kids, *5000 Miles Underground* (1908), was written by one of the all-time champions of the pseudonym—Howard Garis. Born in Binghamton, New York, in 1873, his first writing job was as an editor on *Sunnyside*—a trade magazine for undertakers. In 1896 he went to work for the *Newark Evening News* and began writing children's stories on the side. He resigned the newspaper job in 1908 to work for the Stratemeyer Syndicate—a juvenile fiction factory that turned out series titles by the dozens, using writers who worked under various ongoing house pseudonyms. As Victor Appleton, Garis wrote the first thirty-five Tom Swift novels himself, and that was just a drop in his bucket. He also wrote a number of the early Bobbsey Twins books, as well as titles in numerous series now forgotten. And in 1910, under his own name, he created Uncle Wiggley, that wise old rheumatic gentleman rabbit, as a daily feature for the *Newark Evening News*—averaging a story a day (except Sunday) until 1947. Uncle Wiggley was a hit from the start, leading to many books, tie-in merchandising (much of it designed by Garis himself) that included clothes and dishes, a board game, as well as a popular radio show. Garis' cumulative output is positively staggering. Altogether it's estimated that during his long life—Garis died at the age of 89 in 1962—he wrote more than 15,000 stories and about 500 books. Even more remarkable is the fact that for the form, much of it is really quite good.

Written under the pseudonym Roy Rockwood, *5000 Miles Underground* was the third in a series called Marvel Tales and featured an eccentric inventor, two plucky teenage orphan boys, a taciturn big-game hunter descended from Jules Verne's Hans, and a "comic" black servant named Washington White who murders English and is afraid of everything.

As the story opens, the Professor has cobbled together an all-purpose dirigible/boat fit for going down under. His Rube Goldberg wizardry is quintessentially American and emblematic of the period. A fictional mega-Edison, he can invent anything, out of anything. His *Flying Mermaid* incorporates and fancifully improves on many of the ideas and devices that were new at the time—flight, electrical gadgetry, and so on—as well as a few that have yet to be worked out, such as his secret "anti-gravity gas," five times lighter than hydrogen, that allows his cigar-shaped double-hulled 150-foot *Mermaid* to scoot along at high speed using blasts of electrically generated compressed air as fuel.

After a successful test run, the chipper all-male contingent (not a single girl in this one—presumably perfect for the target readership of twelve-year-old boys) heads toward the South Pole to the hole where the ocean pours into the earth's interior. But first, they're attacked by a whale, which Andy the hunter, without a moment's hesitation, shoots in the eye, understandably distracting the creature from going after them. Right after that, they fly over a burning ship and rescue its crew—a major mistake, since they prove to be vicious pirates who take over the *Mermaid.* By faking a near crash, they con the pirates into jumping ship near an uninhabited island and are again safely on their way. During the voyage, one of the boys begins to suspect that they have a mysterious stowaway aboard, but the Professor pooh-poohs the idea. They find the hole leading inside, and it's down the dark wet scary drain, for hundreds of miles, until, as you might expect, they plop into a sunny beautiful land. One more unspoiled paradise down there—where, as in *The Smoky God* and others, conditions are so salubrious that everything grows on a gigantic scale. It's just so darn great there that everything's bigger, too!

They've come to rest in a field of grass and clover as tall as a house, with red and yellow flowers the size of easy chairs. The Professor decides it's due to some unusual quality of the atmosphere and quickly produces a cosmological theory: "I believe we are on a sort of small earth that is inside the larger one we live on. This sphere floats in space, just as our earth does, and we have passed through a void that lies between our globe and this interior one. I think this new earth is about a quarter the size of ours and in some respects the same. In others it is vastly different."

Mark, one of the boys, says he thinks he saw a strange figure fleeing the ship after they landed, but nobody pays attention to him. Soon they begin exploring, and it's trouble right away. Jack stumbles down a steep hill into the cup of an enormous pitcher plant—those gently carnivorous plants best known on the surface as the Venus flytrap. Jack's fallen in and is covered with its sweet digestive goo. But they chop him out before any harm is done. Ants the size of "large rats" come swarming to the mess, as the intrepid explorers move on to an orchard where six-foot peaches grow on vines and several grasshoppers the size of motorcycles are pushing a ripe one along. Andy characteristically wants to blast a couple to kingdom come but is dissuaded on the grounds that they probably aren't very good to eat.

After many days of travel and a close encounter with a deadly half-plant, half-animal "snake tree," they come upon something truly weird—a delirium tremens monstrosity that "had the body of a bear, but the feet and legs were those of an alligator, while the tail trailed out behind like a snake, and the head had a long snout, not unlike the trunk of an elephant. The creature was about ten feet long and five feet in height." Andy is eager to shoot it, but it's suddenly caught in a geyser and drops to the ground dead—not far from a twelve-foot giant. Only Mark sees him before he disappears into the underbrush. Can it be their stowaway?

They continue for several days more, until they come upon a village, whose buildings consist of mounds rudely made from clay—dwellings of a half-civilized Mud Age people. Suddenly, "seeming to rise from the very ground, all about the ship, there appeared a throng of men . . . Not one was less than ten feet tall, and some were nearly fifteen! 'The giants have us!' cried Bill, as he saw the horde of creatures surrounding the ship."

A brief battle ensues, and the giants prove to practically be made of mud themselves. A peculiarity of increased gravity has made the giants' bodies soft and pliant, unmuscular. "They look like men made of putty! They're soft as snow men!" Our explorers prevail for a while, but sheer numbers do them in and they're finally captured. The Putty People are about to execute them, when a figure even taller than the rest appears wearing golden armor and bearing a golden sword. He orders everyone to stop! It's the Putty People's long-lost king, who was the mysterious stowaway on the *Mermaid*. He got stuck on the surface after riding a waterspout up, and he is eternally grateful to the Professor and his crew for bringing him back home. His land is their land.

He directs them to an abandoned temple heaped with diamonds and gold, telling them to take as much as they like. They find it and load up, but then realize their entry hole has been closed by an earthquake. The only way back to the surface is to ride the waterspout. Luckily the Professor has brought along a waterproof escape cylinder that's just the ticket for riding the waterspout, but they'll only have room for a few token diamonds in their pockets during the return ride. So it's up, up, and away in an exit borrowed from Verne. They float in the Atlantic until they're picked up by a passing ship and soon are back on the island in Maine. In an ending duly in keeping with the American Dream, those pocketfuls of diamonds they brought back make them all rich: "There was money enough so that they all could live in comfort, the rest of their lives." The Professor feels it's time to hang up his inventor's cap and retire. The rest, in a true sign of the times, decide to invest the money they get for the jewels "in different business ventures, and each one did well." They all live happily ever after through business savvy!

The number of hollow earth novels dropped off precipitously after 1910. One likely factor was increased scientific knowledge. Information has a way of dousing the fires of dreams. By then repeated expeditions seeking both poles had failed to confirm Symmes' Holes, so closely tied to the notion of a hollow earth. Until 1910 or so, the hollow earth conceit remained a terrific vehicle for adventure and utopian speculation. It provided a handy alternate world very much like our own and at least a marginally believable one. As polar exploration advanced and increasingly established that there were no inviting holes at the poles surrounded by a temperate open polar sea, the required suspension of disbelief became more difficult.

Nevertheless, a few true believers continued to hold on, despite all evidence to the contrary, and two nonfiction books appeared filled with "scientific" proof of the hollow earth.

In 1906, when William T. Reed's *The Phantom of the Poles* appeared, though Peary had made it to the North Pole, and Reed blithely argued that the poles hadn't been discovered because *they don't exist!* Instead, there are openings into the hollow earth where the poles are supposed to be, so vast, and their inclination so gradual, that various polar explorers have traveled a short way into them without realizing it: "I claim that the earth is not only hollow," Reed wrote, "but that all, or nearly all, of the explorers have spent much of their time past the turning-point, and have had a look into the interior of the earth." He accounts for the aurora borealis as "the reflection of a fire within the earth," and is convinced meteors don't come from outer space, but are rather being spat out by volcanoes in the interior—along with a host of other earnestly misinformed thoughts on the working of the compass, and the origins of glaciers, arctic dust, and driftwood, among others. And what's down there? "That, of course, is speculative . . . It is not like the question, 'Is the earth hollow?' We know that it is, but do not know what will be found in its interior." His guess? "From what I am able to gather . . . game of all kinds—tropical and arctic—will be found there; for both warm and cold climates must be in the interior—warm inland and cold near the poles. Sea monsters, and possibly the much-talked of sea serpent, may also be found, and vast territories of arable land for farming purposes. Minerals may be found in great quantities, and gems of all kinds. We may succeed, too, in finding large quantities of radium, which would be used to relieve the darkness if it should be unusually dark. I also believe the interior of the earth will be found inhabited. The race or races may be varied, but some at least will be of the Eskimo race, who have found their way in from the exterior." Like Symmes, he urges immediate exploration and colonization. "[The interior] can be made accessible to mankind with one-fourth the outlay of treasure, time, and life that it cost to build the subway in New York City. The number of people that can find comfortable homes (if it not already be occupied) will be billions." His whole case, presented in 283 obsessive pages, is little more than a rehash of Symmes' ideas from a hundred years earlier.

Marshall Gardner's *A Journey to the Earth's Interior; or, Have the Poles Really Been Discovered?* (1913) covers the same hollow ground. Gardner, who made his living as a maintenance man in an Aurora, Illinois, corset factory, posits a central sun six hundred miles across, a leftover bit of nebula from the time the earth was first formed. Reflected light from this inner sun accounts for the aurora borealis. Gardner was most fired up about the possibilities of developing this interior world (particularly mining), which he was certain contained a bonanza of diamonds, platinum, and gold. And this should be done not out of greed but as a patriotic act. Writing on the eve of World War I, he asked, "Do we want one of the autocratic countries of Europe to perpetuate in this new world all the old evils of colonial oppression and exploitation?" Not on your life. America, "with her high civilization, her free institutions, her humanity," has a "duty" to get there first. And "our country has the men, the aeroplane, the enterprise, and the capital" to pull it off.

With Gardner and Reed we enter the modern phase of hollow earthology —earnest believers marshaling increasingly desperate (and increasingly detailed) evidence to support a theory increasingly at odds with the growing weight of scientific data. But as we'll see, even today a few true believers continue to hang in there, despite all evidence to the contrary.

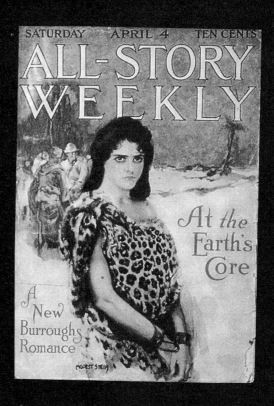

7

EDGAR RICE BURROUGHS
AT THE EARTH'S CORE

THE NUMBER OF HOLLOW EARTH NOVELS dropped off drastically after 1910, largely because polar exploration revealed no Symmes' holes. Consequently it was harder for readers (and writers) to create the suspension of disbelief needed to make such stories work. Something similar happened in the 1960s in regard to Venus. Its thick atmosphere and proximity to the sun had allowed generations of science fiction writers to create stories set in a steamy tropical wonderland of mysterious jungles and strange creatures. But then the facts intruded: under all those clouds Venus is too hot for life and too dry. And so the fetching bosomy Venusian maidens that routinely adorned pulp magazine covers from the 1930s through the 1950s disappeared. And although they didn't disappear completely, stories set in the hollow earth began to seem too far-fetched once science established the geophysical impossibility of a hollow earth.

But one writer remained undaunted by facts to the contrary.

Edgar Rice Burroughs liked the idea of a hollow earth well enough to set

(opposite) "At the Earth's Core," published in *All-Story* magazine, which featured a pensive-looking Dian the Beautiful on the cover. (© Edgar Rice Burroughs, Inc.)

six novels and several short stories in what he called Pellucidar, starting with *At the Earth's Core,* first published serially in 1914 in *All-Story Weekly.*

Burroughs's life before turning to writing at the age of thirty-five was like Baum's compounded for the worse—a study in lack of direction and repeated failure. He was born into a prosperous Chicago family in 1875. His father was a wealthy whiskey distiller, which proved ironic given Burroughs's later struggle with alcoholism. As a teenager he'd been sent to the prestigious Phillips Academy in Andover, Massachusetts, and was elected class president in 1892—but got yanked out of school by his father that same year for low grades and was forcibly relocated to the Michigan Military Academy north of Detroit, where he remained for five years. In 1896, he joined the army, but soon found himself bored stiff at the Arizona fort where he was stationed and began writing to his father, begging him to get him out. Special discharge papers signed by the secretary of war arrived early in 1897.

Years of upheaval followed. His brother Harry owned a cattle ranch in Idaho, and Burroughs's first job after leaving the army was as a cowboy, helping his brother drive a herd of starving Mexican cattle from Nogales to Kansas City. By summer he had enrolled as a student at Chicago's Art Institute, but it didn't last. Early in 1898, with things heating up in Cuba, Burroughs wrote Teddy Roosevelt offering to join his Rough Riders—but was rejected. By June of that year he'd opened a stationery shop in Pocatello, Idaho, but he was back to cowboying with his brother the following spring, and then landed in Chicago again in June as treasurer of his father's American Battery Company—the distillery burned down in 1885, and his father, resilient, had shifted to supplying the nascent automobile industry.

Burroughs married Emma, his longtime sweetheart, in 1900, and stayed with dad's battery company for three more years—but then a roller-coaster ride of jobs followed. By then he was beginning to do some writing and cartooning, but hadn't figured out how to make a living at it. He joined his brother Harry in an Idaho gold dredging operation in 1903, but that went bust in less than a year. On to Salt Lake City, where he became a railroad policeman for a time, and then it was back to Chicago. There, for the next seven years, poor Burroughs tried everything he could think of to support Emma and his growing family: high-rise timekeeper, door-to-door book salesman, lightbulb salesman, accountant, manager of the stenographic department at Scars, partner in his own short-lived advertising agency, office manager for a firm selling a supposed cure for alcoholism called Alcola, and a sales agent for a pencil sharpener company. This last job involved monitoring ads in pulp magazines—but Burroughs found himself more interested in reading the stories in these magazines than the ads he was supposed to be tracking. And the lightbulb lit. *I can do this!* In 1911, as the company was heading under, using the backs of letterhead stationery from his former failed businesses, Burroughs began handwriting what became *Under the Moons of Mars,* featuring John Carter, the first of his invincible heroes. He sent it out, and in August came a letter of acceptance from the editor of *All-Story.* Though Burroughs was still writing in his spare time—or stealing time from his latest job, working for brother Coleman's stationery

manufacturing company on West Kinzie Street, Chicago—by December 1911, he'd started writing *Tarzan of the Apes,* which he also sold to *All-Story* (for $700).

He began work on the first of his Pellucidar novels in 1912 while the manuscript of *Tarzan of the Apes* was still making the rounds of book publishers, collecting rejection slip after rejection slip as it went. His working title was "The Inner World." *All-Story* ran it serially in four issues starting on April 4, 1914. It didn't appear as a book until 1922, when A. C. McClurg, Burroughs's publisher for many years, brought it out with a wonderful cover, both menacing and sexy, by J. Allen St. John, the best illustrator of Burroughs's early work.

(above) The first edition of *At the Earth's Core* (1922) was illustrated by J. Allen St. John; the cover shows David Innes rescuing Dian the Beautiful. (© Edgar Rice Burroughs, Inc.)

His hollow earth story's most obvious debt was to Jules Verne's novel *A Journey to the Center of the Earth* (1864). Another likely influence was Sir Arthur Conan Doyle's *The Lost World,* which was a best seller in 1912. In Doyle's novel, the lost world, discovered by British explorers, lay not in the hollow earth but on a vast plateau surrounded by cliffs rising above the South American jungle, isolated for eons, unchanged since the Jurassic Period. This remote, unapproachable tableland was crawling with prehistoric life—huge, scary dinosaurs in particular. The clashing prehistoric reptiles in Verne's *Journey* played only a minor part in the novel overall. As we've seen, dinosaurs had captured the popular imagination ever since their "invention" in the early nineteenth century and the coining of the term by Sir Richard Owen in 1841. Life-size reconstructions featured at the 1851 Great Exhibition in London (and the splashy formal dinner thrown by sculptor/promoter Waterhouse Hawkins inside a half-constructed Iguanodon) cemented popular interest, which Verne drew on for his prehistoric novel.

In 1884 the discovery of a fossil herd of articulated Iguanodon skeletons in a Belgian coal mine further heightened dinosaurmania, as did the 1886 publication of *Le monde avant la creation del'homme,* by Camille Flammarion (1842–1925), which pictured an Iguanodon rampaging in the streets of Paris—the precursor to all those Godzilla movies. In the late 1890s, the New York Museum of Natural History bought famed dinosaur hunter Edward Drinker Cope's collection and commenced creating dramatic displays that were enthusiastically attended. Dinosaurs hadn't been used much in literature except by Verne, and then only in a minor role. In *The Lost World* they take center stage for the first time. Although Verne was the first to use them in fiction, the real origins of our ongoing pop cult love affair with dinosaurs—which reached an apotheosis of sorts in the *Jurassic Park* movies—can be traced to Doyle's novel, which remains so popular that an adventure series based on it ran for several years on television starting in 1999. While *The Lost World* was still on top of the best-seller lists, Burroughs was casting around for a new writing project. He seems to have combined Verne's hollow earth premise with Doyle's teeming prehistoric world, adding quite a few brainstorms of his own.

The landscape, ecology, and cosmology of Pellucidar are delightfully wacky and definitely all-American, starting with the way mining magnate David Innes and inventor Abner Perry got there: in an experimental mining machine run amok. Perry has invented an "iron mole," a "mechanical subterranean prospector" consisting of "a steel cylinder a hundred feet long, and jointed so that it may turn and twist through solid rock if need be. At one end is a mighty revolving drill." It's a sort of segmented steam locomotive with a huge Roto-Rooter attached to the front. Burroughs may well have been inspired to create this curious device based on his gold mining days, and also by reading the *Chicago Tribune* comics page. Dale R. Broadhurst says in an article in *ERBzine*,

> A likely source for the "Iron Mole" may be found in 1910 issues of the Sunday *Chicago Tribune*, where cartoonist M. L. Wells chronicled in color his "Old Opie Dilldock's Stories." In one of these 1910 illustrated Sunday full-pages, Opie plans a trip to the south pole and constructs an "earth borer" in his secret workshop, in order to make the trip there by way of a straight line through the Earth. Utilizing a hydrogen-oxygen fuel cell for power, the ingenious inventor propels his contraption to "the center of the earth." There he discovers strange intelligent beings . . . one of which he takes with him on his return to the planet's surface. While I doubt very much that Edgar Rice Burroughs sat down with a pile of "Opie Dilldock's Stories," in order to write out his 1913 "Inner World" adventure, some story elements from this set of locally published cartoons may well have entered into the would-be author's inner fantasies, and from there flowed out onto his pages of fiction, probably more by happenstance than through his conscious design.[1]

---

1. From an article by Dale R. Broadhurst titled "The Sword of Theosophy Revisited" on the *ERBzine* web-site (http: www.erbzine.com/mag11/1107.html). Bill and Sue-On Hillman's *ERBzine* site is a terrific re-source for Burroughs fans, whether the interest ranges from mild to total fanatic. Articles, novel summaries, etexts, and tons of mouthwatering graphics scanned from most of his works—a true ERB treasure trove.

Innes and Perry have built this machine not to advance knowledge and exploration, but to extend the frontiers of coal mining beyond those of mortal men—and make tons of money while they're at it. But on its trial run, the steering freezes and the damn thing won't stop—commencing to bore its way like crazy straight for the center of the earth.

After tearing through five hundred miles of rock, the iron mole pops out in sunny, tropical Pellucidar. "Together we stepped out to stand in silent contemplation of a landscape at once weird and beautiful." But in nothing flat, "there came the most thunderous, awe-inspiring roar that ever had fallen upon my ears." It's a colossal bearlike creature the size of an elephant—a dyryth—and it's after them. But it's distracted by the sudden appearance of a wolf pack a hundred strong, quickly followed by their masters, black "manlike creatures" with dracula teeth and long, slender tails, "grotesque parodies on humanity." These are but one of several races of varying intelligence inhabiting Pellucidar. They capture Innes and Perry and race through the treetops to their arboreal bough-village high in the trees.

Pellucidar is a busy, complicated place. As the *ERBzine* puts it, "The land teems with plant and animal life. A veritable melting pot where animals of nearly all the geological periods of the outer crust exist simultaneously. The land's races are just as varied as its animal life." Burroughs seems to have adopted the kitchen sink theory of the hollow earth, throwing in everything he can think of. More is more.

Innes and Perry escape from the tree creatures only to be captured by another vaguely hominid species called the Sagoths. They look like gorillas and are slave masters to yet another species—Stone Age humans. Innes and Perry are added to the chain gang and get to know a few of the enslaved humans—Ghak the Hairy One, Hooja the Sly One, and Dian the Beautiful. They're on a forced march to the village of the evil Mahars.

The dominant species on Pellucidar, the Mahars are a master race of super-intelligent lizards. They "are great reptiles, some six or eight feet in length, with long narrow heads and great round eyes. Their beaklike mouths are lined with

sharp, white fangs, and the backs of their huge lizard bodies are serrated into bony ridges from their necks to the end of their long tails, while from the fore feet membranous wings, which are attached to their bodies just in front of the hind legs, protrude at an angle of 45 degrees toward the rear, ending in sharp points several feet above their bodies."

Voiceless and unable to hear, the Mahars "communicate by means of a sixth sense which is cognizant of a fourth dimension." Whatever that may mean. Their capital is an underground city called Phutra, where they're served by the gorilla-like Sagoths and keep crowds of humans as cattle, since the Mahars consider

(above) A Mahar in flight, in a drawing by St. John from the first edition of *At the Earth's Core*. (© Edgar Rice Burroughs, Inc.)

human flesh quite a delicacy. They enjoy watching Roman-style combat in their great amphitheater between vicious beasts and lowly humans, on whom they also perform "scientific" experiments à la Joseph Mengele. A really nasty bunch, the Mahars, sort of like brainy flying Komodo dragons with Nazi proclivities.

But oddest about them—and telling in regard to Burroughs, whether he intended it or not—is that the Mahars are an *all-female* society. These reptilian incarnations of evil are all girls! Like the Mizorans, many generations ago the Mahars learned how to procreate without the unnecessary complication of having males around—"a method whereby eggs might be fertilized by chemical means after they were laid." The implication, however unintentional, is that the twisted evil Mahars are what you get if women are left to their own devices. There's a definite undercurrent of misogyny here, despite all the praises heaped on noble, pure-as-the-driven-snow Dian the Beautiful (whose characterizing epithet is also revealing in regard to Burroughs' ideas about women—she's not Dian the Smart, or Dian the Resourceful, or Dian the Independent).

The secret of the Mahars' parthenogenesis is kept in a single book stored in a vault deep beneath Phutra. There's only one copy, and none of the high-I.Q. Mahars seems to have memorized the formula, which gives Perry an idea. As they wait around in their cell, Perry prays continually and has a flash: "David, if we can escape, and at the same time take with us this great secret, what will we not have accomplished for the human race within Pellucidar!"

"Why, Perry! You and I may reclaim a whole world! Together we can lead the races of men out of the darkness of ignorance into the light of advancement and civilization. At one step we may carry them from the Age of Stone to the twentieth century."

"David, I believe that God sent us here for just that purpose!"

"You are right, Perry. And while you are teaching them to pray I'll be teaching them to fight, and between us we'll make a race of men that will be an honor to us both."

Note the grandiosity—they'll be doing this to honor themselves. Probably just hasty, imprecise writing (at another point Burroughs has a character say he won't "stand supinely" watching), but also revealing of what's to come.

By this time Perry has figured out Pellucidar's cosmology. Its provenance encompasses hollow earth thinking going all the way back to Edmond Halley. Centrifugal force has caused the hollowness. As the spinning earth cooled, matter was thrown out to the edges, except for a "small superheated core of gaseous matter" that remained in the center as Pellucidar's never-setting sun. This is a slap in the face of Newtonian physics, of course, since a sun existing in the center of the earth would either burn the whole globe to a cinder, and/or its gravity would cause the hollow sphere to collapse. But it's both futile and somehow unfair to insist on plausibility in such a mixed bag of fantasy. There is no mention of a polar opening in *At the Earth's Core,* but Burroughs uses it in the third book, *Tanar of Pellucidar,* to explain the presence of the dastardly Korsars, yo-ho-ho descendants of seventeenth-century Spanish pirates who accidentally sailed over the rim into Pellucidar and have been wreaking havoc there ever since. He also uses the polar opening in *Tarzan at the Earth's Core* to get Tarzan down there to help rescue David Innes, who's been captured for about the nineteenth time.

Since the interior cooled more slowly than the surface, life started later on Pellucidar, making it "younger" than our world—thus all the prehistoric flora and fauna running riot there. The weird twists life has taken on Pellucidar can be explained by alternate evolution. Life forms from different geologic periods exist simultaneously owing to the absence of the cataclysms that have affected life on the surface. Pellucidar has considerably more land; the proportions of ocean to earth are reversed, so that the land area there is three times greater than above, "the strange anomaly of a larger world within a smaller one!" But the greatest anomaly—which Burroughs never successfully explains—is that time doesn't exist on Pellucidar. Nobody can tell how long anything takes. It's supposedly because the sun never sets, but why that would make a difference defies explanation, even though Burroughs insists on it again and again, in book after book. Why this was so important to his conception of Pellucidar is a mystery. But it's his world, and he can do what he wants.

Toward the end of *At the Earth's Core*, after his second escape from the Mahars, while wandering through uncharted territory, Innes comes on a lovely valley that he describes as a "little paradise." The chapter is titled "The Garden of Eden." But Eden wouldn't be complete without an Eve—or a serpent of sorts. Innes comes across a girl standing terrified on a ledge—his long-lost Dian the Beautiful—who's being attacked by "a giant dragon forty feet in length," with "gaping jaws" and "claws equipped with terrible talons." Never a dull moment on Pellucidar. Innes saves her, realizing, finally, that he loves her. Their brief idyll is interrupted by Jubal the Ugly One, who's been sniffing after Dian from the beginning. In their bloody duel to the death, crafty Innes prevails and has an inspiration in the moment of triumph: "If skill and science could render a comparative pygmy

the master of this mighty brute, what could not the brute's fellows accomplish with the same skill and science. Why all Pellucidar would be at their feet— and I would be their king and Dian their queen."

The sociopolitics of Pellucidar from here on are an eccentric amalgam of Arthurian legend, liberal Progressivism, and Teddy Roosevelt–style speak-softly-and-carry-a-big-stick democratic imperialism—an ideological stew representing Burroughs's own jumbled worldview.

Innes and Dian make their way back to Sari, her homeland, and in nothing flat everyone agrees to his plan. An intertribal council is called and "the eventual form of government was tentatively agreed upon. Roughly, the various kingdoms were to

(above) Dian the Beautiful as shown being menaced by Mahars on this 1970s Ace Paperback covers by Frank Frazetta. (© Frank Frazetta)

remain virtually independent, but there was to be one great overlord, or emperor. It was decided that I should be the first of the dynasty of the emperors of Pellucidar."

His goal? Freedom for enslaved humanity, achieved by the extermination of the Mahars. "How long it would take for the race to become extinct was impossible even to guess; but that this must eventually happen seemed inevitable."

And how would this ethically dubious end be achieved? Superior weaponry. Perry has been experimenting with "various destructive engines of war— gunpowder, rifles, cannon and the like" but hasn't been as successful as he hoped. Still, "we were both assured that the solution of these problems would advance the cause of civilization within Pellucidar thousands of years at a single stroke."

In bringing civilization to Pellucidar, they plan to start with guns and genocide.

Innes will make a return trip to the surface in the iron mole to bring back weapons—along with books on such useful subjects as mining, construction, engineering, and agriculture. An arsenal of information to bring Pellucidar into the twentieth century, for better or worse. Works of literature do not appear on the wish list.

"What we lack is knowledge," Perry exclaims. "Let us go back and get that knowledge in the shape of books—then this world will indeed be at our feet." Yet another revealing slip. For all their supposed humanitarianism, Perry and Innes talk like megalomaniacs.

Innes plans to take Dian to the surface with him and show her the sights, but Hooja the Sly One, living up to his cognomen, pulls a switch, and Innes finds himself boring headlong upward with a creepy Mahar as a companion, not Dian the Beautiful. The iron mole comes out in the Sahara, and the novel ends with Innes and the bewildered Mahar waiting for someone to find them.

Nearly two years passed before Burroughs began work on *Pellucidar,* the second book in the series. Innes returns to Pellucidar in the iron mole with its cargo of guns and knowledge, but the steering *still* isn't working right, so when he gets there, he's lost. More captures, escapes, battles with terrible creatures. Hooja is on a rampage; he has raised a rebel force and has again kidnapped Dian. Innes is paddling away from Hooja's ships in a small dugout. All seems hopeless, as usual, when the empire's new fleet, fifty ships strong, sails onto the scene and defeats Hooja's inferior forces. Ecstatic, Innes cries, "It was MY navy! Perry had perfected gunpowder and built cannon! It was marvelous!" They cream Hooja's inferior forces. Plans for the empire shift into high gear and progress, of a sort, strikes poor Pellucidar.

Like every boy of his time, Burroughs grew up on the medieval romances of Sir Walter Scott, but unlike most, he apparently hadn't outgrown them by 1915—at the age of forty. Part of his charm, I guess. It seems safe to consider Innes an alter ego for Burroughs, and he indulges in some knights-in-shining-armor dreamin' here. After the battle, Emperor David's "fierce warriors nearly came to blows in their efforts to be among the first to kneel before me and kiss my hand. When Ja kneeled at my feet, first to do me homage, I drew from its scabbard at his side the sword of hammered iron that Perry had taught him to fashion. Striking him lightly on the shoulder I created him king of Anoroc. Each captain of the forty-nine other feluccas I made a duke. I left it to Perry to enlighten them as to the value of the honors I had bestowed upon them."

Perry updates Innes on the improvements he's made at Sari. Everyone has joined the cause against the Mahars, but beyond that Perry says, "they are simply ravenous for greater knowledge and for better ways to do things." They mastered many skills quickly, and "we now have a hundred expert gun-makers. On a little isolated isle we have a great powder-factory. Near the iron-mine, which is on the mainland, is a smelter, and on the eastern shore of Anoroc, a well equipped shipyard."

So the Pellucidarians, in a single bound, have leaped into the Industrial Age, and have been introduced to the joys of mines scarring the landscape, factories billowing smoke, and long, tedious work days.

Innes responds, "It is stupendous, Perry! But still more stupendous is the power that you and I wield in this great world. These people look upon us as little less than supermen. We must give them the best that we have. [You can practically hear the patriotic music begin to swell and see the flag proudly flapping in the breeze.] What we have given them so far has been the worst. We have given them war and the munitions of war. But I look forward to the day [music really swelling now, possibly a visionary tear in his eye] when you and I can build sewing machines instead of battleships, harvesters of crops instead of harvesters of men, plow-shares and telephones, schools and colleges, printing-presses and paper! When our merchant marine shall ply the great Pellucidarian seas, and cargoes of silks and typewriters and books shall forge their ways where only hideous saurians have held sway since time began!"

But before this grand vision can be realized, first they have to deal with those "haughty reptiles"—the evil Mahars. A council of kings convenes and decides to commence "the great war" against them immediately.

As Burroughs was writing this in January 1915, the real Great War was spreading like a terrible brushfire on the surface. In 1912–1913 small wars in the Balkans had begun bursting into flames out of seeming spontaneous combustion. Then on June 28, 1914, Archduke Ferdinand, heir to the Austrian throne, was assassinated in Sarajevo. By summer's end, declarations of war flying like dark, dry leaves, country after country found itself involved, and within months the fighting was burning its way through Europe with a ferocity unprecedented in history.

One might expect to see at least a glimmer of these events in "the great war" against the Mahars; and there is, though not much more, beyond the fact that Burroughs decided to make it part of the story in the first place. The main parallel is that Emperor David quickly gains many allies—nearly all the known tribes of Pellucidar are united for the first time against one enemy. The plan? "It was our intention to march from one Mahar city to another until we had subdued every Mahar nation that menaced the safety of any kingdom of the empire"—starting with Phutra, the Mahar capital.

The Battle of Phutra is a pretty good one. Burroughs didn't entirely waste those years in military school and the army. A phalanx of Sagoths and Mahars engages the Empire's forces outside the city but is "absolutely exterminated; not one remained even as a prisoner." On to the city and its "subterranean avenues," where the allies are temporarily stymied—the morally corrupt Mahars are using poison gas. But Perry jury-rigs a few cannon bombs, dumps them down the holes like oversize grenades, and *blam!* Mahars by the hundreds come streaming out of their underground lair like dazed wasps and, taking wing, flee to the north. After the fall of Phutra, victory follows victory—the Mahars are less tenacious than the Germans. Emperor David's armies march "from one great buried city to another. At each we were victorious, killing or capturing the Sagoths and driving the Mahars further away." The menace isn't eliminated—"their great cities must abound by the hundreds and thousands [in] far-distant lands" —but they've at least been forced far from the Empire.

At the end of *Pellucidar,* David and Dian settle in to enjoy royal life in their "great palace overlooking the gulf." Perry is working like a beaver on further "improvements," laying out a railway line to some rich coalfields he wants to exploit. Sea trade between kingdoms proceeds apace, the profits going "to the betterment of the people—to building factories for the manufacture of agricultural implements, and machinery for the various trades we are gradually teaching the people."

Today we have nearly a hundred years of hindsight to wonder about the ultimate value of what Burroughs clearly sees as progress for Pellucidar. As Emperor David sums it up at the novel's close, "I think that it will not be long before Pellucidar will become as nearly a Utopia as one may expect to find this side of heaven."

Burroughs took fourteen years off from writing about Pellucidar, but in 1928–1929, in a burst, he produced *Tanar of Pellucidar* and *Tarzan at the Earth's Core.* Both represented a falling-off from the earlier books. Whatever improbable coherence this inner territory had in the first two begins flying apart in these. Pellucidar increasingly seems less an intact world than an imperfect collection of shards, broken pieces lacking cohesion. Part of this is due to overcomplication. Savage countries, races, and creatures multiply like prehistoric rabbits in Burroughs's attempts to ever increase the excitement by concocting yet another new kind. As Brian W. Aldiss observes in *Billion Year Spree*, "Burroughs never knew when enough was enough." Just among the races, by series end there are Stone Age men, Sagoths (gorilla men), Mahars (brainy evil reptiles), Horibs (lizard or snake men), Ganaks (bison men, humanoid bovines), Gorbuses (humanoid cannibalistic albinos), Coripies (or Buried People; blind underground dwellers with no facial features, large fangs, webbed talons), Beast Men (savage vegetarians with faces somewhere between a sheep and a gorilla), Ape Men (black hairless skins, long tails, tree dwelling), Sabretooth Men, Mezops (copper-colored island dwellers), Korsars (descendants of pirates who accidentally sailed into the polar opening), Yellow Men of the Bronze

Age—and I may be leaving some out. The overcomplication diminishes their impact. It is impossible to keep all these creatures and their various domains straight, and it's arguable whether or not Burroughs managed to do so himself. With all these races always at odds with each other, there's a growing feeling of fragmentation. Here in the center of the earth there's no center, as one or the other of these squabbling races takes the stage to provide trouble for our various heroes, and everything else all but disappears from view. In both *Tanar* and *Tarzan at the Earth's Core*, for instance, the evil Mahars, the chief scourge of Pellucidar in the first two novels, are hardly mentioned, even though they were only driven off, not exterminated as Perry had hoped. And the Empire that Perry and Innes have forcibly cobbled together also remains far offstage in these later two novels. Most of *Tanar*, essentially a rock 'em sock 'em adventure-filled love story between the title character and imperious Stellara, takes place among the Korsars, and in *Tarzan at the Earth's Core*, everybody spends most of their time lost in the jungle, fighting off one

(above) Cover art for *Tanar of Pellucidar*, the third Pellucidar novel. (© Edgar Rice Burroughs, Inc.)

or another prehistoric monster—which Burroughs multiplies right along with the savage races. Especially in *Tarzan at the Earth's Core* there's a sameness to the attacks, captures, escapes, followed by more attacks, captures, and escapes—as if Burroughs were operating more on autopilot than not.

In *Tarzan at the Earth's Core,* young Jason Gridley of Tarzana, California, has a special radio that receives signals from Pellucidar. He hears that David Innes has been captured by the Korsars and is being held captive by them, and decides that only Tarzan can free him. Gridley goes to Africa to plead his case, saying that he's just learned about an opening at the pole that leads to Pellucidar. Tarzan says, hmm, we'll need a Zeppelin, and just happens to know of an ultralight, ultrastrong

(above) Splendid St. John cover for *Tarzan at the Earth's Core.*
(© Edgar Rice Burroughs, Inc.)

metal in nearby mountains that no one else has discovered, so they have a bunch of it mined and go to Germany to construct the airship. As the Zeppelin drops through the polar opening and drifts lower toward Pellucidar's surface, Tarzan looks approvingly over the landscape and exclaims, "This looks like heaven to me." As soon as they land, Tarzan decides to take a jungle stroll, and doesn't reconnect with the others until the book's end, when almost as an afterthought Innes is sprung from the Korsars' captivity. Tarzan wasn't kidding about heaven. Pellucidar is even more unspoiled and primitive than his own jungle at home. And Tarzan loves it:

> In the first flight of his newfound freedom Tarzan was like a boy released from school. Unhampered by the hated vestments of civilization, out of sight of anything that might even remotely remind him of the atrocities with which man scars the face of nature, he filled his lungs with the free air of Pellucidar, leaped into a nearby tree and swung away through the forest, his only concern for the moment the joyousness of exultant vitality and life. On he sped through the primeval forest of Pellucidar. Strange birds, startled by his swift and silent passage, flew screaming from his path, and strange beasts slunk to cover beneath him. But Tarzan did not care; he was not hunting; he was not even searching for the new in this new world. For the moment he was only living.

This is a beautiful existential moment, in some ways a crystallization of the ethos running throughout all of Burroughs's work. Tarzan is *somewhere else*, in a place of beauty and adventure, with no noise or bus fumes or electric bills—or responsibilities. Born free . . .

Seconds after this peaceful epiphany, *thwap!* Tarzan is caught in a rope snare, and finds himself hanging upside down, slowly spinning, as a ferocious sabre-tooth tiger slinks toward him. But even facing death, Tarzan is not afraid. "He had looked upon death in so many forms that it held no terror for him." He is, however,

moved to rare metaphysical introspection. The interior lives of Burroughs's characters go largely unexplored beyond visceral reactions to whatever the situation is at
hand. But here, dangling, about to be a sabre-tooth's lunch, Tarzan thinks of First
and Last Things. It's the closest to a spiritual creed I've found in the Tarzan books
and presumably isn't too far from Burroughs's own views on these matters:

> Tarzan of the Apes would have preferred to die fighting, if he must die;
> yet he felt a certain thrill as he contemplated the magnificence of the
> great beast that Fate had chosen to terminate his earthly career. He felt
> no fear, but a certain sense of anticipation of what would follow after
> death. The Lord of the Jungle subscribed to no creed. Tarzan of the Apes
> was not a church man; yet like the majority of those who have always lived
> close to nature he was, in a sense, intensely religious. His intimate knowl-
> edge of the stupendous forces of nature, of her wonders and her miracles
> had impressed him with the fact that their ultimate origin lay far beyond
> the conception of the finite mind of man, and thus incalculably remote
> from the farthest bounds of science. When he thought of God he liked to
> think of Him primitively, as a personal God. And while he realized that he
> knew nothing of such matters, he liked to believe that after death he
> would live again.

Maybe it's just as well Burroughs kept this sort of thing to a minimum.
Tarzan reveals a sort of homegrown deism combined with a vaguely born-again
fundamentalism—Thomas Jefferson meets George Bush. Naturally Tarzan doesn't
have to worry about the next life because just as the sabre-tooth strikes, *upsy-
daisy*—the Sagoths who had set the snare yank him upward into the trees.

We get another glimpse into Burroughs's attitudes a little farther on from
young Jason Gridley, who's cowering in a tree himself, watching "hundreds" of
sabre-tooths slaughtering the game they've herded into a deadly roundup circle.

Gridley sees in this a development of intelligence on the cats' part that will lead to their extinction—in their cunning savagery they will eventually wipe out all their prey, and then turn on each other—which leads him to reflect on the future of mankind:

> Nor did Jason Gridley find it difficult to apply the same line of reasoning to the evolution of man upon the outer crust and to his own possible extinction in the not far remote future. In fact, he recalled quite definitely that statisticians had shown that within two hundred years or less the human race would have so greatly increased and the natural resources of the outer world would have been so depleted that the last generation must either starve to death or turn to cannibalism to prolong its hateful existence for another short period . . . What would be next? Gridley was sure that there would be something after man, *who is unquestionably the Creator's greatest blunder,* combining as he does all the vices of preceding types from invertebrates to mammals, while possessing few of their virtues.

Italics mine. This pessimistic blast comes out of the blue, and has a ring of conviction, all the more so because it seems so uncharacteristic of youthful gung-ho boy scientist Gridley, and feels like a peek behind the curtain into Burroughs himself. Burroughs, among his often wacky enthusiasms, was an early Greenie, ahead of his time in realizing the earth's fragility. He gave a speech on ecology to a group on Arbor Day, 1922, and discussed conservation issues in a 1930 radio interview, so it was a lifelong concern. And "the Creator's greatest blunder" business—well, Burroughs carried a weight of bitterness despite his huge popular success. His drive to produce—writing, movie ideas, moneymaking schemes, endless Tarzan spin-offs (among them comic strips, kids' clubs, Tarzan bread, Tarzan ice cream cups, Tarzan belts, Tarzan bathing suits, Tarzan jungle helmets, Tarzan yoyos, Tarzan candy, etc.,

etc.) has in it a nervous mania, a constant thirsty seeking for *something* that none of this frantic activity ever managed to quench. In 1934 as his long marriage to Emma crumbled, largely due to her drinking, compounded by his own fondness for the stuff, he decided learning to fly would be just the thing, commenced taking lessons, and bought his own airplane, while also courting Florence Ashton, his second wife-to-be, and scribbling away (well, dictating away) at his nineteenth Tarzan novel, *Tarzan and Jane (Tarzan's Quest),* which on completion on January 19, 1935, was rejected by *Liberty, Collier's,* and others before *Blue Book* finally bought and began serializing it in October. It's interesting that just as the Tarzan manuscript was being rejected, Burroughs turned again to Pellucidar, starting on *Back to the Stone Age* in late January. Possibly just a coincidence, but possible, too, that thinking about Pellucidar was a pleasant retreat for him, more fun than grinding out yet more Tarzan. (He said in a 1938 radio interview that he had originally planned to write only *two* Tarzan novels.) *Back to the Stone Age* marks a further drop in quality. A long flashback to the Tarzan expedition, it relates the adventures of Von Horst, a crew member who becomes separated from the others. However, Von Horst's story is anything but memorable—just another sequence of near-death scrapes, captures, and escapes, with the usual beautiful prehistoric maiden as a love interest. This manuscript collected rejection slip after rejection slip before being bought by *Argosy* magazine for $1,500 and serialized as *Seven Worlds to Conquer* from January 9 through February 13, 1937, then published in book form under its original title by ERB in September of that year.

In 1938 Burroughs again returned to Pellucidar, writing the 60,000 words of *Land of Terror* between October and April 1939 while juggling other projects. The story was rejected by every magazine it was sent to. It wasn't published until 1944, when it appeared as a book under ERB's own imprint.

Land of Terror is told by David Innes, who begins by reflecting on how *old* he and Perry are, something that may have been on the author's mind, since he was sixty-three while writing this amiable nonsense, still churning it out. David is on his way back home to Sari with some of his minions as the story opens, and, wouldn't you know it, they are attacked as they're crossing a river, and *captured*. "They were heavy-built, stocky warriors with bushy beards, a rather uncommon sight in Pellucidar where most of the pure-blood white tribes are beardless." Odder still, "As I looked more closely at my bearded, hairy captors, the strange, the astounding truth suddenly dawned upon me. These warriors were not men; they were women." One of these he-women comments, "Who wants any more men? I don't. Those that I have give me enough trouble—gossiping, nagging, never doing their work properly. After a hard day hunting or fighting, I get all worn out beating them after I get home."

Yes, we're hearing an echo of *Pantaletta*, with Burroughs indulging in the same role-reversal comedy found in the earlier novel, without superior results. Innes is dragged to Oog, their primitive village, where he encounters "a hairless, effeminate little man," the husband of Gluck, the leader, she of the "legs like a pro-football guard and ears like a cannoneer." Away from the women, hubby and a few other men grouse about the women. "'If I were bigger and stronger than Gluck, I'd beat her with a stick every time I saw her.' 'You don't seem very fond of Gluck,' I said. 'Did you ever see a man who was fond of a woman?' demanded Foola. 'We hate the brutes.'" David is tossed under guard into a hut, where he meets Zor, a fellow prisoner, who tells him, "'They have none of the natural sensibilities of women and only the characteristics of the lowest and most brutal types of men,'" another sentiment that might be straight out of *Pantaletta*. A few sleeps later (no one ever knows what time it is in Pellucidar) David, slaving and starving in Gluck's garden, can't resist grabbing a tuber and gnawing ravenously on it. This enrages a female sentry, but he manages to coldcock her before she can do him in with her bone knife. Gluck turns up, angered that the sentry tried to beat one of her men, and they struggle—until at last Gluck kills the other woman. David watches it all and is moved to philosophy:

There followed one of the most brutal fights I have ever witnessed. They pounded, kicked, clawed, scratched and bit one another like two furies. The brutality of it sickened me. If these women were the result of taking women out of slavery and attempting to raise them to equality with man, then I think that they and the world would be better off if they were returned to slavery.

One of the sexes must rule; and man seems temperamentally better fitted for the job than woman. Certainly if full power over man has resulted in debauching and brutalizing women to such an extent, then we should see that they remain always subservient to man, whose overlordship is, more often than not, tempered by gentleness and sympathy.

At the time Burroughs's second marriage was in trouble. And despite his tireless effort and the ubiquity of Tarzan (published in thirty-five countries, translated into fifty-eight languages), he still struggled financially; the dark shadows of the coming war were falling as well over his little empire and sales were dropping. Soon paper rationing and shortages would force major cutbacks in his book publications. Perhaps worse, Burroughs was losing faith in himself as a writer. I can think of no other writer of his established popularity whose work was so routinely rejected; and it galled him, too, that he was little more than a joke to the literary community—his would-be peers. All this wore on him, led him into bouts of depression and the dubious fleeting solace of whiskey. In June 1939 Florence underwent major surgery, and, in August of that year, primarily to cut down expenses, they decided to move to Hawaii. Then in November Burroughs suffered several minor heart attacks. Arriving in Hawaii in April 1940, Florence seems to have hated it from the start, possibly since they had left a fairly luxurious Beverly Hills apartment for a scruffy Hawaiian beach shack also semi-inhabited by rats and scorpions. Burroughs made the garage his office. Friends began noticing the tension between him and Florence, along with signs of increased drinking on Burroughs's part. Still he amassed stacks of pages, knocking off a new Pellucidar short story, "Hodon and O-AA," in one week during September.

Burroughs would live until 1950, but for all practical purposes his writing career sputtered to an end right here. He would continue to write the occasional Tarzan novel or stray short story, but never again at the manic pace he had maintained since 1911. The marriage to Florence ended in March 1941 when she and the children sailed back to California; they were divorced and she remarried not long afterward. Depressed, turning even more to the bottle, he gained a reprieve of sorts when the Japanese bombed Pearl Harbor on December 7, 1941—soon he had gotten himself a gig as a war correspondent, and spent the war years reporting from all over the Pacific. After the war he moved back to the L.A. area, but his health was so shattered by angina, Parkinson's, and arteriosclerosis that from 1947 on, when he bought his first television set, he spent much of his time in front of it watching sports. In 1948 he experienced severe painful angina. As the Hillman site puts it, "When the nitro-glycerine doesn't work he turns to bourbon. Over the coming months there is a reliance on bourbon for all ills." He spent much of 1949 rereading all his books—"to see what I had said and how I'd said it." He died March 19, 1950, after breakfast in bed, while reading the Sunday comics. Shortly before his death he said, "If there is a hereafter, I want to travel through space to visit the other planets"—a dreamy kid to the very end.

Burroughs's final (and forgettable) tales of Pellucidar were published in the early 1940s, in a sci-fi pulp magazine called *Amazing Stories,* then newly under the editorship of Ray Palmer—who in 1945 began using his magazine to create a major league flap about the hollow earth that came to be known as "The Shaver Mystery."

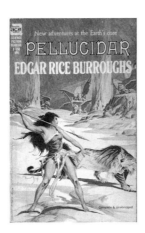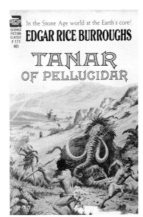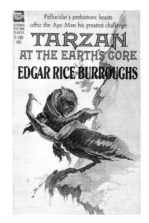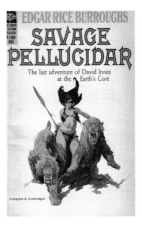

(above) These Ace paperbacks from the 1960s of the Pellucidar series, published decades after they were written, are tangible examples of its continuing appeal. (© Edgar Rice Burroughs, Inc.)

MOON OF DOUBLE TROUBLE *by* A. R. Steber

AMAZING
STORIES

See BACK COVER

MARCH
25¢
IN CANADA 30¢

SENSATIONAL "RACIAL MEMORY" STORY...

I REMEMBER LEMURIA

By RICHARD S. SHAVER

8

THE HOLLOW EARTH LIVES:
EVIL NAZIS, FLYING SAUCERS,
SUPERMAN, NEW AGE UTOPIAS

IN THE EARLY 1940S, *Amazing Stories* had an energetic new editor. Ray Palmer was a gnomish young man slightly over four feet tall, and he had been hired in 1939 to breathe life into a magazine that had been launched in April 1926 as the first all–science fiction magazine by Hugo Gernsback, the pioneering editor who coined the term. But by the time Palmer took over, the magazine was moribund, sluggish editorially, circulation dropping.

Palmer was a fan of the *biff! zap! pow!* space opera branch of science fiction—as embodied by Burroughs, the elder statesman of the form—and began filling the magazine with such stuff. It didn't earn him any critical praise. About the same time, *Astounding Science Fiction*, which had been around since 1930, had become a more highbrow competitor, and the young writers published regularly there (including Isaac Asimov, Ray Bradbury, Robert Heinlein, and Theodore Sturgeon) became the now-legendary icons whose work began the so-called Golden Age of science fiction, while most writers of the boisterous trash in *Amazing Stories*

(opposite) The so-called Shaver Mystery was kicked off with "I Remember Lemuria" in this March 1945 issue of *Amazing Stories*.

are long forgotten. But Palmer's gambit of appealing to a younger, less sophisticated audience paid off in sales—and with the Shaver Mystery, circulation, well, skyrocketed.

As Palmer later told it, it all started

> when one day a letter came in giving the details of an 'ancient alphabet' that 'should not be lost to the world.' It was opened by my managing editor, Howard Browne, who read it with the typical orthodox attitude, and tossed it into the wastepaper basket with the comment "The world is full of crackpots." . . . I retrieved the letter from the wastebasket, examined the alphabet, and made a few casual experiments. I went about the office to those who were familiar with other languages than English, and came up with a few more interesting results. That was Enough. I published the letter in *Amazing Stories*.[1]

The letter, appearing in the December 1943 issue, was from Richard S. Shaver. In it he—with some help from Palmer—claimed that the ancient alphabet he had discovered embedded in many English words was "definite proof of the Atlantean legend . . . suggesting the god legends have a base in some wiser race than modern man." And this race, of course, had lived inside the hollow earth.

To Palmer's considerable surprise, the letter drew a huge response from readers; and Shaver followed up with a 10,000-word manuscript titled "A Warning for Man"—which became, after Palmer got done rewriting and embellishing it, the 31,000-word "I Remember Lemuria!" This first Shaver Mystery story, detailing Shaver's "actual" experiences with remnants of an advanced subterranean race, ran in the March 1945 issue of *Amazing Stories*. The press run of 125,000 sold out. Shaver had other manuscripts on hand. Drastically rewritten by Palmer, "Thought Records of Lemuria" ran in the next issue—which sold 200,000 copies, according to Palmer, at any rate. Actual circulation numbers were never released. Letters poured

---

1. From "Invitation to Adventure" in the first issue of Palmer's *Hidden World* magazine, Spring 1961.

in by the thousands—50,000 in response to the first piece, Palmer said—nearly all testifying to similar experiences of encounters with bizarre beings living in vast labyrinthine caves. Related as *true* experiences, it should be emphasized. Palmer's Shaver stories had struck some strange unexpected chord, and Palmer cheerfully played chorus after chorus. Nearly every issue of *Amazing Stories* for the next two years featured a Shaver story, peaking with an all-Shaver issue in June 1947.

Dennis Crenshaw, who for some years has produced *The Hollow Earth Insider*, both as a print and more recently an online journal, provides a good short summary of Shaver's claims:

> Over 12,000 years ago a race known as the Titan-Altans came from a distant planet and settled on earth. They first settled on the continent of Atlantis and their culture spread all across the new planet. These extraterrestrial aliens communicated by thought transference and had spaceships that could travel at the speed of light. They also understood genetics far beyond our knowledge today and constructed "robot races" to do their dirty work. One of these "robot races" are our ancestors. . . . They also created fabulous machines that could have taken care of their every want and need. Then their top scientists discovered the sun and its harsh radioactive rays was causing them to age. They began to construct huge cave-cities underground, using existing caverns when possible and then using huge machines to excavate even larger ones. Over a long period of time these cavern realms grew until they covered twice as much area as the exterior lands. However, moving underground didn't help. The whole planet was contaminated and Titans were only living for a few hundred years. The decision was to abandon the planet. According to Shaver their population was "more than fifty million" . . . and "There wasn't enough spacecraft to transport all the Titans. . . . So many of the robots were left behind to fend for themselves; those who became our

ancestors returned to the surface, adjusting to the sun's radiation, and after many generations forgot about the caves beneath them." But many other robots remained in the cavern cities. . . . Although they survived and reproduced, most of them degenerated into a race of psychotic dwarfs Shaver called *dero*, short for *detrimental robots*. There were others in the caves who managed to stave off the mental and physical deterioration of the *dero*, and did all they could to defeat them; they were the *tero* (integrative robots). However the deros were in control of all the wonderful machines left behind by the departing Titans and they used them to cause trouble for the humans on the exterior of the planet, everything from train, plane and car accidents to stubbing toes and misplaced house keys, according to Shaver, was the fault of the deros.[2]

While Palmer was in this chiefly to sell magazines, poor Shaver was apparently deeply sincere about it all. He believed he was telling the truth. He had been born in 1907 in Berwick, Pennsylvania, and had a history of mental illness. As a young man in the Philadelphia area he had worked as a meat cutter, and assistant to a tree surgeon. By 1929 he was in Detroit, studying art at the Wicker School of Art, and working as a nude model there to help pay tuition. For a time during Prohibition he'd also supplemented his income by making a little bathtub gin—but then practically everybody was doing it. In 1930 he joined the communist John Reed Club (named for the radical American journalist); by 1932 he was working in an automobile factory as a spot welder on an assembly line, and in 1933 he married and had a daughter. But in 1934 his brother died suddenly, and Shaver took it very badly. Six months later he was institutionalized for insanity at the Ypsilanti State Hospital in Michigan at the request of his wife; according to the physician's certificate he claimed "people are watching him, following him around," and "physicians

---

2. *The Hollow Earth Insider*, http://www.thehollowearthinsider.com/news/wmview.php?ArtID=20. This site, maintained and largely written by Dennis Crenshaw, contains many articles on hollow earth and related phenomena.

are trying to poison" him. An article by Doug Skinner in the June 2005 issue of *Fate* magazine adds:

> He insisted that a demon called Max had killed his brother, and was now after him as well. He must have responded to treatment, since he was released to visit his parents for Christmas in 1936. It was there that he learned of another tragedy: Sophie [his wife] had been killed, electrocuted when she moved a heater in the bathtub. Her family took custody of their daughter. Shaver did not return to Ypsilanti. He was certain now that devils were persecuting him. Over the next few years, he wandered aimlessly and compulsively, trying to shake off the creatures that he believed had killed his wife and brother. He often reminisced about this period later, but his accounts are confused and contradictory; he confessed that he had trouble separating reality from dreams and visions. He tried to stow away in a ship to England; he was imprisoned a few times; he was tormented by giant spiders; he returned to a mental hospital at some point. Max was always after him.

(above) A few samples of Shaver Mystery cover stories that ran in several magazines during the 1940s and early 1950s.

It is a sad story, and Palmer exploited him to the hilt. Once his association with Palmer began in 1943, Shaver continued to add writings to the Shaver Mystery until he died of a heart attack in 1975.

It was of course a dark paranoid sci-fi recasting of ancient ideas about evil spirits, goblins, and things that go bump in the night. In these modern times, they were transformed into rays from weird machines created by aliens from outer space. Scary old wine in new bottles.

That the Shaver Mystery elicited such a response seems remarkable now. In 1947, Palmer added a twist that really put it over the top: flying saucers. On June 25, a short news item had gone out on the AP wires:

> PENDLETON, Ore., June 25 (AP)—Nine bright saucer-like objects flying at "incredible speed" at 10,000 feet altitude were reported here today by Kenneth Arnold, a Boise, Idaho, pilot who said he could not hazard a guess as to what they were.
>
> Arnold, a United States Forest Service employee engaged in searching for a missing plane, said he sighted the mysterious objects yesterday at 3 P.M. They were flying between Mount Rainier and Mount Adams, in Washington state, he said, and appeared to weave in and out of formation. Arnold said he clocked and estimated their speed at 1,200 miles an hour.

The story got it slightly wrong. Arnold hadn't actually said the objects were saucer-shaped. Rather, he'd said they "flew erratic, like a saucer if you skip it across the water"—and that they "were not circular." But apparently the reporter misunderstood—and flying saucers were born.

It should be said that Arnold was a four-square regular guy. He'd been an Eagle Scout, was a high school All-State football player in North Dakota in 1932 and 1933, and since the early 40s had been a pilot, flying from place to place in the Northwest selling fire control equipment, occasionally moonlighting as a relief federal U.S. marshal and flying federal prisoners to various penitentiaries. He'd also been a field representative for the Red Cross for many years. He was no kook—he'd just seen these strange flying objects.

Ray Palmer jumped on Arnold's story like a dog on a bone. Early in July he contacted Arnold to do an article about his sighting for *Amazing Stories* and hired him to investigate another one reported three weeks after his.

Soon flying saucers became a major component of the Shaver Mystery—since Shaver had earlier talked about spacecraft built by the Elder Ones. In the new formulation, there were still a few Elders left in their subterranean kingdom, along with some of their spaceships, and they sometimes used these flying saucers to check out the upper world.

Yes, the *true* origin of flying saucers lay in the hollow earth!

In the late 1940s and early 1950s sightings multiplied, and a certain flying saucer mania swept the United States, spreading far beyond the community of true-believer sci-fi fans and others susceptible to embracing fringe phenomena. Back then *Life* was one of the highest-circulation magazines, and a good indicator of everyday American interests. Its April 7, 1952 issue featured a fetching picture of Marilyn Monroe on the cover, with the cover line "Marilyn Monroe The Talk of Hollywood." The only other cover line was "There Is A Case For Interplanetary Saucers"—and this not in some screwy oddball publication but in what was arguably the most mainstream general interest magazine in the country. In a lengthy examination complete with photos of supposed saucers, after marshaling considerable evidence pro and con, the article has this portentious ending:

...the real depths of the saucer mystery bemuse penetration, as the night sky swallows up a flashlight beam. . . . Why do the things make no sound? How to explain their eerie luminosity? What power urges them at such terrible speeds through the sky? Who, or what, is aboard? Where do they come from? Why are they here? What are the intentions of the beings who control them? Before these awesome questions, science—and mankind—can yet only halt in wonder. Answers may come in a generation—or tomorrow. Somewhere in the dark skies there may be those who know.

Palmer played this story in his magazine for all it was worth, and in 1952 he and Kenneth Arnold collaborated on a book, *The Coming of the Saucers*. Palmer is often credited—perhaps blamed is a better word—for creating the flying saucer hysteria that swept the country back then. Certainly, and almost single-handedly, using Shaver and then Arnold, he established the premises and vocabulary that have formed the basis of so-called UFOlogy ever since, essentially defining the mind-set exemplified by *The X-Files*. Without Palmer, we wouldn't have had Scully and Mulder.

The whole Shaver Mystery idea, especially with the addition of flying saucers, is yet another example of how ideas of the hollow earth—and thoughts of what might lie within—mutated with the times. The advent of the atomic age, signaled by the dropping of the atomic bomb in August 1945, brought with it previously undreamed-of possibilities, including previously undreamed-of terrors. The Shaver Mystery can be considered an incarnation of these new fears in a contemporary sci-fi costume. In Burroughs, evil took the form of soulless flying reptiles and thuggish Stone Age villains—but with the Shaver Mystery, the horror is more cosmic and more incomprehensible, like the atomic bomb itself. And unlike previous forays into the hollow earth, which were often scary but charming and ultimately life-affirming, here the suggestion is that things are deeply, irrevocably *wrong* in ways that cannot be understood or rectified. The Elder Ones—who can be read as

God—have all but abandoned us, leaving behind wreckage and vicious mutants. Only evil remains.

Speaking of evil, according to some sources, another hollow earth believer in the 1940s was Adolph Hitler. It's not mentioned in *The Rise and Fall of the Third Reich*, but during the 1930s, Hitler supposedly heard some lectures on Koreshanity—yes, Cyrus Teed's hollow earth religion—and became a convert. This has only the slimmest substantiation, if it can even be called that. Along with other more virulent ideas he held, Hitler is said to have entertained Teed's notion that our earth is concave, and we're all living on the inside. In 1941 he supposedly had a go at putting the idea to some military use, sending a small expedition to the Baltic island of Hogan, armed with powerful telescopes, which they aimed in the general direction of England. The reasoning? If the earth curved upward, then properly aligned telescopes could spy on the movements of the British fleet. Probably none of this is true—it comes from current hollow earth websites on the Internet—but it's somehow pleasing to think of Hitler being dumb or desperate enough to try it.

A variant supposition holds that "Hitler and his chief advisers escaped the last days of the Third Reich by going through the opening at the South Pole." As one website recounts it,

> According to the hollow earth Research Society in Ontario, Canada, they are still there. After the war, the organization claims, the Allies discovered that more than 2,000 scientists from Germany and Italy had vanished, along with almost a million people, to the land beyond the South Pole. This story gets more complicated with Nazi-designed UFOs, Nazi collaboration with the people who live in the center of the Earth, and the explanation for "Aryan-looking" UFO pilots.[3]

So Hitler may be down there yet, basking under an antiaging machine left behind by the Elder Ones, plotting his next move.

---

3. For more of this weirdness, the website address is http://paranormal.about.com/library/weekly/aa011199. htm?once=true&terms=hollow+earth+nazi. You can also check out "Paranormal Basics," "Lost Worlds," and "Time and Dimension Travel" while you're there.

In 1947, Admiral Richard E. Byrd became another unlikely player in what was turning into the unintentional comedy of the hollow earth.

If anything, you'd think his explorations of both poles would have provided discouraging facts for the hollow earthers. In 1926, he'd been the first to fly over the North Pole and had repeated the feat in 1929 with the first flyover of the South Pole. He'd established the famous base, Little America, during the 1928–1930 Antarctic expedition, and had led a second expedition there from 1933–1935, a third in 1939–1940 (during which four exploratory flights were made), and then a fourth from 1946 to 1947, during which Byrd explored and mapped nearly a million square miles of territory and made his second flight over the South Pole, as well as another over the North Pole that same year. He went back to Antarctica yet again in 1956, and flew over the South Pole once more.

And in all this time, Byrd *never* mentioned seeing a single polar opening.

Did this stop the hollow earthers from adopting him as their poster child? Not on your life. They leaped on a few casual remarks he'd made and performed a maniacally close reading that would make Talmudic scholars shake their heads in wonder. In February 1947 Byrd stated, "I'd like to see that *land beyond the Pole* [italics courtesy of hollow earthers]. That area beyond the Pole is the center of the *Great Unknown.*" The significance read into this by the hollow earthers, and a few other equally ambiguous remarks by Byrd, is positively daffy.

The most "definitive" (or at least exhaustive) recent elucidation of hollow earth theory came in a 1963 book titled *The Hollow Earth* by Dr. Raymond Bernard. His real name was Walter Siegmeister, and he wrote his master's thesis on Rudolph Steiner, anthroposophist founder of the Waldorf Schools. Bernard was also a higher-up in the Rosicrucian Society. Biographical information about him is fuzzy at best. He appears to have had a lifelong dedication to esoteric ideas of every sort. Born in New York City, as a biochemistry student in Germany he became interested in the therapeutic possibilities of lecithin. On returning to the United States he began manufacturing a patent medicine containing it and writing articles for health magazines promoting its benefits—until the FDA charged him with fraud and forced him to shut down the operation. Around this time he changed his name to Bernard and moved to Lorida, Florida, continuing to write tirelessly about his "fruitarian" (eating mainly fruits) and "breatharian" (breathing air for food) interests. A former sometime secretary, Guy C. Harwood, recalled: "He would type all day and, sometimes half the night on these manuscripts. [He would] eat baked sweet potatoes and a lot of kelp . . ."[4] Typical output from this time is a booklet called *The New Race*, "Devoted to the Creation of a Superior Race through Scientific Vegetarianism, Regeneration, Colonization and Eugenics." Sometime in the 1940s he got word the government was after him, and split for parts south, Mexico then Central and South America. It was around this time that his interest shifted to the hollow earth, subterranean caverns, and related "philosophical" subjects.

The Hollow Earth was first published in 1963 in a down-home edition printed as an offset copy of the original typescript, and republished the next year in a regular hardback edition. It has since been through at least four more editions with three different publishers. The book's subtitle pretty much says it:

> *The Greatest Geographical Discovery in History* Made by Admiral Richard E. Byrd in the Mysterious Land Beyond the Poles—The True Origin of the Flying Saucers

Truly wonderful in its way, deeply earnest, the book is a distillate of virtually every crackpot theory about the hollow earth that had been accumulating for a hundred years or more—presenting it all dead seriously. If there's a single "bible" for current Hollow Earthers, this is it. In the best syllogistic fashion, an early section is headed "WHAT THIS BOOK SEEKS TO PROVE." Which is, that the earth is hollow, with two polar openings; that Byrd "was the first to enter the polar openings"; that the Poles have never really been reached "because they do not exist"; that the hollow interior "has a land area greater than that of the earth's surface"; that the

---

4. Quoted in *The Hollow Earth Insider* at http://thehollowearthinsider.com/news/wmprint.php?ArtID=19.

"hollow interior, which has a warmer climate than on the surface," is "the home of plant, animal and human life"; and "that the mysterious flying saucers come from an advanced civilization in the hollow interior of the earth."

Most telling in this list is the final point: "That, in event of a nuclear world war, the hollow interior of the earth will permit the continuance of human life after radioactive fallout exterminates all life on the Earth's surface; and will provide an ideal refuge for the evacuation of survivors of the catastrophe, so that the human race may not be completely destroyed, but may continue."

A little farther on, the same idea is given a more optimistic turn. Like Symmes nearly 150 years before, Bernard proposes an expedition—but the reasons have changed from finding an unexploited frontier to the expression of atomic-age cold-war collywobbles. He says we need to do it to "establish contact with the advanced civilization that exists there, whose flying saucers are evidence of their superiority over us in scientific development. Perhaps this elder wiser race may save us from our doom, preventing a future nuclear war and enabling us to establish a New Age on earth, an age of permanent peace, with all nuclear weapons outlawed and destroyed by a world government representing all the peoples on earth."

At least his heart is in the right place—if not his science. The hollow earth is still viewed as a handy nearby utopia, only now it contains a beneficent advanced race that will save us from ourselves and nuclear holocaust—the implication being that we're too dumb to do it on our own, and that there is no God around to help out. So we have to make do with the next best thing—wise alien elders living underground.

In the 1950s the hollow earth began appearing in movies. It was a natural for low-budget science fiction melodramas. In 1951 *Unknown World* was released featuring Victor Kilian (best known as Grampa Larkin on the 1970s soap opera send-up, *Mary Hartman, Mary Hartman)*. Kilian plays celebrated geologist Jeremiah Morley, founder of the Society to Save Civilization. He's worried sick that mankind is about to destroy itself in nuclear holocaust. In an echo of Edgar Rice Burroughs's "iron mole," he builds a powerful device called the Cyclotram to dig to the center of the earth in hopes of finding a safe refuge. Sixteen hundred miles down, as critic Jeff Berkwits describes it, "they finally discover their subterranean Shangri-La, a colossal cavern with a huge sea, a phosphorescent ceiling and clouds created by volcanic vapors. But just as everyone begins to feel comfortable, the team's physician realizes that their newfound home holds a dark and potentially deadly secret."[5] Seems like heaven, but then they learn something in the atmosphere down there renders people sterile—and what good is a refuge that will only save one generation? So it's back up to the surface. Berkwits notes, "In 1951, the newly developed H-bomb, combined with the increasingly pervasive influence of Communism, had made the Earth a tremendously scary place. So it's not terribly surprising that, with the ever-present threat of atomic annihilation, [the] film essentially sought to envision the ultimate bomb shelter."

The hollow earth also figured as a motif in the first Superman feature film, *Superman and the Mole Men,* which hit theater screens in 1951 with the tagline, "The All-Time ACE OF ACTION! in his FIRST Full-Length Feature Adventure!" The movie starred television Superman George Reeves in his trademark outfit that looked like flannel pajamas with sewed-on decals and cape, with Phyllis Coates as Lois Lane. A yawner by today's standards, the story has Clark and Lois out in Silsby, somewhere in the generic far Midwest, where a local oil company is completing the drilling of the

(above) Look! Up on the screen! It's the first Superman movie, *Superman and the Mole Men.* (©1951 by National Comics Publications, Inc.)

---

5. Review of *Unknown World* by Jeff Berkwits at http://www.scifi.com/sfw/issue110/cool.html.

world's deepest well—which cuts into an underground realm inhabited by tiny radioactive "Mole Men," two of whom decide to come up to the surface for a look around, causing, of course, widespread panic up top. They're harmless, just pretty funny-looking, but the racist lynch-happy locals want to string them up anyway, and nearly do so before Superman steps in and makes peace. This epic was *so* low-budget that Superman isn't even seen flying in it once (there are a few "Look! Up in the sky!" moments, but we never see what they're looking at), but it did well at the box office, and was even recycled on the television show as a two-parter titled "The Unknown People."

Another semi-hollow earth movie from around the same time, also featuring misunderstood little fellows, was the 1956 subterranean epic, *The Mole People*, which still turns up occasionally on late-late television shows of the Insomniac Stoned Teen Theater variety. This one starred chiseled wooden John Agar, with supporting turns from Hugh Beaumont, later to become Ward Cleaver on *Leave It to Beaver*, and Alan Napier, best remembered as Alfred the butler on television's *Batman* series in the 1960s.

Agar and his colleagues are archaeologists excavating a site in a remote mountainous part of Asia. They stumble into a hole and find the lost city of Sumeria, ruled by unfriendly albino descendants of ancient Sumer who've been living underground since an earthquake relocated their city downward five thousand years earlier. When a tremor clogs their hole with boulders, the archaeologists become trapped and discover that the Sumerians have enslaved an abject and ugly troglodyte-like subterranean race of Mole People, who can dig their way around with a certain ease. The Sumerians, who sacrifice beautiful women to practice birth control and are otherwise downright nasty, have one weakness—they're pathologically afraid of light. So a single

(above) The tiny, subterranean Mole People. (©1956 by Universal Pictures, Inc.)

flashlight becomes the archaeologists' most powerful weapon, until the batteries give out. Elinu, the head Sumerian villain, is about to kill them all. But by then they've befriended a few of the Mole People and beautiful Adad, a Sumerian princess. Fortuitously, the Mole People, after suffering thousands of years of oppression, decide right then to stage a slave rebellion. During the chaos, Adad, now in love with Agar, leads the archaeologists to the surface and safety but is killed when a rock pillar falls on her. This, incidentally, was an alternate ending. In the first one they shot, she leaves her underground world hand in hand with Agar; but the studio execs (and this is *really* 1956-think) decided that having such a racially mixed couple—both of them white, technically, but she was a little *too* white, I guess—live happily ever after was too controversial, so they killed her off instead. Amazing but true. The story has absolutely no socially redeeming value, or intellectual resonance, except maybe to say that slavery isn't nice.

Perhaps most memorable about *The Mole People* is the five-minute introduction, featuring Dr. Frank Baxter. Those of a certain age will remember him as the young people's television intellectual during the 1950s, genially expounding on matters of presumed scientific interest to kids. That the Dr. before his name came from a Ph.D. in English didn't seem to matter. Here we find him standing behind a desk in a generic book-lined "academic" office, frequently fondling a globe on the desk in an oddly sensual way, like he's stroking his girlfriend's hair, and, yes, delivering a short lecture on the history of the hollow earth—the idea, of course, being to validate and make more believable what's to come in the movie. He starts with the Sumerians, talks about beliefs regarding subterranean worlds in cultures worldwide, mentions Halley's theory, and even tells us about John Cleves Symmes and Symmes' Holes—definitely a movie first, and pretty funny.

Even more so, though, was the 1959 movie version of *A Journey to the Center of the Earth*. The movie stars James Mason as the Professor, and throughout he looks like playing in such a campy production is giving him a migraine headache. Possibly in part because his costar, as his eager young assistant, is Pat Boone.

Pat Boone was very big with the teen audience in 1959—the squarer portion of it, at any rate—so casting him, even though he could hardly act, made a certain amount of box office sense. But it would be wasting him if he couldn't sing, so several *songs* were interspersed into the story. The movie opens, in fact, with Mason being knighted, and a choir of academics, led by Boone, saluting him by singing "Here's to the Professor of g-e-o-l-o-g-y . . ." The setting has been moved from Germany to Edinburgh. After two world wars, better to have them be Scotsmen than Germans—though it means having Pat Boone wrestling with a Scottish accent throughout.

Verne's plot was fairly bare-bones, too much so for Hollywood, so several entirely new complications were added—starting with a rival professor who will spare no dastardly deed, including attempted murder, to beat the Professor to the center of the earth. And there has to be a love interest, of course. But in Verne's novel it was an all-male expedition. Easily fixed. The rival professor is killed off early on, but his sweet wife, played by Arlene Dahl, insists on going along in return for donating all her dead husband's equipment to the enterprise. She flounces through all the adventures in fancy Victorian dresses, perfect makeup, and carefully coiffed hair. She and Mason hate each other at first, but guess what happens by the end? Taciturn Hans is given a beloved pet duck named Gertrude as a companion, which also cutely quacks her way through the center of the earth with them—until she's snatched and eaten by minions of the dead evil professor who've continued dogging them.

During their trip, they wander into visually splendid additions to Verne's story—a shining crystal grotto, another that's phosphorescent, and a remnant of Atlantis replete with fallen pillars and broken temples. Instead of encountering a dinosaur or two, they face herds of them. They escape on a great alabaster bowl left over from Atlantis, which they ride up a lava flow until *plop!* they're on the surface again. Pat Boone seems to be missing—no, there he is, clothes in tatters, surrounded by a bunch of giggling nuns! Mason observes, "This I know: the spirit of man cannot be stopped."

The changes are a perfect example of how the hollow earth idea has been repeatedly adapted to suit the needs of the time—in this case, adding elements to make the story conform to movie conventions of the day.

Edgar Rice Burroughs fared even worse. *At the Earth's Core* seems like Pulitzer Prize material compared to the movie version made in 1976, starring Doug McClure as David Innes and Peter Cushing as Abner Perry. At least *A Journey to the Center of the Earth* had good production values. But the scenery and so-called special effects in *At the Earth's Core* are so lame they're almost painful to watch. And Doug McClure has a bonked-on-the-head quality as an actor, generally looking like he's just coming out of a daze and wondering where he might be, that's also unfortunate—as are his *very* 70s hair and sideburns. The story line remains fairly true to the novel—I think. I confess that I was unable to sit through the whole movie.

And 1991 saw the release of the animated *Teenage Mutant Ninja Turtles at the Earth's Core,* which is probably enough said about that one. The dated feel of the title alone is a reminder of how quickly kid culture fads come and go.

In the past fifteen years or so there's been a minor resurgence in hollow earth novels. As a literary device it lands entirely in the realm of fantasy adventure—the utopian hollow earth novel is apparently a thing of the past. The most notable of these recent entries are *Circumpolar* (1984) by Richard A. Lupoff, *The Hollow Earth* (1990) by Rudy Rucker, and *Indiana Jones and the Hollow Earth* (1997) by Max McCoy. All three pay conscious homage to accumulated literary conventions regarding the hollow earth—two of them are deliberately old-fashioned pulp-style adventure stories. Only Rucker's *The Hollow Earth* is particularly memorable, and it is one of the best ever.

Circumpolar is set in the 1930s and deliberately imitates the pulp science fiction stories of the period, tossing most of the hollow earth conventions into the pot and stirring once. It's about a high-stakes airplane race around the poles (ultimately the race leads *through* them) featuring on one team Charles Lindberg, Amelia Earhart, and Howard Hughes; they are up against the unscrupulous von Richtofen brothers, those German flying aces from World War I, and aloof Princess

Lvova, a cousin to the late tsar of Russia. All the elements are thrown in—Symmes' Holes, an underground civilization descended from the progenitors of Norse mythology, prehistoric creatures, ray guns, the works. Clearly meant to be a light-

hearted romp, a send-up of the form, *Circumpolar* mainly shows that by now the idea has become de-generate. Not in any moral sense, but rather artistic. It's pretty much worn out, reality has too far in-truded, and it's now the stuff of parody—and in this case, not an especially successful one.

Max McCoy's *Indiana Jones and the Hollow Earth* belongs to a series of non-movie Indy novels that hearken back to Howard Garis's efforts for the Stratemeyer Syndicate. It is also set in the 1930s, probably a gambit to make the story more believable. Any parody here seems unintentional. An opening epigraph, the final lines of Poe's "Ms. Found in a Bottle," establishes provenance. Indy is at home in Princeton on a bitter winter night when an old man holding a box shows up at his door, on the verge of death. The box contains his journals and an artifact "from an advanced, ancient civilization" found during his explorations of polar re-gions. Evil Nazis are out to get him—and the box. Indy asks why. "'Vril! The vital element of this underground world. Matter itself yields to it. With it, one becomes godlike. All but immortal. Pass through solid rock, heal wounds, build cities in a single day—or destroy them. To possess vril is to be invincible.'" Bulwer-Lytton lives! The Nazis want these journals to locate the lost kingdom and terrorize the world with vril. They manage to wrest them from Indy, and the chase is on. Indy is asked to lead an expedition to beat them to it. In the end the Nazis are dead, and the secret of the lost civilization is buried back where it belongs.

(above) *Indiana Jones and the Hollow Earth*

The Hollow Earth by Rudy Rucker is fresher and more imaginative. Set in the 1830s, it features Edgar Allan Poe as one of the main characters. In the novel he is Eddie, an endearingly disreputable reprobate. Poe's child bride Virginia appears as well, although she dies early on. Eventually Eddie is discovered to have pulled her teeth as grisly souvenirs, just as Poe's narrator does in "Berenice." Rucker clearly did his research and wasn't afraid of a certain amount of black humor.

The story is told by Mason Reynolds, a Virginia teenager who's on the lam from the law with his pal Otha, a black youth about his age who's technically his slave (echoes of Huck Finn). Soon both are working for Eddie at the *Southern Literary Messenger,* with Mason sometimes handling the writing chores when Eddie's too stoned or hung over to hit his deadlines. Eddie's all fired up about the hollow earth, Symmes, and J. N. Reynolds, who shows up with counterfeit paper money plates that they use to print enough bogus cash to finance a polar expedition. They construct a hot-air balloon to descend into the Symmes' Hole, charter a schooner, and head for the Antarctic. Resemblances to previous hollow earth novels end not long after the southern polar ice cracks and they're falling toward the inside—except perhaps a distant kinship to John Uri Lloyd's hallucinogenic *Etidorhpa,* with the large difference that Rucker's trippy comedy is deliberate and deft.

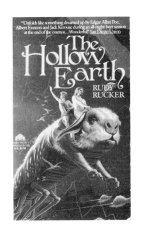

They tumble slowly for hours down the center of a vast tunnel through strangely thick air, past yellow-hot cliffs gushing lava, and a curious round metal thing with a "shape something like a fried egg." On leaving the tunnel they're becalmed in nearly zero gravity. And still below? "The appearance of the sphere's very center was as puzzling as before. All lines of sight near the center were warped and distorted, surrounding the center's blobs of blue with weird halos and mirages. The light there was bright and chaotic and lacked all coherence. Central sun? Perhaps not. I resolved to call it the Central

(above) Rucker's *Hollow Earth*

Anomaly. Earth's interior was illuminated not so much by the Anomaly proper as by the branching pink streamers of light that stretched from the Anomaly to the inner surface of the planetary rind we'd fallen through." Psychedelic!

Spotting a thick green jungle in the distance, they get to it by hitching a ride on one of the many flying creatures inhabiting the pinkish air. In the low gravity, water collects in great pond-size drops, some of which contain fish. Mason swims through one, poking his head up occasionally for air, to spear dinner for them, and then finds he has to build his cooking fire in midair, something of a trick. Making their way to the jungle's edge, they come upon, floating in space, an enormous sunflower half a mile across, inhabited by spritelike flower people who like to ingest the juice of a seed that takes them higher and higher—lotus-eaters living right on their own giant lotus—and the whimsy goes on from there. Huge flying shrigs—shrimp–pig creatures that move on jet flames of methane produced by what they eat (practically everything) blasting out of their rear ends—a telepathic all-knowing black race living near the Central Anomaly, and the anomaly itself, gateway to a Mirrorworld—it's all a lot of fun.

By now you'd think the hollow earth would be little more than this—the stuff of science fiction. We all know that the earth *isn't* hollow, don't we?

Apparently not all of us—at least judging from the amount of hollow earth weirdness alive and well on the Internet. The hollow earth even has its own newsletter—*The Hollow Earth Insider.* Editor Dennis Crenshaw is less of a strict constructionist than I've tried to be here—which is to say, looking only at hollow earth ideas chiefly derived from Halley's original notion and skipping the material about underground civilizations in general—but anything subterranean or UFOlike seems to fit his purview, which gives him *plenty* to write about.

There's also the New Agey "2012 Unlimited" website at http://www.eu .spiritweb.org/Spirit/hollow-earth.html, which has a section about Agartha. This is the name certain Buddhists give to the underground world they believe in, but here it refers to a subterranean New Age utopia of the same name. This Agartha has very specific entrances, which include Mammoth Cave, Argentina's Iguassu Falls, and Mt. Shasta in California—to name a few of "over 100 subterranean cities that form the Agartha Network." The site gets quite specific about what's going on under Mt. Shasta. Over a million people living there in Telos, on five different levels. Here's the rundown from the website:

> The dimensions of this domed city are approximately 1.5 miles wide by 2 miles deep. Telos is comprised of 5 levels.
>
> LEVEL 1: This top level is the center of commerce, education and administration. The pyramid-shaped temple is the central structure and has a capacity of 50,000. Surrounding it are government buildings, the equivalent of a courthouse that promotes an enlightened judicial system, halls of records, arts and entertainment facilities, a hotel for visiting foreign emissaries, a palace which houses the "Ra and Rana Mu" (the reigning King and Queen of the royal Lemurian lineage who are Ascended Masters), a communications tower, a spaceport, schools, food and clothing dispatches and most residences.
>
> LEVEL 2: A manufacturing center as well as a residential level. Houses are circular in shape and dust-free because of it. Like surface living, housing for singles, couples and extended families is the norm.
>
> LEVEL 3: Hydroponic gardens. Highly advanced hydroponic technology feeds the entire city, with some to spare for intercity commerce. All crops yield larger and tastier fruits, veggies and soy products that make for a varied and fun diet for Telosians. Now completely vegetarian, the Agartha Cities have taken meat substitutes to new heights.
>
> LEVEL 4: More hydroponic gardens, more manufacturing and some natural park areas.
>
> LEVEL 5: The nature level. Set about a mile beneath surface ground level, this area is a large natural environment. It serves as a habitat for a wide

variety of animals, including those many extinct on the surface. All species have been bred in a non-violent atmosphere, and those that might be carnivorous on the surface now enjoy soy steaks and human interaction. Here you can romp with a Saber-Toothed Tiger with wild abandon. Together with the other plant levels, enough oxygen is produced to sustain the biosphere.

Hard to resist quoting just a bit more detail:

COMPUTERS: The Agarthean computer system is amino acid-based and serves a vast array of functions. All of the sub-cities are linked by this highly spiritualized information network. The system monitors inter-city and galactic communication, while, simultaneously, serving the needs of the individual at home. It can, for instance, report your body's vitamin or mineral deficiencies or, when necessary, convey pertinent information from the akashic records for personal growth.

MONEY: Non-existent. All inhabitants' basic needs are taken care of. Luxuries are exchanged via a sophisticated barter system.

TRANSPORTATION: Moving sidewalks, inter-level elevators and electromagnetic sleds resembling our snow mobiles within the city. For travel between cities, residents take "the Tube," an electromagnetic subway system capable of speeds up to 3,000 m.p.h. Yes, Agartheans are well versed in intergalactic etiquette and are members of the Confederation of Planets. Space travel has been perfected, as has the ability for interdimensional shifts that render these ships undetectable.

ENTERTAINMENT: Theatre, concerts and a wide variety of the arts. Also, for you Trekkies, the Holodecks. Program your favorite movie or chapter in Earth history and become a part of it!

CHILDBIRTH: A painless three months, not nine. A very sacred process whereby, upon conception, a woman will go to the temple for three days, immediately welcoming the child with beautiful music, thoughts and imagery. Water birthing in the company of both parents is standard.

It goes on like this. Apparently it was premature of me to think hollow earth utopias were dead.

So the old hollow earth is still with us.

And why not? It's been an appealing dream for centuries.

And . . . uh, wait a minute. I'm just getting an incoming message from one of the fillings in my teeth. Um . . . yes, unhuh, no kidding? That was Yzxrnth, my own personal channeler from—well, I'd better not say. The CIA will be after me. He finally got through all the static from my computer. He just gave me the true scoop on the hollow earth. Those dreary scientists *do* have it wrong. And Symmes was *almost* right. The earth *is* hollow, and there's an opening—but it's not at the poles. It's on a lovely uninhabited island in the Pacific, and Yzxrnth has given me the specific coordinates.

Gotta run. Time to hit the lecture circuit, petition Congress, and begin raising money for The Dave Expedition To The Hollow Earth.

BIBLIOGRAPHY

Primary Sources

Adams, Jack [Alcanoan O. Grigsby and Mary P. Lowe]. *Nequa; or, The Problem of the Ages.* Topeka, KS: Equity, 1900.

Aikin, Charles. *Forty Years with the Damned; or, Life Inside the Earth.* Chicago: Regan Printing House, 1895.

Anonymous. *Relation d'un voyage du pole arctique au pole antarctique par le center du monde.* Paris: Pissot, 1723.

———. *A Voyage to the World in the Centre of the Earth, Giving an Account of the Manners, Customs, Laws, Government & Religion of the Inhabitants, their Persons & Habits Described, with several other particulars: In which is introduced the History of an Inhabitant of the Air, written by Himself, with some account of the planetary worlds.* London: Crowder & Woodgate, 1755; London: Fisher and Hurst, 1802.

Arnold, Kenneth, and Ray Palmer. *The Coming of the Saucers.* Boise, ID; Amherst, WI: Privately published by the authors, 1952.

Atkins, Rev. E. C. [pseud.]. "My Bride from Another World: A Weird Romance Recounting Many Strange Adventures in an Unknown World" in *Physical Culture,* June 1904.

Baum, L. Frank. *Dorothy and the Wizard in Oz.* Chicago: Reilly and Lee Co., 1908.

Beale, Charles Willing. *The Secret of the Earth.* New York: Neely, 1899; New York: Arno Press, 1975.

Bell, George W. *Mr. Oseba's Last Discovery.* Wellington, New Zealand: New Zealand Times, 1904.

Bennet, Robert Ames. *Thyra, A Romance of the Polar Pit.* New York: Holt, 1901; New York: Arno, 1978.

Bernard, Dr. R. W. [Walter Seigmeister]. *The Hollow Earth, the greatest geographical discovery in history made by Admiral Richard E. Byrd in the mysterious land beyond the poles—the true origin of the flying saucers.* New York: Fieldcrest Publishing Co., 1964.

Bradshaw, William Richard. *The Goddess of Atvatabar: Being the History of the Discovery of the Interior World & Conquest of Atvatabar.* Introduction by Julian Hawthorne. New York: Douthitt, 1892; New York: Arno, 1975.

Bulwer-Lytton, Edward. *The Coming Race.* London: Blackwood, 1871; New York: Francis Felt, 1871.

Burnet, Thomas. *Archaeologie Philosophicae: sive Doctrina antiqua de rerum originibus.* London: Kettilby, 1692.

———. *The Sacred Theory of the Earth.* London: 1684.

Burroughs, Edgar Rice. *At the Earth's Core.* Chicago: McClurg, 1922; originally serialized in *All Story Weekly,* April 4–14, 1914.

———. *Back to the Stone Age.* Tarzana: Burroughs, 1937; originally serialized in *Argosy,* January 9 through February 13, 1937, as "Seven Worlds to Conquer."

———. *Land of Terror.* Tarzana: Burroughs, 1944.

———. *Pellucidar.* Chicago: McClurg, 1923; originally serialized in *All-Story Cavalier,* May 1–29, 1915.

———. *Savage Pellucidar.* New York: Canaveral Press, 1963. Made up of four connected novellas first published in *Amazing Stories:* "The Return to Pellucidar" (February 1942); "Men of the Bronze Age" (March 1942); "Tiger Girl" (April 1942); and "Savage Pellucidar" (November 1963, though written in 1944).

———. *Tanar of Pellucidar.* New York: Metropolitan, 1930; originally serialized in *Blue Book,* March through August 1929.

———. *Tarzan at the Earth's Core.* New York: Metropolitan, 1930; originally serialized in *Blue Book,* September 1929 through March 1930.

Casanova, Jacques. *Icosameron.* Prague: 1788; Translated by Rachel Zurer. New York: Jenna Press, 1986.

DeMille, James. *A Strange Manuscript Found in a Copper Cylinder.* New York: Harper, 1888.

DeMorgan, John. *Under the World.* New York: Street & Smith, 1906; previously serialized in *Golden Hours,* July 7 through September 8, 1894, as "Into the Maelstrom."

De Plancy, Jacques-Auguste-Simon Collin. *Le voyage au centre de la terre, ou Aventures diverses de Clairancy et de ses compagnons dans le Sptizberg.* Paris: Caillot, 1821.

De Tarde, Gabriel. *Underground Man.* Translated by Cloudesley Brereton. Introduction by H. G. Wells. London: Duckworth, 1905; Westport, CT: Hyperion Press, 1974.

Dumas, Alexandre. *Isaac Laquédem.* Paris: 1852–1853.

Emerson, Willis George. *The Smoky God; or, A Voyage to the Inner World.* Chicago: Forbes, 1908.

Fairman, Henry Clay. *The Third World, A Tale of Love & Strange Adventure.* Atlanta: Third World, 1895; New York: Trans-Atlantic Publishing Company, 1896.

Fawcett, Edward Douglas. *Swallowed by an Earthquake.* London: Arnold, 1894.

Fezandie, Clement. *Through the Earth.* New York: Century Co., 1898.

Gardner, Marshall B. *A Journey to the Earth's Interior; or, Have the Poles Really Been Discovered?* Aurora, IL: published by the author, 1913; revised, 1920.

Halley, Edmond. "An account of the cause of the change of the variation of the magnetick needle, with an hypothesis of the structure of the internal parts of the Earth." *Philosophical Transactions of the Royal Society of London* 17:195 (1692): 563–78.

Harben, Will(iam) N(athaniel). *The Land of the Changing Sun.* New York: Merriam, 1894.

Hodder, William Reginald. *The Daughter of the Dawn.* London: Jarrolds, 1903.

Holberg, Ludvig. *A Journey to the World Under-Ground by Nicholas Klimius.* Translator unknown. London: Astley and Collins, 1742.

Jackson, Frank D., and Mary Everts Daniels. *Koreshan Unity. Communistic and Co-operative Gathering of the People.* Chicago: Guiding Star Publishing House, 1895.

Lane, Mary E. Bradley. *Mizora, A Prophesy.* New York: Dillingham, 1890; edited by Jean Pfaelzer. Syracuse, NY: Syracuse University Press, 2000.

Lloyd, John Uri. *Etidorhpa; or, The End of the Earth. The Strange History of a Mysterious Being & the Account of a Remarkable Journey.* Cincinnati: Lloyd, 1896; Cincinnati: Clarke, with added material, 1896; New York: Dodd Mead, revised and enlarged, 1901.

Lockwood, Ingersoll. *Baron Trump's Marvellous Underground Journey.* Boston: Lee and Shephard, 1893.

Lupoff, Richard A. *Circumpolar!* New York: Timescape Books, 1984.

Lyon, William F. *The Hollow Globe; or, The world's agitator and reconciler. A treatise on the physical conformation of the earth. Presented through the organism of M. L. Sherman, and written by Prof. Wm. F. Lyon.* Chicago: Religio-Philosophical Publishing House, 1871.

Marryat, Captain Frederick. *The Pacha of Many Tales.* Philadelphia: Cary and Hart, 1834.

Marshall, Archibald. *Upsidonia.* London: Hodder and Stoughton, 1915.

Mather, Cotton. *The Christian Philosopher.* Boston: 1721.

———. *Curiosa Americana.* Boston: 1712–24.

[McBride, James]. *Symmes's theory of concentric spheres; demonstrating that the earth is hollow, habitable within, and widely open about the poles.* By a citizen of the United States. Cincinnati: Morgan, Lodge and Fisher, 1826.

McCoy, Max. *Indiana Jones and the Hollow Earth.* New York: Bantam Books, 1997.

McKesson, Charles L. *Under Pike's Peak; or Mahalma, Child of the Fire Father.* New York: Neely, 1898.

Miller, William Amos. *The Soverign Guide: A Tale of Eden.* Los Angeles: George Rice, 1898.

Moore, M. Louise, and M. Beauchamp. *Al-Modad; or Life Scenes Beyond the Polar Circumlfex. A Religio-Scientific Solution of the Problems of Present and Future Life.* Shell Bank, LA: M. L. Moore and M. Beauchamp, 1892.

Mouhy, Charles de Fieux, Chevalier de. *Lamekis, ou les Voyages extraordinaires d'un Egyptien dans la terre intérieure avec la découverte de le isle des Silphides.* Paris: L. Dupuis, 1734.

[Paltock, Robert]. *The Life and Adventures of Peter Wilkins A Cornish Man: Relating particularly, His Shipwreck near the South Pole; his wonderful Passage thro' a subterraneous Cavern into a kind of new World; his there meeting with a Gawry or flying woman, whose life he preserv'd, and afterwards married her; his extraordinary Conveyance to the Country of Glums and Gawrys, or Men and Woman that fly. Likewise a Description of this strange Country, with the Laws, Customs, and Manners of its Inhabitants, and the Author's remarkable Transactions among them. Taken from his own Mouth, in his Passage to England from off Cape Horn in America, in the ship Hector. With an INTRODUCTION, giving an Account of the surprizing Manner of his coming on board that Vessel, and his Death on landing at Plymouth in the Year 1739. Illustrated with several CUTS, clearly and distinctly representing the Structure and Mechanism of the Wings of the Glums and Gawrys, and the Manner in which they use them either to swim or fly.* London: J. Robinson, 1751.

Poe, Edgar Allan. "Astounding News by Express" ["The Balloon Hoax"]. *The New York Sun, Extra,* 13 April 1844: 1+.

———. "A Descent into the Maelstrom." *Graham's Lady's and Gentleman's Magazine,* May 1841.

———. "MS. Found in a Bottle." *Baltimore Saturday Visiter,* 19 October 1833: 1+.

———. *The Narrative of Arthur Gordon Pym of Nantucket.* New York: Harper and Brothers, 1838.

———. "The Unparalelled Adventure of One Hans Pfaall." *Southern Literary Messenger,* June 1835: 565–580.

Reed, William T. *The Phantom of the Poles.* New York: W. S. Rockey Co., 1906.

Regnus, C. [Charles Sanger]. *The Land of Nison.* London: Daniel, 1906.

Reynolds, Jeremiah N. *Remarks on a review of Symmes' theory, which appeared in the American Quarterly Review, by a "citizen of the United States."* Washington: Gales and Seaton, 1827.

Rockwood, Roy [Howard Garis]. *Five Thousand Miles Underground, or The Mystery of the Centre of the Earth.* New York: Cupples and Leon, 1908.

Rollins, James. *Subterranean!* New York: Harper, 1999.

Rucker, Rudy. *The Hollow Earth.* New York: William Morrow and Company, 1990.

Scott, G[eorge] Firth. *The Last Lemurian: A Westralian Romance.* London: John Bowden, 1898.

Shaver, Richard S. "I Remember Lemuria." *Amazing Stories* 19:1 (March 1945): 12–70.

———. *I Remember Lemuria* [and] *The Return of Sathanas.* Evanston, IL: Venture, 1948.

Shaw, William Jenkins. *Cresten, Queen of the Toltus.* New York: Excelsior, 1892; originally published anonymously as *Under the Auroras, A Marvelous Tale of the Interior World.* New York: Excelsior Publishing House, 1888.

Sherman, M. L. *The Hollow Globe; or, The world's agitator and reconciler. A treatise on the physical conformation of the earth. Presented through the organism of M. L. Sherman, M.D., and written by*

Prof. Wm. F. Lyon. Chicago: Religio-Philosophical Publishing House, 1871.

Symmes, Americus. *The Symmes Theory of Concentric Spheres, demonstrating that the earth is hollow, habitable within, and widely open about the poles. Compiled by Americus Symmes from the writings of his father, Capt. John Cleves Symmes,* 2ND ed. Louisville, KY: Bradley and Gilbert, 1878.

[Symmes, John Cleves] Seaborn, Adam. *Symzonia, A Voyage of Discovery.* New York: Seymour, 1820; New York: Arno, 1975.

Symmes, John Cleves. ["Purple Martins"] *National Intelligencer,* September 15, 1820.

Taylor, William Alexander. *Intermere.* Columbus, OH: XX. Century Publishing Co., 1901–1902.

[Teed, Cyrus R.], and Ulysses G. Morrow. *The Cellular Cosmogony; or, The Earth a Concave Sphere.* Part 1: "The universology of Koreshanity," by Koresh [pseud.]; Part 2: "The new geodesy," by Professor U. G. Morrow. Chicago: Guiding Star Publishing House, 1899 [c1898]; 1905; edited by Robert S. Fogarty. Philadelphia: Porcupine Press, 1975.

[Teed, Cyrus R.]. *The Illumination of Koresh: Marvelous Experiences of the Great Alchemist Thirty Years Ago, at Utica, N.Y.* Chicago: Guiding Star Publishing House, ca. 1900.

[Teed, Cyrus R.] Chester, Lord. *The Great Red Dragon, or, The Flaming Devil of the Orient.* Estero, FL: Guiding Star Publishing House, 1908.

Thoreau, Henry David. *Walden; or, Life in the Woods.* Boston: Ticknor and Fields, 1854.

Thorpe, Fred. *Through the Earth; or, Jack Nelson's Invention.* New York: Street and Smith. Serialized in *Golden Hours,* June 5 through August 7, 1897, as "In the World Below; or, Three Boys in the Center of the Earth."

Tower, Washington L. *Interior World, A Romance Illustrating a New Hypothesis of Terrestrial Organization &c.* Oakland, OR: Milton H. Tower, 1885.

Verne, Jules. *An Antarctic Mystery (Le Sphinx des Glaces).* Translated by Mrs. Cashel Hoey. Boston:

Gregg Press, 1975.

———. *Journey to the Center of the Earth.* Translated by Robert Baldick. London: Penguin Books, 1965.

Welcome, S. Byron. *From Earth's Center, A Polar Gateway Message.* Chicago: Kerr, 1894.

Wells, H. G. *The Time Machine, An Invention.* New York: Henry Holt and Company, 1895.

Winthrop, Park. *The Land of the Central Sun.* Serialized in *Argosy,* July 1902 through January 1903.

Wood, Mrs. J. [pseud.]. *Pantaletta: A Romance of Hesheland.* New York: American News Co., 1882.

Secondary Sources

Adams, Henry. *The History of the United States of America During the Administrations of Jefferson and Madison.* New York: Charles Scribners' Sons, 1889–91.

Aldiss, Brian W. *Billion Year Spree: The True History of Science Fiction.* New York: Doubleday, 1973.

Allen, Hervey. *Israfel: The Life and Times of Edgar Allan Poe.* New York: George H. Doran, 1926.

Almy, Robert F. "J. N. Reynolds: A Brief Biography with Particular Reference to Poe and Symmes," *Colophon* 2 (1937): 227–245.

Anonymous. "Peter Wilkins." *Monthly Review* (4 December 1750): 157.

Arndt, Karl J. R. "Koreshanity, Topolobampo, Olombia, and the Harmonist Millions." *Western Pennsylvania Historical Magazine* 56 (January 1973): 71–86.

Bailey, J. O. *Pilgrims Through Space and Time.* New York: Argus Books, 1947.

———. "Sources for Poe's *Arthur Gordon Pym,* 'Hans Pfaal,' and Other Pieces." *PMLA* 57 (1942): 513–535.

Barrington, Daines. *The possibility of approaching the North Pole asserted. A new edition with an appendix, containing papers on the same subject, and on a North West Passage, by Colonel Beaufroy.* London: T. and J. Allman, W. H. Reid, and Baldwin, Cradock and Joy, 1818.

Barron, Neil. *Anatomy of Wonder: Science Fiction.* New York and London: R. R. Bowker Company, 1976.

Barrow, Sir John. *A chronological history of voyages into the Arctic regions: undertaken chiefly for the purpose of discovering a north-east, north-west, or polar passage between the Atlantic and Pacific: from the earliest periods of Scandinavian navigation to the departure of the recent expeditions under the orders of captains Ross and Buchan.* London: J. Murray, 1818.

Bassan, Maurice. *Hawthorne's Son.* Columbus, OH: Ohio State University Press, 1970.

Baudelaire, Charles. *Fatal Destinies—The Edgar Poe Essays.* Translated by Joan Fiedler Mele. Woodhaven, NY: Cross Country Press, 1981..

———. *Flowers of Evil.* Translated by George Dillon and Edna St. Vincent Millay. New York: Harper and Brothers, 1936.

Bestor, Arthur. *Backwoods Utopias,* 2ND enlarged ed. Philadelphia: University of Pennsylvania Press, 1970.

Boitard, Pierre. *Paris avant les hommes.* Paris: Passard, 1863.

Broadhurst, Dale R. "John Carter: Sword of Theosophy Revisited." *ERBzine,* vol. 1107. http://www.erbzine.com/mag11/1107.html (accessed 4 February 2006).

Bryer, John, and William Butcher. "Nothing New Under the Earth." *Earth Sciences History* 22:1 (2003): 36–54. http://home.netvigator.com/~wbutcher/articles/nothing%20new.htm (accessed 24 January 2006).

Butler, Samuel. *Erewhon; or, Over the Range.* London: Truebner, 1872.

Carmer, Carl. *Dark Trees to the Wind.* New York: William Sloane Associates, 1949.

Chapman, Walker [Robert Silverberg]. *The Loneliest Continent.* Greenwich, CT: New York Graphic Society Publishers, Ltd., 1964.

Clark, P. "The Symmes theory of the earth." *Atlantic Monthly* 31 (April 1873): 471–480.

Cook, Alan. *Edmond Halley: Charting the Heavens and the Seas.* Oxford: Clarendon Press, 1998.

Cook, J. *Captain Cook's journal during his first voyage round the world, made in H. M. Bark 'Endeavour,' 1768–71: a literal transcription of the original mss; with notes and introd. ed. by Captain W. J. L. Warton.* Adelaide: Libraries Board of South Australia, 1968.

Costello, Peter. *Jules Verne: Inventor of Science Fiction.* New York: Charles Scribner's Sons, 1978.

Cowie, Alexander. *The Rise of the American Novel.* New York: American Book Company, 1951.

Darwin, Charles. *The Origin of Species.* Introduction by Julian Huxley. New York: Mentor, Penguin Books, Ltd., 1958.

Dash, Joan. *The Longitude Prize.* New York: Frances Foster Books, Farrar, Straus and Giroux, 2000.

Davy, Humphrey. *Humphrey Davy on Geology: The 1805 Lectures for the General Audience.* Edited by Robert Siegfried and Robert H. Dott Jr. Madison, WI: University of Wisconsin Press, 1980.

De Camp, L. Sprague, and Willy Ley. *Lands Beyond.* New York: Rinehart and Co., 1952.

Descartes, René. *Principia philosophiae.* Amsterdam: 1644.

Doyle, Sir Arthur Conan. *The Lost World.* London: Hodder and Stoughton, 1912.

Eiseley, Loren. *Darwin's Century.* Garden City, NY: Doubleday and Company, 1958.

Euler, Leonhard. *Letters to a Princess of Germany.* Translated by Henry Hunter. London: 1795.

Evans, Arthur B. "Literary Intertexts in Jules Verne's *Voyages Extraordinaires.*" *Science-Fiction Studies* 23:2 #69 (July 1996): 171–187.

Fiedler, Leslie. *Love and Death in the American Novel.* New York: Criterion Books, 1960.

Figuier, Louis. *La Terre Avant le Deluge.* Paris: L. Hachette, 1863.

Fine, Howard D. "The Koreshan Unity: The Chicago Years of a Utopian Community." *Journal of the Illinois State Historical Society* 68 (1975): 213–227.

Flammarion, Camille. *The monde avant la création de l'homme.* Paris: C. Marpon, 1886.

Fontenelle, Bernard Bovier de. *Conversations on the Plurality of Worlds.* Paris: 1686; London: 1688; Berkeley: University of California Press, 1990.

Fry, B. St. J. "Captain John Cleve Symmes." *The Ladies' Repository* 8:2 (August 1871): 133–136.

Gilbert, William. *De Magnete.* London: Petrus Short, 1600; New York: Basic Books, 1958.

Godwin, Joscelyn. *Arktos: The Polar Myth in Science, Symbolism, and Nazi Survival.* Grand Rapids, MI: Phanes Press, 1993.

Gould, Stephen Jay. *Ever Since Darwin: Reflections in Natural History.* New York: W. W. Norton and Company, 1977.

Gray, Robert. *A History of London.* New York: Taplinger Publishing Company, 1978.

Griffin, Duane. "What Curiosity in the Structure: The Hollow Earth in Science." http://www.facstaff.bucknell.edu/dgriffin/Research/Griffin-HE_in_Science.pdf (accessed 22 January 2006).

Hallam, A. *Great Geological Controversies,* 2ND ed. Oxford: Oxford University Press, 1989.

Hearne, Samuel. *A Journey from Prince of Wales's Fort in Hudson's Bay to the Northern Ocean: In the Years 1769, 1770, 1771, and 1772.* London: A. Strahan and T. Cadell, 1795.

Hicks, Peter. "Cyrus Teed." The Unofficial Site of the Koreshan State Historic Site. http://koreshan.mwweb.org/teed.htm (accessed 1 February 2006).

Hinds, William Alfred. *American Communities and Co-operative Colonies,* 2ND revision. Chicago: Charles H. Kerr and Co., 1908.

A History and Biographical Cyclopaedia of Butler County Ohio, With Illustrations and Sketches of its Representative Men and Pioneers. Cincinnati, Ohio: Western Biographical Publishing Company, 1882.

The History of Clinton County Ohio. Chicago: W. H. Beers and Company, 1882.

"Hollow Earth Cities." 2012 Unlimited website. http://www.2012.com.au/HollowEarthCities.html (accessed 6 February 2006).

The Hollow Earth Insider. Website: www.thehollowearthinsider.com.

Hooke, Robert. *Micrographia.* London: Jo. Martyn and Ja. Allestry, printers to the Royal Society, 1665; Mineola, NY: Dover Publications, 2003.

Howe, Henry. *Historical Collections of Ohio.* Columbus: State of Ohio, 1888.

Howells, William Dean. *A Traveler From Altruria, A Romance.* New York: Harper, 1894.

Jardine, Lisa. *Ingenious Pursuits: Building the Scientific Revolution.* New York: Nan A. Talese Doubleday, 1999.

Kircher, Athanasius. *Magnes sive de arte magnetica opus tripartitum.* Rome: Ex Typographia Ludouici Grignani, 1641.

———. *Mundus Subterraneus.* Amsterdam: Johannes Janssonius van Waesberge, 1665.

Kollerstrom, Nick. "The Hollow World of Edmond Halley." *Journal of the History of Astronomy* 23 (August 1992): 185–192.

Landing, J. E. "Cyrus R. Teed, Koreshanity, and Cellular Cosmogony." *Communal Societies* (Autumn 1981): 1–17.

———. "Cyrus Reed Teed and the Koreshan Unity." In *America's Communal Utopias,* edited by Donald E. Pitzer. Chapel Hill: University of North Carolina Press, 1997.

Leslie, Sir John. *Elements of Natural History: Including Mechanics and Hydrostatics.* Edinburgh: Oliver and Boyd, 1829.

Levin, Harry. *The Power of Blackness: Hawthorne, Poe, Melville.* New York: Alfred A. Knopf, 1958.

Lottman, Herbert R. *Jules Verne.* New York: St. Martin's Press, 1996.

Mackle, Elliott J., Jr. "The Koreshan Unity in Florida: 1894–1910." Master's thesis, University of Miami, 1971.

Madden, E. F. "Symmes and his theory." *Harper's New Monthly Magazine* 65 (October 1882): 740–744.

McBride, James. *Pioneer Biography: Sketches of the Lives of some of the Early Settlers of Butler County, Ohio,* 2 vols. Cincinnati: R. Clarke and Co., 1869–1871.

McDermott, James. *Martin Frobisher Elizabethan Privateer.* New Haven, CT: Yale University Press, 2001.

Miller, Perry, *The New England Mind: From Colony to Province.* Cambridge, MA: Harvard University Press, 1953.

———. *The Raven and the Whale.* New York: Harcourt, Brace and World, 1956.

Milton, John. *Paradise Lost.* London: Samuel Simmons, 1667.

Morison, Samuel Eliot. *Admiral of the Ocean Sea: A Life of Christopher Columbus.* Boston: Little, Brown and Co., 1942.

———. *The Oxford History of the American People.* New York: Oxford University Press, 1965.

Nelson, Victoria. "Symmes Hole, Or the South Polar Romance." *Raritan* 17 (Fall 1997): 136–166.

Nevins, Allan, and Henry Steele Commager. *A Short History of the United States.* New York: The Modern Library, 1945.

Newton, Sir Isaac. *The Principia: Mathematical Principles of Natural Philosophy.* Translated by Bernard I. Cohen and Anne Whitman. Berkeley: University of California Press, 1999.

Nordhoff, Charles. *The Communistic Societies of the United States; From Personal Visit and Observation.* London: John Murray, 1875; New York: Harper and Brothers, 1875.

Nugent, Walter T. K. *From Centennial to World War: American Society 1876–1917.* Indianapolis: Bobbs-Merrill Company, Inc., 1977.

Officer, Charles, and Jake Page. *A Fabulous Kingdom: The Exploration of the Arctic.* New York: Oxford University Press, 2001.

Ogg, David. *Europe in the Seventeenth Century.* New York: Collier Books, 1962.

Peck, John Weld. "Symmes' Theory." *Ohio Archaeological and Historical Quarterly* 18 (January 1909): 28–42.

Pfaelzer, Jean. *The Utopian Novel in America, 1886–1896.* Pittsburgh, PA: University of Pittsburgh Press, 1984.

Philbrick, Thomas. *James Fenimore Cooper and the Development of American Sea Fiction.* Cambridge, MA: Harvard University Press, 1961.

Rainard, Robert Lynn. "In The Name of Humanity: The Koreshan Unity." Master's thesis, University of South Florida, 1974.

Rea, Sara Weber. *The Koreshan Story.* Estero, FL: Guiding Star Publishing House, 1994.

Robertson, Pricilla. *Revolutions of 1848: A Social History.* Princeton, NJ: Princeton University Press, 1952.

Rogers, Katharine M. *L. Frank Baum: Creator of OZ: A Biography.* New York: St. Martin's Press, 2002.

Ross, Sir John. *Narrative of a second voyage in search of a North-West Passage.* London: A. W. Webster, 1835.

Savours, Ann. *The Search for the North West Passage.* New York: St. Martin's Press, 1999.

Siegfried, Robert, and Robert H. Dolt Jr., eds. *Humphrey Davy on Geology: The 1805 Lectures for the General Audience.* Madison: University of Wisconsin Press, 1980.

Silverman, Kenneth. *The Life and Times of Cotton Mather.* New York: Harper and Row, 1984.

Stanton, William. *The Great United States Exploring*

Expedition of 1838–1842. Berkeley: University of California Press, 1975.

Starke, Aubrey. "Poe's Friend Reynolds." *American Literature* 11:2 (May 1939): 152–159.

Steeves, Harrison R., ed. *Three Eighteenth Century Romances.* New York: Charles Scribner's Sons, 1931.

Swift, Jonathan. *Travels into Several Remote Nations of the World in Four Parts by Lemuel Gulliver, First a Surgeon, & then a Captain of Several Ships.* First published by Lemuel Gulliver. London: Motte, 1726.

"Symmes's theory." *American Quarterly Review* 1 (March 1827): 235–253.

Tebbel, John, and Mary Ellen Zuckerman. *The Magazine in America 1741–1990.* New York: Oxford University Press, 1991.

Varma, Devendra P. *The Gothic Flame.* London: Arthur Barker, Ltd., 1957.

Villiers, Alan. *Captain James Cook.* New York: Charles Scribner's Sons, 1967.

Webber, Everett. *Escape to Utopia: The Communal Movement in America.* New York: Hastings House Publishers, 1959.

White, Frederic R. *Famous Utopias of the Renaissance.* New York: Hendricks House Farrar, Straus, 1946.

Wiebe, Robert H. *The Search for Order, 1877–1920.* New York: Hill and Wang, 1967.

Williams, Glyn. *Voyages of Delusion.* London: HarperCollins Publishers, 2002.

Zirkle, Conway. "The Theory of Concentric Spheres: Edmond Halley, Cotton Mather, and John Cleves Symmes." *Isis* 37 (July 1947): 155–159.

INDEX

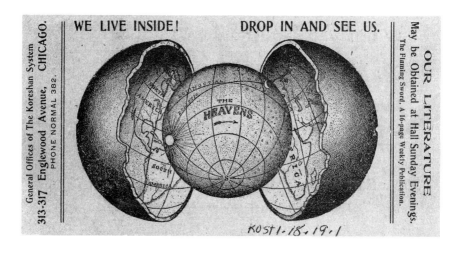

Kost 1·18·19·1

WE LIVE INSIDE! DROP IN AND SEE US.

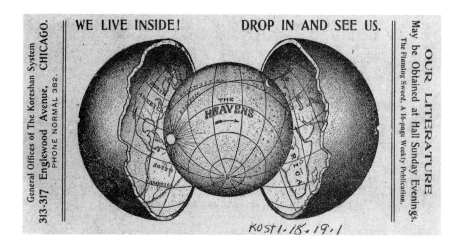

KOST 1·18·19·1